# MILTON STUDIES
# XXIX

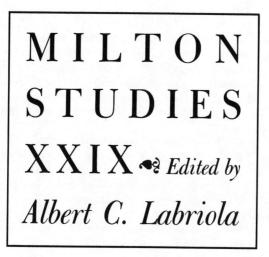

# MILTON STUDIES

## XXIX *Edited by*

## Albert C. Labriola

UNIVERSITY OF PITTSBURGH PRESS
Pittsburgh and London

## MILTON STUDIES

is published annually by the University of Pittsburgh Press as a forum for Milton scholarship and criticism. Articles submitted for publication may be biographical; they may interpret some aspect of Milton's writings; or they may define literary, intellectual, or historical contexts—by studying the work of his contemporaries, the traditions which affected his thought and art, contemporary political and religious movements, his influence on other writers, or the history of critical response to his work.

Manuscripts should be upwards of 3,000 words in length and should conform to the old *MLA Style Sheet*. Manuscripts and editorial correspondence should be addressed to Albert C. Labriola, Department of English, Duquesne University, Pittsburgh, PA 15282-1703. Manuscripts should be accompanied by a self-addressed envelope and sufficient unattached postage.

*Milton Studies* does not review books.

Within the United States, *Milton Studies* may be ordered from the University of Pittsburgh Press, Pittsburgh, Pa. 15260.

Library of Congress Catalog Card Number 69-12335

ISBN 0-8229-3732-8

US ISSN 0076-8820

Published by the University of Pittsburgh Press, Pittsburgh, Pa. 15260

# CONTENTS

# IN MEMORIAM
## O.B. HARDISON, JR., 1928–1990

O N  T H E  O C C A S I O N  of the tercentenary of *Paradise Lost,* O. B. Hardison, Jr., and seven other distinguished Miltonists gave lectures in a series sponsored by the Department of English of the University of Pittsburgh. These lectures were the core of the first volume of *Milton Studies* (1969). Then and thereafter as a member of the Editorial Board, O. B. was involved with *Milton Studies* until his death on August 5, 1990. One of my regrets is that he could not counsel me in my role as editor.

My first close-up of O. B. occurred in August 1975 when I was a short-term fellow doing research on Milton at the Folger Shakespeare Library, where he was the director. At the end of my stay, I dutifully submitted a progress report of my activity. Soon thereafter at my carrel, the director's secretary appeared with a message from O. B. to join him for coffee and conversation in his office. When I joined him, he laid aside the legal pad on which he was writing poetry and held aloft my progress report. He remarked that in my report was the essence of an article for *Milton Studies*. I never anticipated that I would become the editor of the very publication to which he referred, nor did I expect to be memorializing him in its pages.

As a humanist and a Miltonist, O. B. Hardison's achievement is most aptly assessed by citing the title of one of his books: *The Enduring Monument.* As a person, his impact remains profound because the alchemy of his joie de vivre enriched all of us while his affinity for the transcendent was a gentle summons to sublimate our nature. We will continue to remember him.

Albert C. Labriola

# MILTON STUDIES
# XXIX

# "THE FIEND WHO CAME THIR BANE": SATAN'S GIFT TO *PARADISE LOST*

## Hye-Joon Yoon

---

> Gift (gift), sb. [. . . MDu. *gift, gifte*
> (Du. *gift* fem. gift, n. poison), OHG,
> *gift* fem. gift, poison . . .]
> —*Oxford English Dictionary*

ONE OF THE obviously peculiar aspects of Milton's *Paradise Lost* would be its old and familiar subject matter. But the "absolute" anachronism, as it were, of choosing the beginning of human history itself as its theme is countered by a sense of immediacy, a kind of vividness that only an intimate engagement with the present historical moment could bring forth. Hegel finds in this discrepancy between the archaic past and the living present a characteristic symptom of modernity; *Paradise Lost* stands among those "Romantic" epics that are marked with a "cleft between the subject-matter and the personal reflections [*der Zwiespalt des Inhalts und der Reflexion des Dichters*] on which the poet draws when he describes events, persons, and situations."[1] This "cleft" or strife between the subject matter and its poetic representation constitutes a serious problem for Hegel, since a genuine epic subject matter must have an intrinsic value in itself as an "objective presentation of a self-grounded world, made real in virtue of its own necessity" (p. 1047). If so, a modern epic like *Paradise Lost,* lacking a subject matter that has an objectively and inherently epic quality, can give itself only a subjective basis. Or, to put it differently, the specific modernity of *Paradise Lost* that its archaic subject matter paradoxically reveals consists in the subjective attempt to establish an epic necessity for itself.

It should be noted that the rigidly historicized aesthetics of Hegel rules out any real possibility of a postclassical epic: genuine epic poetry belongs, almost by definition, to a "middle period,"

in which a people has awakened out of torpidity, and its spirit has been so far strengthened as to be able to produce its own world and feel itself at home in it, while conversely everything that later becomes firm religious dogma or civil and

3

moral law still remains a living attitude of mind from which no individual separated himself, and as yet there is no separation between feeling and will.(P. 1045)

It would not be very difficult to see that the historical background of
*Paradise Lost* disqualifies it from being an epic in the Hegelian sense: with
all the turmoil and bitter struggle of revolution and counterrevolution,
Milton's England hardly fits into such happy "middle period." But at the
same time it would make fairly good sense to maintain that the English
Revolution does stand for such national awakening, as a radical effort to
"produce its own world" by challenging the old religious, civil, and moral
doctrines and creating new ones. In this regard, one could argue that the
historical experience behind *Paradise Lost*, in particular the English Revolution, meets the essential requirements of an epic age—at least from the
standpoint of those who actively supported and fought for the revolution,
including Milton himself.

But we find, once again, the distinctive feature of *Zwiespalt* in this
historical experience itself. In the first place, there is the rift between the
world-historical novelty of the revolution and the anachronism in the
ideological and rhetorical self-presentation of the revolutionaries. As Marx
points out, "Cromwell and the English people had borrowed speech,
passions and illusions from the Old Testament for their bourgeois revolution."[2] This tension at the level of discursive practice between the borrowed representation and the actual experience of the revolution corresponds to the struggle to save the revolution itself against the internal and
external challenges, at the level of politics proper. In either case, the
outcome is negative; the epic experience of revolution remains merely an
epoch-making attempt, an "epic" failure. In the context of *Paradise Lost*,
of the revolution's ignominious defeat, all the aspirations and glory of the
revolution can only be seen as something irretrievably lost and past.[3]
Those who had a glimpse of the divine awakening of history are again left
homeless, as the "borrowed speech, passions and illusions" are returned
back to the Old Testament. The "cleft," then, is ultimately one between
the defeated revolutionary subject and the subject matter of history itself.
But the rupture or alienation in itself does not have to be seen as definite
and final. Milton refuses to stay within that cleavage between history and
history-making, between the English Revolution and the Old Testament;
in fact, he takes over the very foundation of the Old Testament itself, the
Book of Genesis, to wage his struggle for the epic, to write the epic itself
against the epic failure of the revolution.

Yet the issue of the "cleft" is still not fully settled. Leaving the problem of the poem's internal organization alone for the time being, one

could ask whether a decisive break can be found between *Paradise Lost* and Milton's prose works. That is, if *Paradise Lost* registers a break from the kind of epic overdetermination of theology and politics Milton establishes in his prose pamphlets, a rupture strong enough to make the poem a markedly nonpolitical or even antipolitical text, the primary task of interpretation would consist in spelling out the theological or ethical themes of the text. In other words, the poem would literally be a reflection on the general "ways of God" that would have to remain historically and politically abstract, if not absent. The reader, if so, would be permitted and even obliged to justify the ways of the text both to the theological doctrine that frames it and to his or her own subjective religious and ethical notions. But if any such disjunction of theology from politics proves to be illusory, if the actual articulations of the poem reveal a sustained, if ambivalent, engagement of the poet with the problem of making and changing history, the apparently transparent theological form and content of the text would have to be reilluminated in the light of the historical experience that informs or haunts the text.

This need not imply that an expertise in the historiographical knowledge of the period in question would in itself guarantee a valid approach to the poem. It would be bootless, for instance, to reduce all the specific determinations of the text back to the known or discovered facts of the seventeenth-century English history. Any brand of historical criticism of *Paradise Lost* should not fail to pay full attention to the peculiarities and idiosyncrasies of the text itself, before venturing to make broad generalizations or one-to-one correspondence to historical documents.[4] It may perhaps be better to attempt a categorical delineation of Milton's struggle with the problem of history as such in this epic about the prehistory of human history. All the more so if the real locus of the epic action, as we have already suggested, lies in that strife of the poet to recover or reground history against the odds of the fallen political history. Within the limited scope of our argument, we will try to show how such categorical criticism can be applied to one specific problem of the poem, the significance of Satan for *Paradise Lost*.

The Romantics may very well be credited as the first readers of *Paradise Lost* to have seen Milton's Satan from a standpoint that is free both from the age-old theological and mythical stigma attached to the figure, and from what William Empson calls "the modern duty of catching Satan out wherever possible." One of the most obvious faults of the "satanic" readings of Satan, it is true, lies in their dismissal or willful neglect of the better part of the text where much of Satan's heroism becomes conspicuously diminished. But the Romantic reading, as Kenneth Gross

demonstrates, is something more than a satanic distortion in this sense, at
least with Blake and Shelley. For instance, one recalls Shelley's sober
disapproval of Satan's "desire for personal aggrandisement" in his preface
to *Prometheus Unbound*. Besides, reading Satan sympathetically would
not necessarily be "Romantic" in itself, for even someone as unromantic as
E.M.W. Tillyard admits that Satan "best expresses . . . [the] heroic energy of Milton's mind." As a whole, what the Romantic strategies of
stressing the significance of Satan as a heroic figure or establishing Milton's unconscious or inadvertent alliance with Satan make quite clear is
one significant, if somewhat obvious, fact: Satan in *Paradise Lost* is not the
Satan of Christian myth or the horned devil of medieval morality plays.
Milton's Satan is an articulate and distinct literary figure whose specific
qualities cannot be reduced to preconceived notions about the devil. In
fact, the peculiar role and character of Satan in *Paradise Lost* save the
poem from the apparent tautology and redundancy of merely represent-
ing the given biblical myth. We can call this, then, the first gift of Satan to
*Paradise Lost*.[5]

But we must also add that Milton's Satan is neither Goethe's Mephis-
topheles nor Baudelaire's Satan. The uniqueness of Satan's position in
*Paradise Lost* should equally prevent such Romantic overdeterminations
of Satan.[6] Satan, for one thing, is a Satan after all and not a fellow mortal
like us. Insofar as Satan comes from the Christian mythology, however
revised and altered it may be in Milton's poem, there can be no real
understanding of the figure beyond the dichotomy established by the
myth, the agonistic relationship of Satan to God. Hence it would be quite
natural to look up what Milton had to say about Satan in his theological
writings, notably the *Christian Doctrine*. But we are flatly disappointed in
our expectation to find some detailed theological account of Satan in this
text. Besides the fact that Milton does not even care to individualize the
"author of all wickedness, and the opponent of all good" (p. 992) by giving
him the name Satan, the extremely cursory discussion of the evil angel in
the tract looks quite unusual compared to his detailed treatment of other
issues.[7] Milton deals with the devils in the *Christian Doctrine* not in the
context of the Fall and the Temptation, but simply under the heading "Of
the Special Government of Angels" in general. It turns out, thus, that
Satan in *Paradise Lost* occupies a unique place within Milton's writings as
a whole. Of course, Satan returns as an articulate figure in *Paradise Regained*, but not with the complexity and distinctness of the former. If so,
the point in emphasizing the uniqueness of Satan would lie in detecting
the specific need for Satan in the poem, in locating the categorical or
functional role he plays in the discursive deployment of the poem.

We begin, then, with Milton's God, for Satan exists, in every sense of the word, within the domain of God. But on the other hand, it needs to be emphasized that Milton's God is not the God of Calvinism, the personal God of inscrutable predestination and arbitrary will. For Milton, God is someone who has to justify himself, above all, to the tribunal of human reason: he is not so much the mysterious subject of divine revelation as "that reason which is discernible to the rational inquiring mind," as Andrew Milner aptly observes.[8] It follows from this that the primary faculties of God in Milton's understanding are not his will and predestination but his decree and foreknowledge, neither of which has absolute sway over the subsequent determinations grounded on them. This "theory of contingent decrees," which Milton takes many pains to elaborate in the *Christian Doctrine*, has the effect of exonerating God from any contradictory consequences in the realization of his decree.[9] As Milton clearly perceives, if "the decrees of God" are "understood in an absolute sense, without any implied conditions, God would contradict himself, and appear inconsistent" (p. 912). Thus it is no accident that in the first speech God delivers in *Paradise Lost* we find the following preemptive rationalization:

> whose fault?
> Whose but his own? ingrate, he had of mee
> All he could have; I made him just and right,
> Sufficient to have stood, though free to fall.          (III, 96–99)

In this self-justification of God is established divine justice, which becomes, in turn, the negative premise of human freedom and dignity: to the extent that human beings are free to fall and transgress God's decree they become, in God's expression, "Authors to themselves in all / Both what they judge and what they choose" (III, 122–23). Milton's God, in fact, states quite emphatically that "they / themselves ordain'd thir fall" (III, 128). God himself deconstructs, as it were, the absolute authority of divine conditioning or ordaining, yielding its determining power as the efficient cause of human destiny to that of man's self-determination.

If the divine decree has to be limited by contingent conditioning to be consistent and just, and if the origin of contradiction lies in the created being and not in the creator, God has his own special way of coping with this limitation of himself through his attribute of foreknowledge. God foresees the totality of conditions for the actualization of his decrees sufficiently and absolutely. The creator makes the contingency in his creation a self-sufficient totality and leaves the determinations within that totality to themselves, while reserving the justice of such provision for himself alone. In this regard, Milton's God can be seen as ineluctably tied to his own created order, both to the justice of his own decree and to the practical or contingent conditioning of the consequences of his decrees. This entails nothing less than a full autonomy of the created world as a self-sufficient totality. In this dialectical arrangement the divine justice can be reconciled to human freedom and vice versa through the mediation of God's foreknowledge that stands between the absolute decree and its contingent outcomes.[10] This middle term of foreknowledge, or the "Prevenient Grace" (XI, 3), can then be understood as the realm of provisionary disposition or anticipatory conditioning that precedes or prevents contradictions.

We can now go back to the question of Satan's place and his function in the conceptual economy of *Paradise Lost*. Satan, it can be argued, emerges from this moment or realm of "Prevenient Grace" as the negative supplement and agency of Milton's God who sees to it that his justice is unimpaired by any accident. By taking the preventive measure of allowing the accident of Satan's fall, God provides himself with an indispensable mediator whose (pre)determined negativity takes the entire charge of contradiction to itself, whereas the Son of God is the positive mediator, or God's "dearest mediation" (III, 226). Otherwise there can be found no logical necessity for Satan since Adam's self-sufficient conditioning allows him to stand or fall on his own account.

One can illustrate this mediating function of Satan, at the most obvious level, with the general movement of the narrative. *Paradise Lost*, as an epic about "Man's first Disobedience" (I, 1), does not deal with the proposed theme directly. The actual disobedience, which is depicted only in Book IX, is doubly mediated by the disobedience of Satan that precedes Man's "first" transgression. Not only does the reader dwell with Satan's fall from the beginning of the epic action, but Satan's fall is narrated again by Raphael to Adam before the fatal incident takes place. Although in a fuller account of Adam's fall and Satan's role in it we must also emphasize the other important mediation of the Fall by the differential relationship of Adam and Eve that culminates in the temptation of Eve, the primary axis of mediation in the narrative as a whole centers upon Satan as the precursor of the Fall. Without Satan, Eve would not have fallen; but without Satan, Eve would have had no one to accuse.

Thus far, we have examined the objective necessity of Satan's fall. But there still remains the problem of the subjective dimension of Satan's fall; the concrete cause of his action as a self-willed being has to be clarified in its own terms. This is all the more necessary since God himself strictly denies the ground for any objective cause of Satan's fall. He states, once and for all, that Satan's is a "self-tempted, self-deprav'd" (III, 130) fall. These words of God are less unequivocal than they sound. To begin with, we can understand in the theological terms outlined above that God cannot possibly be the cause of Satan's fall: God did not, and could not, decree it. God's decrees are in general characteristically incapable of involving even an inkling of injustice, much less a fall. On the other hand, if Satan's fall had been "self-tempted, self-deprav'd," it still could not mean that there had been an inherent moral defect or fault on Satan's part that preceded the revolt itself. If such were the case, as the creator and conditioner of Satan, God can be charged with having singled out, if not having made, Satan as a uniquely evil angel beforehand, a situation that would implicate God in Satan's fall at least in his foreseeing capacity. Or if we dismiss the question of what precisely caused or triggered Satan's fall and construct a genealogy of evil by focusing exclusively on the actual event of the revolt and its outcome, *Paradise Lost* would be deprived of its specific meaning and turned into a tautological and redundant exegesis of the Old Testament, which it clearly is not.

Neither the theological notion of the predisposing foreknowledge of God nor the genealogical need for the origin of evil, then, is germane to the issue in question. What looks relatively convincing, if only because the immediate circumstance of the fall is reflected, would be the aspect of power struggle or power politics. Satan's fall, in Book I, is presented as a political defeat of the "Glorious Enterprise" (I, 89) in which Satan and his followers attempted nothing less than to overthrow the power and the glory of God. More precisely, Satan understands the entire business strictly in the context of contingent military might: "so much the stronger prov'd / He with his Thunder: and till then who knew / The force of those dire Arms?" (I, 92–94). This cannot simply be an example of Satan's perverted reasoning, because God and his Son did resort to the "dire Arms" of thunder, and to that extent Satan's fall is a political and military defeat and not a direct outcome of moral depravity. In fact, Satan is not defeated morally at all; if anything, his "fixt mind / And high disdain, from sense of injur'd merit" (I, 97–98) are stronger than ever. Whether such firmness would be acceptable to us or not is a different question altogether. Although we know all too well that much more than thundering and routing are involved in Satan's fall, it is still tempting to follow this satanic reasoning and its peculiarly antinomious implications. If all that mattered were military superiority of "dire Arms," as Satan argues, Satan's fall would also be God's fall into mere force: God's self-justification would have to be based on his thunder alone. Conversely, if we overemphasize the inherent *a priori* superiority of God, in which his thunder plays only an incidental part, it yet remains true that God had to condescend to use the sheer force of his thunder to banish Satan from his heaven.

To clarify the issue fully, we would have to believe Raphael's version of the story, which has it that it all began with the begetting of the Son one day:

> This day I have begot whom I declare
> My only Son, and on this holy Hill
> Him have anointed, whom ye now behold
> At my right hand; your Head I him appoint;
> And by my Self have sworn to him shall bow
> All knees in Heav'n, and shall confess him Lord:
> Under his great Vice-gerent Reign abide
> United as one individual Soul
> For ever happy: him who disobeys
> Mee disobeys, breaks union, and that day
> Cast out from God and blessed vision, falls
> Into utter darkness, deep ingulft, his place
> Ordain'd without redemption, without end.          (V, 603–15)

Thus in this particular decree of God, the Son is begotten and declared as the "Head" of the heavenly host. As a divine decree it has to be rationally justifiable for, as we have seen, Milton's God cannot afford to be contradictory. But one wonders what the grounds are for begetting the Son and privileging him absolutely above the angels, who, for one thing, can also claim to be the sons of God created or fathered by him. In fact, these sons of God precede the newly begotten Son in the order of seniority. Of course, one could cleverly point out that in heaven time sequence itself is meaningless, but the temporality of begetting does not seem to have much of a superhuman quality in itself. Or, one could turn literalist and point out that the angels are only "Progeny of Light" (V, 600) and thus qualitatively different from the "only Son." But unless we make the absurd deduction that somehow "Light," itself a created entity, begot the angels, the qualitative difference between the Son and the angels seems rather ambiguous, since God would be the lone cause of all heavenly beings and begettings. The decree or declaration of God, then, brings about a legitimation crisis, as it were, for other sons of God; one cannot find any rational ground for it beyond the performative act of the declaration itself, with its stipulation of unquestioned obedience and its threat of eternal punishment. Besides, it is not clear whether God swears to his Son upon some mutual agreement, that is, whether the Son had any say in the business. And all the while, we are not told why God has to delegate his reign to his Son in the first place, for apparently God will nonetheless remain as the supreme sovereign. Tested by these questionings and doubts of fallen humanity, the divine wisdom of the decree becomes somewhat suspect.

Or, the point might lie somewhere else than in the act of begetting and delegation per se. It appears, in effect, that the emphasis falls on testing the loyalty of the angels and, more significantly, on stipulating the punishment of dissenters as the banishment from heaven to the "utter darkness." It also seems that hell has already been created precisely for the purpose of engulfing opposition. The decree, if not the will, of God has begotten its own negation and the negative relationship to itself. It is then the timely gift of Satan to have fulfilled that decreed negativity through his revolt and to have justified the reign of the Son, when such justification was crucially lacking in his fall into the "utter darkness, deep ingulft, his place / Ordain'd without redemption, without end" (V, 614– 15). Satan's notorious pride and ambition come only after that primal creation of hell and after the begetting of the Son. The gift of the Son, thus, becomes the bane for Satan, which in turn serves as an indispensable gift for the burden of indeterminacy in the decree itself.

This does not make Satan a virtuous republican hero, as William Godwin, among other Romantic readers, believed: "But why did he rebel against his maker? It was . . . because he saw no sufficient reason, for that extreme inequality of rank and power, which the creator assumed. It was . . . because a sense of reason and justice was stronger in his mind, than a sense of brute force."[11] Satan's revolt in itself is clearly not against "inequality of rank and power" as such, much less against the tyranny of "brute force." There is no warrant for taking Satan out of his proper context and crowning him with democratic virtues. It should not be a matter of giving Satan all the benefit of rationality, in contrast to God who would turn out to be a highly suspicious "neurotic," to quote Empson's rather amusing expression.[12] If any, the rationality of the decree is all on God's side, but God's rationality itself is a dialectical rationality that lives on its own propagated negations. Satan is strictly subject to the decreed relationship of negativity with God and his Son: he is preveniently ordained to finalize and legitimize the decree of God, or God as decree.

If one wants to see the opposition of Satan to God in terms of intersubjectivity, the Hegelian dialectic of self-consciousness gives us a better model as a less personalized or psychological view of a conflict between two irreconcilable positions. In Hegel's *Phenomenology of Spirit*, we come to an important moment in the pilgrimage toward the Absolute Knowing, when consciousness divides itself against itself, or in other words, when it becomes self-consciousness for the first time, only to find another self-consciousness firmly blocking its movement. What ensues from this confrontation is the "life-and-death struggle" between the self-consciousness and its double, in which each strives to realize itself by annihilating the other. By analogy, we could say that God has entered and initiated the dialectic of self-consciousness in begetting and promoting his "only Son" as his "Vice-gerent": God has divided himself in his Son. Satan, on his own part, becomes self-conscious of himself, or in simpler terms becomes proud and ambitious against the self-consciousness of God, the birth of the Son. He becomes thus the other or the double of God's self-consciousness and completes the dialectic in rising against the absolute positivity, or the absolute dictatorship, of God. "They must engage in this struggle," Hegel writes, "for they must raise their certainty of being *for themselves* to truth, both in the case of the other and in their own case."[13]

But the analogy cannot be taken too far since the struggle between Satan and God is also an undialectical, or one-sided, one. Not only is the outcome of the battle predetermined firmly in the decree quoted above, but the interrelationship itself is severed. In the Hegelian plot, the moment of "life-and-death struggle" is superseded by the relationship of "lordship and bondage." But in this case Satan simply falls away from the relationship itself; between him and God there is no mediation subjectively or objectively until, of course, the creation of Adam and Eve. The struggle, or the dialectical interaction, is essentially aimed at achieving proper determination; it is a battle to supplement the indeterminacy of the decree. The upshot of the struggle is a rigid, undialectical separation of the predetermined hell from heaven. In contrast, Adam and Eve fall from the state of one-sided or immediate bliss into mediation or interaction; Adam and Eve are given a share in producing and reproducing their own life through their respective labors. But for Satan, the fall merely consummates and initiates the demonic destiny of unmediated negativity, "ordain'd without redemption, without end."[14]

If Satan, as the immediate, irredeemable negativity, relieves God and heaven of their burden of negation and contradiction through his fall, Adam in his own fall finds a felicitous mediator in Satan as his predecessor in this regard. Insofar as Adam's transgression can be identified as such, that is, as negation, it is in the first place a repetition of Satan's transgression. But to the extent that it is a repetition, the immediacy or the demonic novelty of the first fall of Satan is mediated and canceled. Had there been no Satan's fall, Adam himself would have to be Satan and human history would have to take place in the one-sided *topos* of hell. This has to be seen as Satan's crucial gift to Adam and his descendants: by occupying the irredeemable position of hell in advance and for good, Satan has opened up the possibility and need for the redemption of human history both from the pure positivity of God and from the pure negativity of Satan. It is a curious way of justifying humanity against the alienating forces of human history itself. By going back to the divine or demonic prehistory so as to free human history once again from it, human history is given yet another new beginning just when actual history itself seems to turn irredeemably demonic. One cannot simply call this subtle move an escape from or a transcendence of history, as Milner understands it. [15] What happens in *Paradise Lost* can be better explained as a kind of transcendental deduction of history, transcendental in the specifically Kantian sense, which the philosopher defines as follows: "I entitle *transcendental* all knowledge which is occupied not so much with objects as with the mode of our knowledge of objects in so far as this mode of knowledge is to be possible *a priori*."[16] We could argue, then, using this Kantian formula, that the *a priori* of history has been transcendentally secured for Adam and for us through this prehistory of "Heav'n ruining from Heav'n" (VI, 868).

But there is another side to this issue, one that complicates a merely functional or structural explanation of Satan's role. We begin with the notion of transcendental freedom which, as much for Milton as for Kant, cannot but face its own limitation when it leaves the paradise of pure reason and falls into the world of historical contingency. When Milton's God himself had to divide his attribute into the determinate decree and sufficient foreknowledge as a way of coping with the problem of contingency and contradiction, it would be only too natural that the individual mortal who wills and acts freely should find himself powerless in the objective world of contingent history that opposes him with its own autonomy. One way of solving this aporia will be to conceive of a godly individual whose subjective will corresponds always-already to the will of the objective universe, that is, to the justice of God. This appears to have been Milton's idea during the revolutionary years. But after the Restoration the relationship of the godly individual to the objective order of history necessarily turns into one of rigorous and stringent antagonism. If so, the only guarantee of one's subjective validity can be found nowhere else than in the subjective insistence on subjective validity. Milton's Samson would be the most dramatic example of such stubborn "standing," but *Paradise Lost* has its own specimens of solitary but righteous individuals: Abdiel standing alone "Among the faithless, faithful only hee; / Among the innumerable false, unmov'd, / Unshak'n, unseduc'd, unterrifi'd" (V, 897–99); Enoch, "the only righteous in a World perverse" (XI, 701); Noah, the "One man except, the only Son of light" (XI, 808); finally, the poet himself singing "unchang'd / To hoarse or mute, fall'n on evil days, / On evil days though fall'n, and evil tongues" (VII, 24–26). In this holy and noble war of standing alone, however, the objective world itself stands undisturbed, unmoved, and unshaken. Except for Abdiel, who is after all an angel, the godly individual mortals have to leave the fallen world alone to its own determined doom. His battle is just a struggle to distance himself from the ungodly multitude.[17] This glory of exception, or this stigma of isolation, implies that the vision of human history now becomes a negative vision of eschatology: history has meaning only in its negation, in its end.

In a sense this dialectic of the One against All appears as a mirror image of God's election of his "only Son": the election of the One can only be justified when it originates from God's decree, and it is only in the self-conscious faith in that decree that saves the individual from falling into the dialectic of self-consciousness. Hence the godly human being has the additional burden of having to stand unmediated except through his own subjective will, unlike God who always has his Son to supplement him objectively. Of course, mortals can "believe in" Christ as their mediator, but it nonetheless remains a matter of subjective faith, an act of sheer self-consciousness. One of the implications of such unmediated solitude is the unwelcome parallel to the unmediated opposition of Satan to God, the reflection as it were of the other side of Satan's gift. If the fall of Satan consisted in his standing demonically against the determined decree of God, and if the type of the solitary One isolated in his self-consciousness can only be found in that first rebel, the godly individual in the fallen world would already be enjoying the gift, indeed the bane of Satan, however godly he happens to be.

The specific mission of Abdiel, in this context, seems to be one of erasing the demonic essence from the "only righteous," as the usurper of the usurper and the rebel against the rebel. But it must be noted that Abdiel, as a matter of fact, merely defects to God's camp, without really doing anything much to stem the tide of revolt. Besides, Milton clearly depicts him as an extremely zealous, hot-blooded young angel, whose godly criticism of Satan's rhetoric fails to win over his former comrades to God's cause: "So spake the fervent Angel, but his zeal / None seconded, as out of season judg'd, / Or singular and rash" (V, 849–51). Abdiel does act out effectively by dealing an unforgettable blow to Satan, but by then he had God and his thunder behind his back. One could even argue perversely that Abdiel's "noble stroke" (VI, 189) started the actual physical fighting. At any rate, this angel who seemed to stand for the heroism of the godly individual (and there are as yet no human heroes in this prehistory of human history) does not fit exactly into Milton's definition of true heroism in *Areopagitica:* "He that can apprehend and consider vice with all her baits and seeming pleasures, and yet abstain, and yet distinguish, and yet prefer that which is truly better, he is the true warfaring Christian" (p. 728). This characterization of the "true warfaring Christian," of course, cannot be a direct criterion for the character and actions of a warfaring angel. But it does complete the antinomy of Milton's dialectic of the One against All by reducing the problem of historical praxis to that of passive abstention and of preferring "that which is truly better." If the "true warfaring Christian" is going to materialize his warfare only at the level of subjective choice, he would first have to withdraw from the world of objective contingency where the alternatives themselves are established and abolished. To the extent that he had no share in setting up the choices in the first place, or to the extent that his choice is one of abandoning the objective actuality altogether, the godly individual, unlike Abdiel, will not have the ready alternative in God's camp and God's thunder, but only the trench of subjectivity, the bane and gift of Satan.

It would be wrong, however, to take hastily the passage quoted above as the manifestation of the limit of Milton's subjective historical consciousness. In *Areopagitica* there still was the assurance of the "vast city, a city of refuge, the mansion house of liberty, encompassed and surrounded with his [God's] protection," where the league of godly individuals fashioned out "the plates and instruments of armed justice in defense of beleaguered Truth" (p. 743). Even when the godly nation came to the threshold of the Restoration, Milton found the possibility of saving the revolution in the idea of a perpetual senate of godly individuals. But these instances only highlight the painful sense of the fall in *Paradise Lost* from any such objective politics, from any possibility of making intervention "to speak in season, and to forewarn my country in time" (*The Ready and Easy Way*, p. 898). Such timely forewarning belongs to the domain of God and his angels in *Paradise Lost*, not to the mundane realm of political action. Moreover, the redemption of human history is reserved for God alone, at least in Michael's vision of it:

> so shall the World go on,
> To good malignant, to bad men benign,
> Under her own weight groaning, till the day
> Appear of respiration to the just,
> And vengeance to the wicked, at return
> Of him so lately promis'd to thy aid.            (XII, 537–42)

If this is the destined doom of human history, one is not sure how any "paradise within thee" could be "happier far" (XII, 587). When the determined course of history can only be one of contradiction, and the mode of

existence in that contradiction can only be one of passive, isolated suffering, what real paradise can one cherish within oneself? Would it not rather
be the case that the real paradise within happens to be the poet's act of
writing *Paradise Lost,* his having redeemed history from utter absurdity
through the narrative of divine and demonic prehistory? If Milton's *Paradise Lost* in itself serves as the "plate and instrument" of "Prevenient
Grace" in its dialectical sublation of Satan's gift/bane, would not that be a
more significant intervention than the messianic redemption promised by
Michael?

Perhaps the real meaning of the informing mood behind the last moment of the poem is nothing else than the contentment and relief arising
from the completion of this great poetic labor. When Michael ends his
divine forewarning and departs from Adam, Milton likens the scene to an

> Ev'ning Mist
> Ris'n from a River o'er the marish glides,
> And gathers ground fast at the Laborer's heel
> Homeward returning.                    (XII, 629–32)

It is an unexpected beauty, this serenity and calmness of description
painted with a tincture of mild melancholy. But this serene beauty, it must
be stressed, is one that is punctuated by a human figure, a laborer at that,
whose toil and sweat transform the created nature, the gift of God, to a
humanized drama of secular history. The great poem about the prehistory
of human history closes itself with the tread of a laboring man whose
weary and lonely steps are opening up human history proper. Of course,
the inscription of the poet's self-gratifying reflection on his own work can
be seen in these lines. But more important is the fact that between these
lines the economy of divine or demonic gift/bane has been overcome by
the economy of human labor; with the curse of Adam, with human toil,
the soil of human history has been broken.[18] The issue is not, as Terry
Eagleton has put it, about facing "Eden with the horror-stricken face of
Benjamin's *Angelus Novus,*" but turning away from Eden altogether.[19]

Hence we find a sense of soothing, though inarticulate, hope in the
last four lines of the poem:

> The World was all before them, where to choose
> Thir place of rest, and Providence thir guide:
> They hand in hand with wand'ring steps and slow,
> Through *Eden* took thir solitary way.           (XII, 646–49)

Almost abruptly the "World" is given to us as an infinite possibility whose
indeterminacy itself becomes its greatest gift to our first parents and to us.

Are we then to see here a forgetfulness of Adam and the poet regarding the determined doom of history decreed by Michael? Or is it the Christian hope in the end of the world that presents the fallen world in its allegorical transvaluation? Of course, they have "Providence thir guide" and each other to rely on. But Providence is something that has already been embedded with the Fall in the secular course of history and contingency; it is no more the actual presence of superhuman beings who come flying from hell or heaven. In the uncertainty and indeterminacy of the "wand'ring steps and slow," and in the sudden freedom of "thir solitary way," the prehistory of history, the Paradise of the supernatural *mythos*, has been superseded.

The release and the freedom of the Fall, however, strictly remain in the negative guarantee of indeterminacy, in its essential nonfinality that opens up, in Milton's epic, the entire past of human history itself. Ernst Bloch summed up this dialectic of indeterminacy in the following maxim: "Mankind is not yet finished; therefore, neither is its past."[20] At the moment in which Paradise is lost, human history can always be seen as eternally unfinished, its past as the eternally new beginning. This, finally, can be said to be the ultimate gift of "the Fiend / Who came thir bane" (IV, 166–67) to *Paradise Lost:* the prehistory of humanity finds in Satan the timely Other that saves human history from the hopeless eternity of Satan's determined fate, the saving indeterminacy that keeps human history fresh in its very inception, even in its negative beginning as irredeemable loss.

Seoul, Korea

### NOTES

1. G.W.F. Hegel, *Aesthetics: Lectures on Fine Art*, 2 vols., trans. T. M. Knox (Oxford, 1975), vol. II, p. 1075; *Vorlesungen über die Äesthetik III* in *Werke*, 20 vols., eds. Eva Moldenhauer and Karl Markus Michel (Frankfurt am Main, 1969–71), vol. XV, p. 370.

2. Karl Marx, *The Eighteenth Brumaire of Louis Bonaparte* (New York, 1963), p. 17.

3. On the historical context of Milton's writings see Christopher Hill, *Milton and the English Revolution* (New York, 1977).

4. For example, see James A. Freeman, *Milton and the Martial Muse: "Paradise Lost" and European Traditions of War* (Princeton, 1980), and Robert Thomas Fallon, *Captain or Colonel: The Soldier in Milton's Life and Art* (Columbia, 1984). These critics tend to rely more on their range of historiographical knowledge than on their reasoned account of the relationship between the poem and the historical facts they constantly enumerate. In some respects, Hill, *Milton and the English Revolution*, pp. 365–75, can be held responsible

for initiating this tradition of empiricist historicism, which in fact bases itself on a simplified view of analogy between the revolutionary history and Milton's poems. Andrew Milner, *John Milton and the English Revolution: A Study in the Sociology of Literature* (Totowa, N.J., 1981), who adopts Lucien Goldmann's theory of homology, stands in a rival position to Hill.

5. William Empson, *Milton's God* (London, 1961), p. 74; Kenneth Gross, "Satan and the Romantic Satan: A Notebook," in *Re-membering Milton: Essays on the Texts and Traditions,* ed. Mary Nyquist and Margaret W. Ferguson (London, 1988), pp. 318–42. Gross also uses the expression "Satan's gift" (p. 340), although in a different sense and within a different context; Percy Bysshe Shelley, *Poetical Works,* ed. Thomas Hutchinson, corrected by G. M. Matthews (Oxford, 1970), p. 205; E. M. W. Tillyard, *Milton,* rev. ed. (London, 1966), p. 236.

6. Harold Bloom's chapter on Milton in his *Ruin the Sacred Truths: Poetry and Belief from the Bible to the Present* (Cambridge, Mass., 1989), pp. 91–113, would certainly rank among the most interesting overdeterminations of Satan to date. Bloom's strategy of personalizing Satan by at once praising "Satan's superb personality" (p. 99) and impersonating a superb personality himself reflects his resentment at the way present "literary academies" forget poetry and get "converted into temples of societal resentment" (p. 91). Against this tendency, Bloom's "Uncle Satan" (p. 92) would shine as "the morning and evening star of the poetry in our language" (p. 113).

7. Quotations of Milton's prose and poetry are from *John Milton: Complete Poems and Major Prose,* ed. Merritt Y. Hughes (New York, 1957).

8. Milner, *John Milton and the English Revolution,* p. 115. Milner's term for Milton's rationalist understanding of God is "logical atheism" (p. 116). See also William B. Hunter, Jr., "The Theological Context of Milton's *Christian Doctrine,*" in *Achievements of the Left Hand: Essays on the Prose of John Milton,* ed. Michael Lieb and John T. Shawcross (Amherst, 1974), pp. 269–87; Hill, *Milton and the English Revolution,* part IV.

9. For a slightly different understanding of the "exoneration" of God, see Hill, *Milton and the English Revolution,* p. 352.

10. Throughout this paper I use the infinitive "to mediate" and its derivatives in the logical, Hegelian sense. For a semiotic and theological application of the term to *Paradise Lost,* see R. A. Shoaf, *Milton: Poet of Duality: A Study of Semiotics in the Poetry and the Prose* (New Haven, 1985), pp. 30–39.

11. William Godwin, *Enquiry Concerning Political Justice and Its Influence on Morals and Happiness,* 3 vols., ed. F. E. L. Priestley (Toronto, 1946), vol. I, pp. 323–24.

12. Empson, *Milton's God,* p. 116.

13. G. W. F. Hegel, *Phenomenology of Spirit,* trans. A. V. Miller (Oxford, 1977), p. 114.

14. Hegel's self-consciousness, after falling into the position of the bondsman, acquires individuality and independence through labor which "forms and shapes the thing." Hegel, *Phenomenology,* p. 118; Gross's analysis of the one-sided essence of Satan should be a fair alternative to what we propose here: "Satan cannot give himself over so as to give himself back to himself. . . . He cannot . . . divide himself against, isolate himself from, and empty himself out before an image of authority so as to receive himself and his power back from that authority." Gross, "Satan and the Romantic Satan," p. 332.

15. Milner, *John Milton and the English Revolution,* pp. 144–47.

16. Immanuel Kant, "Introduction," in *Critique of Pure Reason,* trans. Norman K. Smith (New York, 1965), p. 59. In fact, Kant also deduces the *a priori* ground of man's rational historical existence from the Fall itself. See Immanuel Kant, "Conjectural Beginnings of Human History," in *On History,* ed. Lewis W. Beck (New York, 1963), pp. 53–68.

17. David Loewenstein makes a similar argument in *Milton and the Drama of His-*

*tory: Historical Vision, Iconoclasm, and the Literary Imagination* (Cambridge, 1990), pp. 101–105.

18. It is not entirely fortuitous that Milton's contemporary, Sir William Petty, came up with the idea that labor is the foundation of all material wealth in *A Treatise of Taxes and Contributions* (1667), and thus laid the conceptual foundation for modern political economy. See *The Economic Writings of Sir William Petty*, 2 vols., ed. Charles Henry Hull (Cambridge, 1899), vol. I, p. 68.

19. Terry Eagleton, "The God That Failed," in *Re-membering Milton*, p. 344. See also Herman Rapaport, *Milton and the Postmodern* (Lincoln, Neb., 1983), chap. 2, for an interesting use of Walter Benjamin for an analysis of *Paradise Lost*.

20. Ernst Bloch, "Dialectics and Hope," trans. Mark Ritter, *New German Critique* IX (1976), 8.

# LOSING A POSITION AND TAKING ONE:
# THEORIES OF PLACE AND *PARADISE LOST*

## Jon Whitman

---

I NTERPRETING AN object, it is often argued, may reveal as much about the orientation of the interpreter as about the object that he seeks to interpret. Since Kant, even apparently "objective" conditions like the spatial organization of the world have frequently seemed dependent on the intuitions applied to that world by the perceiver. From such a perspective, an interpreter not only responds to the world's design; he is in one sense responsible for it.

Interpretive responsibility of this kind, however, has not always been claimed. In one of its forms, the view that changes in the location of an observer may alter his account of the very position of an object, the argument does not develop systematically until attitudes toward space as a whole undergo radical transformation between antiquity and the early modern period. One of the critical turning points in that transformation occurs in the sixteenth and seventeenth centuries with the shift from an earth-centered model of the universe to a model in which there is no fixed physical center by reference to which an object can be placed. In such a universe, to specify where something is requires clarifying the perspective from which it is assessed.

The intellectual crisis associated with this interpretive shift has frequently been discussed.[1] Its imaginative implications, however, remain difficult to define. Perhaps a sign of the difficulty is that the seventeenth-century poem most carefully delineated in terms of cosmic space, Milton's *Paradise Lost*, is nearly framed by two statements which seem to challenge the value of spatial distinctions. "The mind is its own place, and in itself / Can make a heaven of hell," proclaims a fallen angel in Book I. Although one Paradise is to be lost, declares an upright angel to Adam in Book XII, there can be a "paradise within thee, happier far."[2] It is provocative to find two such opposed figures making such apparently related claims about individual placement; more generally, it is not easy to reconcile the poet's insistent turning toward the interior world with his intricate mapping of exterior space.[3] Such difficulties seem to me to pass beyond the poem itself into the broader problem of what it means to take a position in a cosmos undergoing rapid revaluation. By definition no critical formula can fully account for this problem, but an exploration of changing notions of "place" in Milton's period may help to clarify the very terms of the dilemma.

Those terms develop against the background of several contrasting attitudes toward place in antiquity. Among these views, three perhaps have a special bearing on the context of Milton's work, although it should be stressed that other early approaches to place have their own influence and that there are internal variations within each of the three general attitudes themselves.

One of these attitudes is the Aristotelian concept of "place" (topos) as the boundary between an enclosing body and an enclosed one. For Aristotle, "place" is not a realm of empty space—a notion he rejected in general—or an interval occupied by a body, but the set of outlines, as it were, specifying the limits of various bodies. Such a treatment of place as a series of distinct enclosures complements the Aristotelian view that there are distinct places in the cosmos toward which heavier and lighter elements, like earth and fire, naturally tend. "Place" of this kind implies the discrete positions of an ordered cosmos.[4]

A rival conception is the Neoplatonic view that the material cosmos as a whole belongs to an immaterial "place" (topos) that gives bodies their dimensions and coherence. This view, partly based on earlier developments in the Platonic and Stoic traditions, treats place not as the boundary between objects but as the boundless space in which things are located. Such an unlimited space is a kind of transcendent counterpart to Plato's underlying room or "place" (khōra), the chaotic realm in which all things take shape. Neoplatonic theories of this kind emphasize less an Aristotelian array of specific positions than a comprehensive order of reference that situates objects in the universe.[5]

A third conception is the Jewish view that God himself is the "Place" (Makom) in which the world is sited. Though this approach overlaps with the Neoplatonic concept of transcendent space, its orientation is less strictly cosmological than theological, stressing the intimate, organizing presence of the all-encompassing God. "Place" in this sense implies not an Aristotelian hierarchy nor a Neoplatonic field of reference, but the spiritual meeting ground between the divine Absolute and the interior of individual creatures.[6]

The interaction of such attitudes in antiquity and the Middle Ages produces considerable tension in early Jewish, Christian, and Moslem accounts of the properties and contours of space. Already in the speculations of Philo and Clement of Alexandria, who try to alter the Platonic notion of intelligible "place" to accord with the belief in an omnipresent God, there are tendencies to give spiritual place varying degrees of transcendence. As long as the concept of spiritual place remains strictly otherworldly in orientation, it can coexist (on its own level) with the Aristotelian concept of place as a physical boundary. Indeed, even a theologian as insistent on God's omnipresence as Augustine supports the Aristotelian view that beyond the finite cosmos there is no "place" (*locus*), by specifying that this world, the only one created, is wholly pervaded by God.[7] By the late Middle Ages, however, there is a growing sense that an infinite God cannot be so limited by a finite cosmos. Fourteenth-century philosophers such as Bradwardine and Oresme envision a kind of unlimited spiritual place (*situs, espace, lieu*) surrounding the enclosed world. Along with Moslem, Christian, and Jewish qualifications of the Aristotelian concept of place as a boundary, such attitudes contribute in the late Middle Ages and the Renaissance to a full-scale interpretive crisis about the very shape of the universe. In the course of this crisis, the prevailing model of a finite cosmos arranged in a hierarchy of spheres is gradually displaced by theories of an indeterminate universe extended in a uniformity of space.[8]

The theories themselves develop unevenly in a variety of disciplines. In Christian philosophy of the fifteenth century, Nicholas of Cusa argues that the spiritually charged universe is *interminatum;* because it lacks a physical center, even designations of up and down are relative to the placement of the perceiver. To the philosopher-poet Giordano Bruno in the sixteenth century, cosmic space is infinite in scope and homogeneous in character; it contains not higher and lower regions, but countless vantage points that constantly alter the sense of center and circumference. Such a decentering of the cosmos takes a highly speculative form in these writers. An increasing sense of relativity about place, however, develops in quite different quarters—in the sixteenth-century natural philosophy of theorists such as Telesio and Campanella, who deny the very notion of Aristotelian "natural place," and in the mathematical and observational work of Copernicus, Kepler, and Galileo, who help to systematize the critique of an earth-centered cosmos.[9] The broad tendency in this period to open the enclosed cosmos, in any case, is due to no single movement or discovery. In several respects, it draws deeply upon Neoplatonic concepts of boundless space and upon associations between place and the boundless God which are as old as the Jewish concept of *Makom*. It is significant that Campanella, indirectly influenced by cabalistic lore, nearly divinizes the "immortal" space of his universe, and that the seventeenth-century Cambridge Platonist Henry More supports his treatment of space as end-

less spiritual extension—in contrast to Descartes's material extension—
by arguing that "the very Divine Numen is called, by the Cabalists,
MAKOM, that is, Place."[10]

That statement appears in 1671, a few years after the first edition of
*Paradise Lost* (1667). Neither More's approach nor any other theory of
place, it should be emphasized, defines the terms of Milton's universe,
which is fundamentally allusive—and notoriously elusive. A few decades
ago it was argued that, already in Milton's time, his cosmic model was
somewhat old-fashioned, largely based upon early philosophic and poetic
accounts of the heavens and occasionally varied for special purposes. More
recently it has been claimed that Milton's universe is boldly new-
fashioned, deeply influenced by contemporary scientific and imaginative
views of panoramic space, and highly sensitive to the diversity of perspectives in such a world.[11] *Paradise Lost,* I think, fits wholly into neither of
these categories. The space it delineates seems to change in design over
the very course of the poem. More importantly, that change appears to be
implicated with an ethical argument to which the poem gives shape and
direction. Milton's work thus suggests not only the conceptual dilemma of
locating a stable position in a "decentered" universe, but the moral problem of finding a position of value in such a world.

Already in its early stages, Milton's poem is playing subtly with the
concept of a determinate cosmos, scarcely evoking it before qualifying it.
Not only does a fallen angel flamboyantly announce that "place" is relative
to his own mind (I, 252–55)—his testimony, after all, is dubious, and both
he and his party are soon debating the value of changing places.[12] More
broadly, the formal debate itself (Book II) suggests that a hierarchical
concept of "natural" places is becoming problematic in a universe where
heavenly spirits have slipped into hell. "In our proper motion we ascend"
(II, 75), contends one of those fallen spirits in a speech that fails to convince even his own comrades. A second spirit counters by urging his
cohorts to remain in hell, offering the strange prospect that they may be
"to the place conformed / In temper and in nature" (II, 217–18). When a
third spirit proclaims that the satanic party may thrive "in what place so
e're"—the very torments of hell, he proposes, may become "our elements" (II, 260–61, 274–75)—it is as if the gradual lowering of sights in
the debate is dramatically reenacting the original dissolution of celestial
elements into infernal ones. Such an elemental change could hardly have
been imagined by Aristotle, to say nothing of such a shift in place.

When the debaters finally turn their attention to a new place, they
project this disorder into the closed cosmos itself. "There is a place,"
announces Beelzebub, "another world, the happy seat / Of some new race

called Man . . . / . . . this place may lie exposed" (II, 345–60). "There is a place . . . exposed": the speaker here cleverly manipulates an ancient rhetorical *topos*, the formal introduction of a new place, to undermine the very notion of discrete cosmic domains. As the fallen spirits endorse the proposal to subvert this place, their plot, like the poet's, largely turns on the breaking of boundaries.[13] As if to exhibit that breakage—and with it the challenge to "natural" places, distinct locations, and the enclosed cosmos as a whole—Satan in his journey toward the cosmos first passes through a region not included on any Aristotelian map, a chaotic realm "without bound" where "time and place are lost" (II, 892–94). In Milton's universe, a boundless chaos is not just the primeval substratum for the orderly cosmos; it is a perpetual threat to it.

A different kind of expansiveness counters that disorder. Passing from hell and chaos to the "pure empyrean," the poet pictures God "High throned above all highth," surveying the universe from heaven to earth to hell, locating Satan about to descend on "the bare outside of this world" (III, 56–76). The divine realm of Milton's poem is not the immaterial "place" of Neoplatonic speculation; it is at once loftier in status and more intimately spiritual in character. Like that place, however, it offers a comprehensive frame of reference according to which different regions of the universe can be authoritatively placed. Taking over the poetic foreground as Satan prepares to infiltrate the cosmos, it serves at once to broaden and to realign the space of Milton's world.

Compared to the panoramic perspective of the empyrean, every other vantage point is only provisional. Plunging through the enclosed cosmos, Satan traverses "innumerable stars," distant points of light which, as he approaches them, "seemed other worlds" (III, 565–66). Something of the relativity of position theorized by advocates of an open universe seems to have entered Milton's vast enclosed cosmos. Whether Satan's course is "up or down," the poet comments, is "hard to tell" (III, 574–75). Significantly, this kind of vertigo is not the same as that of chaos, where there are hardly distinct points of reference at all. Inside the ordered cosmos, the shifting perspective of the individual observer locates and dislocates him in turn. Such variability of perspective increasingly dominates the poem, from the scene of Uriel leaving earth by gliding *down* the upraised beam of a sun already set (IV, 589–92), to the account of fallen angels seeing the "bottom" of upturned mountains approaching them in the war in heaven (VI, 648–49)—a war, it is stressed, that is itself described only in perceptual terms which need to be revised.[14] By the time the angel Raphael conspicuously refuses to specify whether the sun revolves around the earth or vice versa (VIII, 64–178), it has become clear that every assessment of position in

Milton's universe is finally subject to an absolute framework inaccessible to human perception. Wherever God's creatures are "placed," says Raphael to Adam, "let him dispose" (VIII, 170).

Such advice may seem reassuring enough in the Garden. It is deeply complicated, though, after the Fall when Sin and Death pave a passage from hell through chaos toward a "now fenceless world," and finally reach the very area where, "in little space," the "confines" of the empyreal heaven itself and the cosmos meet (X, 282–324). Satan gloats that "so near heaven's door" hell and this world have become "one realm, one continent / Of easy thorough-fare" (X, 389–93). Not only is an Aristotelian theory of "natural" place or a Neoplatonic notion of transcendent place liable to be inadequate in a continuum of this kind, but Milton's universe seems to have opened so widely as to endanger the very precincts of the divine itself.

Against this background, Milton's approach to space seems to change conspicuously at the close of the poem. Critical discussions of *Paradise Lost* frequently note differences in approach between Books XI–XII and the rest of the work; they rarely analyze, though, the poet's abrupt shift in spatial orientation. There is a scenic austerity in these final books as the angel Michael informs Adam about human history after the Fall and outside the Garden. Although the angel's account takes place on the highest hill of Paradise (XI, 377–78), it presents not a panoramic vista of continuous space but a series of brief, somewhat detached scenes, adapted in part from the Bible and other religious texts and frequently accompanied by ethical and theological explanation. The sense of spatial restriction intensifies when, after describing the Flood, Michael shifts his method of presentation to Adam from vision to narration (XII, 6–12) and rapidly passes from Babel to Canaan toward "this world's dissolution" and "New heavens, new earth" (XII, 459, 549). The poem of Books I–X, with its breathtaking cosmic trajectories, turns into a poem that barely describes the scene of a sun standing still at Joshua's command; such a story, notes the angel, would be "long to tell" (XII, 260–67).

No single explanation, I think, fully accounts for this deep change in the poet's spatial design. Perhaps even Milton finds it hard to make a smooth transition from the outer reaches of interstellar space to a biblical topography of Middle Eastern locations. Such a consideration might help to clarify and revise the old distinction between "Hellenism" and "Hebraism" in Milton's work. In a stricter sense, perhaps the poet's Protestant emphasis on the belief that no sanctuary is spiritually preferred to "the upright heart and pure" (I, 17–18) inclines him finally to recede from the exotic places explored in his poetry. Such an inclination might be intensified by his disenchantment with a place he once thought privileged, the England of the Puritan Commonwealth; that would-be paradise on earth he had lost. [15]

Perhaps, at least implicitly, the poet is also responding to a related but different disjunction. Somewhat like Adam in an altered cosmos, Milton is situated in a world where determinations of physical place have become ambiguous. Even when such determinations are made, it has become increasingly uncertain whether they correspond reliably to distinctions of value. The developing tendency in the final books to subordinate physical scenes to moral and doctrinal interpretation suggests a pressing need to reshape the space of the world, to turn *topoi* into *typoi*, shapes or types of a spiritual design. Michael himself hardly speaks of the movement from "types" to truth (XII, 303) before shifting typologically from the account of Joshua leading Israel into Canaan to the prospect of Jesus bringing man to "eternal paradise" (XII, 307–14). [16] More generally, the radical displacements which conclude the poem's vision—Adam exiled from Paradise after the Fall (XI, 259–62), Paradise pushed "Out of his place" on earth by the Flood (XI, 829–31), earth as a whole finally dissolved and transformed into a "far happier place" (XII, 463–65)—convey something of the pressure, as well as the promise, in the poet's effort to shift into a different dimension, to develop a sense of spiritual place not only in Adam's universe but in his own.

The distinctive turn in this shift seems to me not the broad appeal to an all-pervasive Deity, even if, shortly after announcing the expulsion, Michael calls attention to God's "omnipresence" (XI, 336). It is, rather, the ethical stance implied in that appeal. In contrast to Augustine, who in discussing divine omnipresence tends to stress that no individual, good or bad, can escape God's pervasiveness, Milton, who emphasizes more keenly the constructive capacity of the will, suggests that good individuals can in one sense bring God's presence into effect. Announcing that Paradise itself will change its place, Michael explains to Adam that "God attributes to place / No sanctity, if none be thither brought / By men" (XI, 836–38). It is as if the character of place depended not just on divine omnipresence, but also on human orientation. [17]

Such a link between human disposition and the position of God draws upon a wide variety of religious and philosophic influences. But perhaps it is significant that a striking discussion of divine "Place," the *Pirkei de-Rabbi Eliezer*—with its related argument that God is called *Makom* because "in every place where the righteous stand He is found with them"— was translated into Latin (1644) as Milton was planning *Paradise Lost*. [18] Whether or not Milton knew the text, in Latin or in Hebrew, he adapts the general sentiment to his own needs. In a poem that elaborately charts the coordinates of the physical universe, he finally suggests that space itself can be "bent" according to the spiritual attitudes of its human inhabitants. Such a reshaping not only occurs with the Fall, which prompts God (conventionally) to alter the very alignment of the cosmos (X, 649–707); it also applies to a yet unfulfilled future. "The world was all before them," Milton writes of Adam and Eve near the end of the poem, "where to choose / Their place of rest, and providence their guide" (XII, 646–47). "Providence" itself can be the object of "choose" in these lines, but the fluidity is not only between "place" and "providence." By its end, *Paradise Lost* is suggesting that even the most objective Place has its subjective counterpart in the realm of human responsibility.[19]

As in many contemporary controversies, Milton adopts no single approach to the dilemma of placement in his time. If he casts doubt on Aristotelian boundaries and "natural places" in a fallen world, he nonetheless refrains from renouncing, with Copernicus and Galileo, an earth-centered model of the universe. While he speaks of an "immeasurable abyss" from which emerges an "almost immense" cosmos (VII, 211, 620), he does not enthusiastically proclaim, with Bruno, a uniformity of space containing an infinity of worlds. Even his approach to spiritual place is less cosmological than that of More; he stresses more intently an ethical dimension. Writing a number of years before Newton propounds the concept of "absolute," immovable space—and a number of centuries before the Newtonian concept begins seriously to break down in physical theory—Milton brings his own kind of relativity into the universe. He finds himself in a world that has been breached not only primordially by Satan, but recurrently by disruptions of individual and political order. Significantly, he does not just turn inward, to the "paradise within"; he turns the uncertainty he perceives about space into an opportunity to remake it. In the end, his poem itself is an imposing figure of the mind's effort to reconstruct the world.[20]

From this perspective, perhaps *Paradise Lost* finally explores a kind of place that differs somewhat from the conditions of physical or spiritual space on which I have been concentrating. This is a kind of imaginative or intellectual place, the realm of *topoi* or reference points by which an argument is constructed—ranging from the evocative places of memory to the organizing frameworks of rhetoric and dialectic.[21] Referring to dialectical places near the opening of his own *Art of Logic*, Milton writes that the "invention of arguments" is called *topica* because it contains "*topous*, that is, places from which arguments are taken."[22] Almost as if he were discussing the "great argument" about "eternal providence" in *Paradise Lost* (I,

24–25), Milton adds in the treatise that the "first of all arguments is *cause*" and that "providence is the first cause of all things."[23] In an essay largely devoted to places of a different kind, I do not want to investigate the complex role of dialectical and other *topoi* in the general argument of the poem.[24] Even the brief adaptation of a traditional *topos* by Beelzebub in the infernal debate, as I have suggested, turns in more than one direction. Before closing a discussion about *Paradise Lost* and space, though, I want at least to open the question of how the poet's drive to find the "places" of his argument eventually converges with his effort to clarify the physical and spiritual dimensions of his universe.

Perhaps nothing more strikingly suggests that convergence than the four invocations in which Milton considers the sources and settings of his own inspiration (Books I, III, VII, and IX). Initially designing his song to soar "with no middle flight" above "the Aonian mount" while it pursues "Things unattempted yet in prose or rhyme" (I, 14–16), the poet claims by the following invocation to have flown "Through utter and through middle darkness" and to "revisit" the divine light that inspires him (III, 13, 16, 21). Unlike the muses of Homer and Virgil, Milton's Muse does not just tell the poet about faraway places, but seems to take him there.[25] In what sense, though, can the blind poet visit these "places"? Confronted with a "universal blank," he can only implore "celestial Light" to illuminate his "mind" (III, 47–55). For all the spatial maneuvers of the following books, he asks in his next invocation to be "guided down" (VII, 15), and finally, just before the Fall, it is no longer he who comes to "visit" places, as in an early invocation (III, 32), but the Muse who deigns "Her" nightly "visitation" to him (IX, 21–24).[26] With a retrospective reference to himself "long choosing" the subject of heroic song (IX, 25–26), he concludes that his own "higher argument" justly gives "heroic name / To person or to poem" (IX, 40–47). In effect, the poet is no longer so much exploring "places" to find his argument as choosing the argument that establishes his place, a place now coextensive with the design of his poem. A poet once transported by the physics of space has turned into a poet transformed by the ethics of choice. From such a perspective, the poetics of his "great argument" is where he takes his stand.

Yet there is a sense in which the poet himself remains internally divided about the efficacy of this stance, and finally about the broader relation between mind and place. The world at large, after all, is not just the product of his poetic vision, however inspired. It has palpable dimensions of its own, and to Milton it provides the setting for events of cosmic importance. *Paradise Lost* remains unclear about the precise degree to which that world is manipulable by the mind. The poet's shift from the cosmic spectacle of Books I–X to the spiritual concentration of Books XI–XII perhaps suggests something of the dilemma. For all his religious faith, the anxiety the poet expresses in his invocations about physical blindness (III, 21–50), political dangers that encompass him (VII, 25–28), and threatening forces in the world at large (IX, 44–46) gives that dilemma a deeply personal intensity. Perhaps it is a particularly urgent dilemma in a post-Cartesian world, the difficulty of clarifying how a realm of spiritual value can inform a world of material extension.

Milton himself offers no single-minded answer to that question. He offers, rather, a way of posing the question—the poetic argument that place itself needs to be constantly "placed" and reassessed if human activity is to be properly oriented. Conscious of critical tendencies that leave an individual's position undetermined, Milton posits the perpetual act of determining a standpoint. Whatever its limitations, *Paradise Lost* is a *locus classicus* of that interpretive process.

The Hebrew University of Jerusalem

### NOTES

I dedicate this article to the memory of my father-in-law, Rabbi Meyer Passow, who with his learning and generosity offered me not only valuable assistance with this study of "place," but orientation of a much deeper kind.

1. See, e.g., Arthur O. Lovejoy, *The Great Chain of Being: A Study of the History of an Idea* (1936; rpt. Cambridge, Mass., 1974); S. L. Bethell, *The Cultural Revolution of the Seventeenth Century* (London, 1951); and Marjorie H. Nicolson, *The Breaking of the Circle: Studies in the Effect of the "New Science" Upon Seventeenth-Century Poetry*, rev. ed. (New York, 1960).

2. See *Paradise Lost* I, 254–55, and XII, 585–87, in *The Poems of John Milton*, ed. John Carey and Alastair Fowler (London, 1968), from which all quotations of the poem are taken; line references to this edition are hereafter cited in the text. In my discussion of *Paradise Lost* I am indebted to the notes and commentary in this edition.

3. For the critical difficulty of clarifying the degree to which Satan's claim may be valid, see Arnold Stein, *Answerable Style: Essays on "Paradise Lost"* (Minneapolis, 1953), pp. 10–11, 22, 31, 36–51; Merritt Y. Hughes, "Myself Am Hell," *MP* LIV (1956), 80–94; Isabel Gamble MacCaffrey, *"Paradise Lost" as "Myth"* (1959; rpt. Cambridge, Mass., 1967), pp. 70–72; Joseph H. Summers, *The Muse's Method: An Introduction to "Paradise Lost"* (London, 1962), pp. 42, 160, 222; and G. K. Hunter, *Paradise Lost* (London, 1980), pp. 144–45. On approaches to space in earlier epic poetry, see Theodore M. Andersson, *Early Epic Scenery: Homer, Virgil, and the Medieval Legacy* (Ithaca, N.Y., 1976). On some spatial designs in seventeenth-century English poetry, see James G. Turner, *The Politics of Landscape: Rural Scenery and Society in English Poetry, 1630–1660* (Cambridge, Mass., 1979).

4. See Aristotle's *Physics* IV, chaps. 1–5, with David Ross, *Aristotle*, 5th ed. (1949; rpt. London, 1977), pp. 85–87; John Herman Randall, Jr., *Aristotle* (New York, 1960), pp. 146, 194–97; and Ernst Cassirer, *The Individual and the Cosmos in Renaissance Philosophy*, trans. Mario Domandi (Oxford, 1963), pp. 174–85.

5. On the development of Neoplatonic theories of "place," see Shmuel Sambursky, *The Concept of Place in Late Neoplatonism* (Jerusalem, 1982), pp. 11–29. On Plato's *khōra*, see my discussion in *Allegory: The Dynamics of an Ancient and Medieval Technique* (Oxford and Cambridge, Mass., 1987), pp. 170–72, with the references in the notes; compare Sambursky, *The Concept of Place*, p. 13.

6. See Ephraim E. Urbach, *The Sages: Their Concepts and Beliefs*, trans. Israel Abrahams (Cambridge, Mass., 1975), pp. 66–79; Max Jammer, *Concepts of Space: The History of Theories of Space in Physics* (Cambridge, Mass., 1954), pp. 25–50; Sambursky, *The Concept of Place*, pp. 14–15; and Harry Austryn Wolfson, *Philo: Foundations of Religious Philosophy in Judaism, Christianity, and Islam* (1947; rpt. Cambridge, Mass., 1982), I, pp. 247–51.

7. Concerning Philo and Clement, see the attribution of "place" (*topos* or *khōra*) to the Logos or Nous, with particular reference to modulations of the Christian Logos, analyzed in the following studies by Harry Austryn Wolfson: *Philo*, I, pp. 227–52; *The Philosophy of the Church Fathers: Faith, Trinity, Incarnation*, 3rd ed. (1970; rpt. Cambridge, Mass., 1976), pp. 209–10, 266–69, 285; and "Extradeical and Intradeical Interpretations of Platonic Ideas," *JHI* XXII (1961), 3–32, and in Wolfson, *Religious Philosophy: A Group of Essays* (Cambridge, Mass., 1961), pp. 33–49. For Augustine on omnipresence, see, e.g., *Confessions* I.2–5; III.6–7; IV.12; V.2; VII.1, 5, 15; VIII.3; X.27; XI.5; XII.28; XIII.7–9. For his view that there is no "place" beyond the world, see *De Civitate Dei* XI.5, with the studies of Edward Grant cited in note 8. Cf. the different levels of *locus* in the early medieval work of John the Scot Eriugena, discussed in Marta Cristiani, "Le problème du lieu et du temps dans le livre Ier du 'Periphyseon,'" in *The Mind of Eriugena*, ed. John J. O'Meara and Ludwig Bieler (Dublin, 1973), pp. 41–48, esp. p. 46.

8. On Bradwardine, Oresme, and spiritual place, see Edward Grant, "Medieval and Seventeenth-Century Conceptions of an Infinite Void Space Beyond the Cosmos," *Isis* LX (1969), 39–60, and "Place and Space in Medieval Physical Thought," in *Motion and Time, Space and Matter: Interrelations in the History of Philosophy and Science*, ed. Peter K. Machamer and Robert G. Turnbull (Columbus, 1976), pp. 137–67. On various qualifications of the Aristotelian concept of place, see Jammer, *Concepts of Space*, pp. 60–82; Grant, "Medieval and Seventeenth-Century Conceptions," 39–60, "Place and Space," pp. 137–67, and "Cosmology," in *Science in the Middle Ages*, ed. David C. Lindberg (Chicago, 1978), pp. 270–75; and Harry Austryn Wolfson, *Crescas' Critique of Aristotle: Problems of Aristotle's "Physics" in Jewish and Arabic Philosophy* (Cambridge, Mass., 1929), pp. 34–69, 114–27.

9. On Nicholas of Cusa, see Alexandre Koyré, *From the Closed World to the Infinite Universe* (1957; rpt. New York, 1958), pp. 6–24; Jammer, *Concepts of Space*, pp. 80–82; Cassirer, *The Individual and the Cosmos*, pp. 20–29, 176–82; and Lovejoy, *The Great Chain of Being*, pp. 112–15. On Bruno, see Koyré, *From the Closed World*, pp. 39–55; Jammer, *Concepts of Space*, pp. 85–88; Cassirer, *The Individual and the Cosmos*, pp. 187–91; and Lovejoy, *The Great Chain of Being*, pp. 116–21. On Telesio, Campanella, Copernicus, Kepler, and Galileo, see Jammer, *Concepts of Space*, pp. 33–34, 70–71, 83–84, 88; Koyré, *From the Closed World*, pp. 28–35, 58–99; and Cassirer, *The Individual and the Cosmos*, pp. 162–65, 173, 180–87.

10. See Jammer, *Concepts of Space*, pp. 32–33, 38–46, 88, and Koyré, *From the Closed World*, pp. 99–154, whose translation of More's statement, p. 148, is used. For the statement itself, see More, *Enchiridion Metaphysicum* VIII.8, p. 167, in *Henrici Mori Cantabrigiensis*

*Opera Omnia* (London, 1679): "ipsum Divinum Numen apud *Cabbalistas* appelari MAKOM [printed in Hebrew letters], id est, *Locum.*" On *Makom*, cf. pp. 168–70, 173.

11. For such differing attitudes, see Kester Svendsen, *Milton and Science* (Cambridge, Mass., 1956), pp. 39–85, 235–43, esp. pp. 42, 85, 237; Walter Clyde Curry, *Milton's Ontology, Cosmogony, and Physics* (Lexington, Ky., 1957); and Murray Roston, *Milton and the Baroque* (London, 1980).

12. For certain plausible and implausible features of Satan's argument, see D. C. Allen, *"Paradise Lost,* I, 254–5," *MLN* LXXI (1956), 324–26; J. B. Broadbent, *Some Graver Subject: An Essay on "Paradise Lost"* (London, 1960), pp. 78–85; the references above in note 3; and my discussion below. On the debate and the question of changing places, see Stein, *Answerable Style,* pp. 38–51.

13. On the formal introduction of a new place, see, e.g., Virgil's "est . . . locus," *Aeneid* I, 159, in *The "Aeneid" of Virgil,* 2 vols., ed. R. D. Williams (Basingstoke, England, 1972–73), with Williams's note to I, 159f., in vol. I, p. 173. On the breaking of boundaries and *Paradise Lost,* see Regina Schwartz, "Milton's Hostile Chaos: '. . . And the Sea Was No More,'" *ELH* LII (1985), 337–74; cf. *PL* X, 738–41.

14. See *PL* V, 563–76, 748–54, and VI, 893–96. Compare MacCaffrey, *"Paradise Lost" as "Myth,"* pp. 48–73; Stein, *Answerable Style,* pp. 17–37; and Roston, *Milton and the Baroque,* pp. 80–145.

15. On "Protestant" tendencies in seventeenth-century literature, see Barbara Kiefer Lewalski, "Typological Symbolism and the 'Progress of the Soul' in Seventeenth-Century Literature," in *Literary Uses of Typology from the Late Middle Ages to the Present,* ed. Earl Miner (Princeton, 1977), pp. 79–114, and Lewalski, *Protestant Poetics and the Seventeenth-Century Religious Lyric* (Princeton, 1979). On disenchantment with England and Milton's treatment of place, see Louis L. Martz, *Poet of Exile: A Study of Milton's Poetry* (New Haven, 1980), pp. 160–68, and David Loewenstein, *Milton and the Drama of History: Historical Vision, Iconoclasm, and the Literary Imagination* (Cambridge, 1990), pp. 107–09.

16. *Typos* in a different sense, involving the shaping function of cosmic space, is explicitly associated with *topos* already in ancient Neoplatonic thought; see Sambursky, *The Concept of Place,* pp. 21–22, 68–69, 94–95. The reshaping of space in the final books of *Paradise Lost* differs from the poet's more general strategy of giving physical placement moral overtones; see MacCaffrey, *"Paradise Lost" as "Myth,"* pp. 64–73. On early Christian approaches to "typology," see my *Allegory,* pp. 3n1, 6n4, 51, 64n8, 67–68, 77–78, 81–91, 107, 127–30, 133–35, 143–44, 167, 215–16, 218, 239, 257, 266–67. On some changing attitudes in Protestant interpretation and in Milton, see Lewalski, "Typological Symbolism," pp. 79–114, and *Protestant Poetics,* pp. 72–144; H. R. MacCallum, "Milton and Figurative Interpretation of the Bible," *UTQ* XXXI (1962), 391–415; and Sanford Budick, "Milton and the Scene of Interpretation: From Typology Toward Midrash," in *Midrash and Literature,* ed. Geoffrey H. Hartman and Sanford Budick (New Haven, 1986), pp. 195–212.

17. For Augustine's sense of God's pervasiveness, see, e.g., *Confessions* I.2–5; III.6–7; IV.12; V.2; VII.1, 5, 15; VIII.3; X.27; XI.5; XII.28; XIII.7–9; *Enarratio in Psalmum LXXIV,* in *Patrologiae Cursus Completus, Series Latina* 36, 952–53; and *Sermo LXIX,* in the same series, 38, 442. Certain phrases in these discussions, however, suggest a more variegated relationship between the divine and human orders. For Milton's emphasis on the capacity of the will, see, e.g., Arnold Stein, "The Paradise Within and the Paradise Without," review of *The Paradise Within: Studies in Vaughan, Traherne, and Milton,* by Louis L. Martz, in *MLQ* XXVI (1965), 595–600, and Dennis Richard Danielson, *Milton's Good God: A Study in Literary Theodicy* (Cambridge, 1982).

18. On *Makom* in *Pirkei de-Rabbi Eliezer,* see Urbach, *The Sages,* p. 75. My transla-

tion of this passage from chapter 35 of the work is based in part on Urbach's translation, p. 716n38. For the Hebrew, see *Pirkei Rabbi Eliezer* (Jerusalem, 1973–74), p. 126: "b'khol makom shehatzadikim sham, hu nimtza imahem." For the Latin translation, see *Capitula R. Elieser,* trans. Guilielmus Henric. Vorstius (Leiden, 1644), p. 87: "Cur autem vocatur nomen eius MAKOM [printed in Hebrew letters] *locus?* quia in omni loco, ubi iusti sunt, ipse existit cum illis." On the possible influence of *Pirkei de-Rabbi Eliezer* on *Paradise Lost,* see Golda S. Werman, "Midrash in *Paradise Lost: Capitula Rabbi Elieser,*" in *Milton Studies* XVIII, ed. James D. Simmonds (Pittsburgh, 1983), pp. 145–71.

19. On the relation between "choose" and "providence" in the poem's closing lines, see the note to XII, 647 in Carey and Fowler, and Martz, *Poet of Exile,* pp. 187–88.

20. On the scope of Milton's universe, see, with caution concerning the philosophic claims, Curry, *Milton's Ontology,* pp. 33–44, 50–65, 88, 144–57; compare J. H. Adamson, "The Creation," in W. B. Hunter, C. A. Patrides, and J. H. Adamson, *Bright Essence: Studies in Milton's Theology* (Salt Lake City, 1973), pp. 99–100. On Bruno, see Koyré, *From the Closed World,* pp. 39–54. On Newton, see Koyré, pp. 159–79, and Jammer, *Concepts of Space,* pp. 93–100. On Milton and the subject of cosmic disorder, see the note to *PL* IX, 44–47 in Carey and Fowler, and Schwartz, "Milton's Hostile Chaos," 368–69.

21. On diverse but overlapping traditions of mnemonic, rhetorical, and dialectical *topoi,* see Frances A. Yates, *The Art of Memory* (1966; rpt. Harmondsworth, 1978); Eleonore Stump, trans., *Boethius's "De topicis differentiis"* (Ithaca, N.Y., 1978); and Ernst Robert Curtius, *European Literature and the Latin Middle Ages,* trans. Willard R. Trask (London, 1953), esp. pp. 70–71, 79–105, 452–53; compare Louis L. Martz, *The Poetry of Meditation: A Study in English Religious Literature of the Seventeenth Century,* rev. ed. (1962; rpt. New Haven, 1965), pp. 27–32, 37–40. For some perspectives on *topoi* and the early development of narrative, see Eugene Vance, *From Topic to Tale: Logic and Narrativity in the Middle Ages* (Minneapolis, 1987).

22. See Milton, *Artis Logicae Plenior Institutio, ad Petri Rami Methodum Concinnata,* ed. and trans. Allan H. Gilbert, in *The Works of John Milton,* 18 vols., ed. Frank Allen Patterson et al. (New York, 1931–38), vol. XI, pp. 22–23: "Argumentorum itaque inventio *Topica Graecè* nominatur; quia *topous* continet, i.e. locos unde argumenta sumuntur." Translations from this work are based on Gilbert's edition and translation and on *A Fuller Course in the Art of Logic Conformed to the Method of Peter Ramus,* ed. and trans. Walter J. Ong and Charles J. Ermatinger, in *Complete Prose Works of John Milton,* ed. Don M. Wolfe et al. (New Haven, 1953–82), vol. VIII, p. 219.

23. See Gilbert's edition and translation of *Artis Logicae,* pp. 28–29: "argumentorum autem omnium primum *causa* est," and pp. 48–49: "Sed providentia rerum omnium prima causa est." In the translation of Ong and Ermatinger, *A Fuller Course,* see pp. 221, 229. Compare Leon Howard, " 'The Invention' of Milton's 'Great Argument': A Study of the Logic of 'God's Ways to Men,' " *The Huntington Library Quarterly* IX (1946), 149–73, and Stanley Eugene Fish, *Surprised by Sin: The Reader in "Paradise Lost"* (1967; rpt. Berkeley and Los Angeles, 1971), pp. 67–68.

24. For various approaches, see Howard, " 'The Invention' "; MacCaffrey, *"Paradise Lost" as "Myth"*; and Barbara Kiefer Lewalski, *"Paradise Lost" and the Rhetoric of Literary Forms* (Princeton, 1985).

25. Compare Gordon Teskey, "From Allegory to Dialectic: Imagining Error in Spenser and Milton," *PMLA* CI (1986), 18–19.

26. Compare the transitions in Book VII: "I soar" (3); "I have presumed" (13); "Return me to my native element" (16); "thou / Visit'st my slumbers nightly" (28–29). Compare also MacCaffrey, *"Paradise Lost" as "Myth,"* pp. 55–59.

# "HONIED WORDS": WISDOM AND RECOGNITION IN *SAMSON AGONISTES*

## David Gay

WISDOM, AS Milton understood it, is the virtue which motivates a person to seek God's will. Wisdom literature offers guidance and instruction to the individual searcher. Biblical wisdom literature is characterized by the use of proverbs, aphorisms, and sayings, as well as riddles and parables. The literary devices of wisdom are found throughout the Bible and have a special prominence in the Gospels. The representative texts of wisdom include Proverbs, Ecclesiastes, and Job in the Old Testament, as well as the apocryphal books of Sirach and Solomon. Like other kinds of biblical literature, wisdom finds its orienting focus in creation: "The Lord by wisdom hath founded the earth; by understanding hath he established the heavens" (Prov. iii, 19). The framing of moral instruction in the context of the event of creation carries with it the conviction that the individual is literally born, by virtue of being newly created, in every act of moral decision. Milton maintains and develops the close relationship between conduct and creation in his three major poems. In *Paradise Lost*, for example, Raphael braces Adam against the Fall by telling him the story of creation. In *Paradise Regained*, Jesus is expected to "vanquish by wisdom hellish wiles" (I, 175), creation itself being the conquest of chaos by wisdom. In *Samson Agonistes*, on the other hand, the memory of creation is painful as Samson ponders his sense of exile from God's "prime decree" of light.[1] In each case, the creation event implies grace in the gift of life, law in the obligations of remembrance ("Remember now thy Creator in the days of thy youth," Eccles. xii, 1), and salvation in God's actions in the spheres of nature and history, space and time, which issue for humanity in "the beginning." The relationship between conduct and creation is a conventional feature of biblical wisdom.

In *Paradise Lost*, the Father calls the Son "My word, my wisdom" (III, 170). In Raphael's narrative the Son is the agent of creation; in Michael's narrative he is the culmination of revelation and the agent of recreation. In both his creative and recreative aspects, the Son fulfills his role as divine wisdom. The connection between wisdom and revelation declares Milton's position on the source of true wisdom. The source of wisdom posed difficult questions in the Renaissance, a period which is often represented in terms of the tension between humanists, who locate wisdom in the order of natural human ability and apply it to the demands of public life, and reformers who consider the endowments of reason, will, and understanding to have been irretrievably damaged by the Fall.[2] Eugene Rice summarizes the view of Luther, for whom the dependence of human wisdom on divine grace is unconditional: "The truly wise man . . . thus finds his only adequate foundation in Christ. His roots are in God, and he derives the nourishment of wisdom and goodness through them alone. He seeks the wisdom-giving knowledge of secret, hidden and invisible things in Revelation and is conscious that only the man reformed by faith and divine illumination can attain and contemplate them."[3]

How does Milton's idea of wisdom compare with this position? In the *Christian Doctrine*, Milton defines wisdom as the "VIRTUE BY WHICH WE EARNESTLY SEARCH OUT GOD'S WILL, CLING TO IT WITH ALL DILIGENCE ONCE WE HAVE UNDERSTOOD IT, AND GOVERN ALL OUR ACTIONS BY ITS RULE."[4] Milton's definition echoes the many biblical proverbial expressions concerned with seeking, such as the Gospel proverb "seek, and ye shall find" (Matt. vii, 7). Jesus himself confesses: "I seek not mine own will, but the will of the Father which hath sent me" (John v, 30). One of the supporting texts Milton selects in the *Christian Doctrine,* among several from Proverbs and Ecclesiastes, is James i, 5: "if any one of you is lacking in wisdom, let him ask it of God who gives it to all men liberally" (YP, p. 648). Milton's definition of wisdom values the effort of the seeker, but these scriptural examples and exhortations base the search on divine grace and revelation. Milton accordingly views human effort as being summoned and aroused in a climate of faith which places seeking under the countenance and aid of divine grace. In this respect, he is wholly consistent with biblical writers who frame wisdom in the context of divine creation. It is precisely in this spirit that Milton seeks guidance and enlightenment in the *Christian Doctrine,* which is mainly a searching of the scriptures. He declares the same spirit in his sense of his poetic vocation: individual erudition and effort can only be guided and enriched by divine grace. And in the major poems the human characters are all finally illuminated by their Creator while the devils persist in mazes of error. In *Paradise Lost,* Raphael and Michael descend from heaven bringing to Adam and Eve their enlightening narratives of creation and recreation. In *Paradise Regained,* the heavens open, the dove descends, and a voice proclaims Jesus the Son of God. In *Samson Agonistes,* the story of

Samson's birth concerns a fiery, twice-descending angel who declares Samson's unique relationship with God and who goes with Samson, as the Chorus hopes, to the Temple of Dagon. These symbolic patterns of light, descent, and guidance locate Milton's idea of wisdom in the order of grace. Conduct, creation, and individual identity are inseparable aspects of that virtue "by which we earnestly search out God's will."

I

Wisdom is a central theme in Milton's poetry and prose, but *Samson Agonistes,* by virtue of its compressed action, is perhaps Milton's most concentrated examination of the problem of wisdom. Samson is certainly preoccupied wth the nature of personal as well as political wisdom: "what is strength without a double share / Of wisdom?" (53–54) he asks in the prologue. The poem concludes with the Chorus's meditation on wisdom:

> All is best, though we oft doubt,
> What th' unsearchable dispose
> Of highest wisdom brings about,
> And ever best found in the close.          (1745–48)

The desire for the consolations of wisdom is a notable characteristic of the Chorus. "Many are the sayings of the wise," they observe, "In ancient and in modern books enroll'd" (652–53). The Hebrew title of Proverbs— *mashal*—is usually translated simply as "sayings," and the speeches of the Chorus are rich in allusions to, as well as replicas of, these sayings.[5]

My purpose is to consider the role of the proverbial, aphoristic discourse of wisdom in *Samson Agonistes* with its implications for the structure of the poem. By *structure* I mean specifically the event of recognition which Aristotle defines as "a change from ignorance to knowledge—resulting in love or hate—by those marked out for good fortune or bad fortune."[6] Reversal and recognition distinguish Aristotle's idea of the complex plot and so are defining principles in tragic structure. In *Samson Agonistes,* recognition occurs when Samson experiences the "rousing motions" which reverse his prior intentions and lead him to proceed to the Philistine temple. Milton thus achieves the ideal coincidence of reversal and recognition Aristotle admired in the *Oedipus Rex* (p. 84). Wisdom is an aspect of recognition in *Samson Agonistes* because wisdom provides the clarification of the divine will in the moral and experiential dimensions of a single moment. As in Milton's biblical sources, the moment of Samson's personal illumination is oriented in the event of Creation. In consequence, wisdom and recognition become mutually illuminating as Milton adjusts the structural principle of recognition to the criteria of wisdom as a theological virtue founded on grace.

While the Creator may be the source of Samson's illumination, Milton appoints the Chorus to interpret and even validate the illumination from a tentative and limited human vantage point. The Chorus searches out "th'unsearchable" by *judging* the authenticity of Samson's "rousing motions" at the close of the poem. Prior to Samson's climactic recognition, the Chorus also judges the lesser moments of recognition which occur in each of the middle episodes and which define their separate structures. The recognition of Harapha as a coward is an example of one such lesser moment, and the judgment the Chorus passes upon him comes with hindsight. How these lesser moments of recognition comment on the structure of the larger poem, and vice versa, is a challenging critical problem. My approach to this problem is based on the judgment the Chorus passes on Dalila. While the Chorus recognizes Samson's inner virtue after he destroys the temple, it earlier refuses to recognize Dalila's claim to heroic stature made in her moment of self-recognition. This moment occurs when Dalila compares herself to Jael and, implicitly, to Deborah, two heroines from the early period of the judges, the latter endowed with wisdom and prophetic authority. Comparisons between Dalila and Jael and Deborah have become a focus of debate in Milton criticism through the work of Jacqueline DiSalvo and in biblical studies through the work of Mieke Bal.[7] The typology which connects Dalila to Jael and Deborah, and the debate which now surrounds it, is a necessary focus for the relation between wisdom and recognition in *Samson Agonistes.*

My approach to this typology begins with an allusion to Proverbs contained in the phrase "honied words." The phrase signals the Chorus's rejection of Dalila's identification with Jael and Deborah (that she identifies with both figures is an assumption which this study will support). The phrase occurs in the choral speech which marks the departure of Dalila and the arrival of Harapha. As Dalila makes her exit, the Chorus tells Samson to "Look now for no enchanting voice, nor fear / The bait of honied words; a rougher tongue / Draws hitherward" (1065–67). The "rougher tongue" belongs to the giant Harapha, who should provide an intimidating physical spectacle and who is imagined in Samson's visually descriptive challenge as a heavily armed ancestor of Goliath. Why, then, does the Chorus identify him by his "rougher tongue"? One reason is that *Samson Agonistes,* like *Paradise Regained,* consists of dialogue in which words are the weapons of a spiritual warfare. Speech is perhaps most intensely experienced in the condition of blindness. A more central reason, from the standpoint of this study, is the priority which biblical wisdom literature places on the power of speech. *Samson Agonistes* emulates and interprets biblical injunctions concerning the moral gravity of the spoken word and the power of language to injure or to heal, to edify or to destroy, to frame riddles or to break vows. It is in this context especially that Harapha's "rougher tongue" succeeds Dalila's "honied words."

Honey is frequently the Bible's metaphor for its own laws, precepts, poems, and narratives. Consider Psalm xix, 9–10:

> The fear of the Lord is clean, enduring forever: the judgments of the Lord are true and righteous altogether.
> More to be desired are they than gold, yea, than much fine gold: sweeter also than honey and the honeycomb.

Heather Asals has noted the anagogic meaning of this reference: "Generated out of the tale of the lion and the honeycomb traditional to the Samson story, the 'honied words' of Dalila, in the context of Christian exegesis, identify her with the Word and the Gospel." Dalila, as the former instrument of Samson's destruction and the present agent of his regeneration, has her dual purpose reconciled in a vantage point which includes, as Asals says, the Word and the gospel.[8] I intend to emphasize the significance of "honied words" primarily in the typological frameworks of Judges and Proverbs, with some consideration of important elements in the New Testament. In the typology of Judges, the allusion links Dalila directly to Deborah. In Proverbs, the allusion evokes the dichotomous personifications of wisdom, a woman of understanding and folly, a strange, foreign, and seductive woman. Typology is a necessary focus because it is essential to Milton's poetic strategies and because Dalila's comparison of herself to Deborah amounts to the construction of a typology: her "honied words" connect her to Deborah through the etymological meaning of the name Deborah: "the honey bee."[9] *Samson Agonistes* works out a pattern of history on a scale that is necessarily more limited than that of *Paradise Lost* by emphasizing typology, which is interpretation rooted in history. Samson, Dalila, and the Chorus seek the evidence of that pattern and their location within it by debating the wisdom of human action in time.

The Chorus's exhortation to Samson to fear no more "the bait of honied words" reads like a proverb: the tribal elders are telling Samson what he should do. The immediate source of "honied words" is surely Proverbs v, 1–3:

My son, attend unto my wisdom, and bow thine ear to my understanding:
That thou mayest regard discretion, and that thy lips may keep knowledge.
For the lips of a strange woman drop as a honeycomb, and her mouth is
smoother than oil.

This portrait of the so-called foreign or strange woman of Proverbs, the
temptress whose presence contrasts with the virtuous woman of wisdom,
gives priority to her words, not her looks. The same priority is evident in
Milton's treatment of Dalila. True, the Chorus does dwell on her spectacu-
lar entrance, but their description of her is largely a composite of biblical
allusions, especially to the destruction of the ships of Tarshish in Psalm
xlviii, and when she exits it is her words they remember: her "honied
words." Whatever threat Dalila poses consists in the arguments she con-
structs and the narratives she creates more than in whatever visual erotic
appeal her presence provokes in Samson's memory.

The priority of the verbal over the visual in the case of Proverbs v, 1–
3, is corroborated by James G. Williams: "The theme of language is so
pervasive in older wisdom, as represented in Proverbs, that it may even
be the key to comprehending the image of the 'stranger woman' who
appears as a seductive lure to the man trying to negotiate his way through
life's hazards. . . . Her weapons are not so much her beauty or sexually
seductive wiles as her manner of using language."[10] How does Dalila use
language? Let us assume that "honied words" refers specifically to her
comparison of herself to Jael and Deborah, given the etymology of Deborah's name. Here Dalila uses language to interpret her own position in the
poem. Dalila is perhaps most threatening to Samson in her bold but
defensible and reasonable comparison of herself to Jael, who assassinated
Sisera, the leader of an invading army (Judg. iv), and to Deborah, who
inspired the armies of Israel in the face of invasion and who celebrated
Jael's deed in her famous song (Judg. v). This, then, is Dalila's interpretation, and it appropriates what Samson and the Israelites most prize: the
narratives of their salvation history.

## II

We should now consider the nature of proverbial discourse in terms
of gender and patriarchy. Proverbial discourse is generally characterized
as patriarchal, although the concluding chapters of Proverbs contain maternal wisdom in the prophecy taught to Lemuel by his mother and in the
portrait of the woman of worth in Proverbs xxxi. Proverbs 5, 1–3 begins
with the apostrophe issued from a father to a son: "My son, be attentive to
my wisdom." The patriarchal emphasis is aligned with the wisdom of age

and experience that is passed on from generation to generation. As Northrop Frye puts it, wisdom "goes with the authority of seniors, whose longer experience in the tried and tested modes of action makes them wiser than the young." Wisdom thus becomes an issue of decorum as Aristotle suggests in the *Rhetoric*, where he advises that "the use of maxims is suited to speakers of mature years, and to arguments on matters in which one is experienced. In a young man, uttering maxims is—like telling stories—unbecoming."[11]

The collectors and compilers of proverbs, aphorisms, and maxims in the Renaissance generally viewed their treasures as a paternal legacy. William Camden, speaking of homespun British proverbs that are still with us, proverbs such as "a new broom sweeps clean," describes proverbial sayings "grounded upon long experience" as "beeing worthy to have a place among the wisest Speeches." As John Clarke said of his proverb collection: "herein is couched and contracted the *quintessence,* marrow, *creame,* flower and *pith* of learning, eloquence and *wisedome:* our wise forefathers, and the learned in all ages, *briefely* transmitting to us in *Proverbs*, the treasures of their experience, and knowledge, like gold, *much in litle:* as the confluence of light, in one *Sunne,* of heat in one *fire.*" Authors of proverbs in Clarke's survey include "the gravest senators, the greatest Emperours, the inspired pen-men of sacred oracles . . . our most blessed Saviour himselfe chusing, and using them, upon incidentall occasions."[12]

If moral conduct depends on wisdom, then so too does eloquence. In *Paradise Lost,* for example, after advising Adam to be "lowly wise / Think only what concerns thee and thy being" (VIII, 173–74), the angel Raphael immediately describes speech as the expression of divine grace within the appointed limits of the human condition:

> Nor are thy lips ungraceful, Sire of men,
> Nor tongue ineloquent; for God on thee
> Abundantly his gifts hath also pour'd
> Inward and outward both, his image fair.     (VIII, 218–21)

The relation between eloquence and divinity is summarized in Thomas Wilson's *The Arte of Rhetorique:*

For he that is emonge the reasonable, of all moste reasonable, and emonge the wittye, of all most wittye, and emonge the eloquente, of all mooste eloquente: him thincke I emonge all menne, not onelye to be taken for a singulr manne, but rather to be counted for halfe a God. For in sekynge the excellencye hereof, the soner he draweth to perfection, the nygher he commeth to GOD who is the chiefe wisdome, and therefore called God, because he is most wise, or rather wisdome itself.[13]

Solomon was both a father and a king, and the traditional attribution of Proverbs to Solomon creates an important link between political and personal authority, or between what Dalila calls public and private "respects." This link is important in all of Milton's major poems if we recall that Adam, Jesus, and Samson represent the body politic, either as the "whole created race" (fallen in Adam and redeemed in Jesus), or, in Samson's case, as the immediate destiny of a community of Israelites. Theories of monarchical authority, which Milton clearly opposed, were derived in part from viewing the monarch in a typological perspective. The figure of Solomon was prominent in the iconography of the court of James I, who composed a series of aphorisms for his son, Henry, Prince of Wales, under the title *Basilikon Doron*, the gift of the King. The collection, which contemplates a king's responsibility to God and his subjects, was later converted into seven hundred verse quatrains and published as *Patrikon Doron*, the father's gift. The latter version contains a memorable reference to Samson:

> Frustrate, by wisdom, the Bane-bodeing Charms
> (As did *Ulysses*) of a *Syren*-tongue:
> From thence it was stout *Sampson* took his harms;
> From thence it is our first of mischief sprung. [14]

As a literature of parental instruction, the discourse of wisdom is marked by a conservative, cautious attitude which is featured in the paranoia of sirens noted above. *Caution* means that the father seeks to order the son's conduct in terms of a predictable stability which conserves and consolidates the profits of experience without necessarily seeking to revolutionize the order in which experience unfolds. Concern for stability is characteristic of what Frye calls the "anxiety of continuity" in biblical wisdom (p. 121). When the purveyor of wisdom is an anointed king we might expect that concern to be heightened. A similar concern is equally valid, however, when the writer seeks to preserve a commonwealth from the imminent return of monarchy. Hence, on the eve of the Restoration, in the second edition of *The Readie and Easie Way to Establish a True Commonwealth*, Milton asks his fellow citizens: "Shall we never grow old anough to be wise to make seasonable use of gravest authorities, experiences, examples?" (YP VII, p. 448).

The anxiety of continuity is evident in what James G. Williams calls the "wisdom of order." The wisdom of order shows "an overwhelming preference to affirm and undergird society and tradition rather than the individual and novelty" (*Pondered*, p. 42). The wisdom of counterorder, on the other hand, challenges tradition either through personal experience which may contradict the wisdom of order, as in Ecclesiastes, or through the vision of a higher, renovated order, as in the beatitudes. In both cases, the proverb of counterorder "moves the mind to look into a small aspect of an accepted order or to deconstruct the received state of things on the basis of a vision that requires a counter-order" (*Women Recounted*, p. 21). The tensions between these forms of wisdom emerge in the irreconcilable, competing claims made by Samson, the Chorus, and Dalila. As a judge in Israel, Samson is the supposed successor to Deborah, but he lacks wisdom equal to this strength until he claims valid inspiration and the climax occurs. Dalila defies the "wise fathers" who surround and control her by claiming a valid comparison between herself and Jael and Deborah. The Chorus, siding naturally with Samson, is left to its own judgments concerning the validity of both claims. Succession and comparison are typological: they establish order and continuity in history. By allowing his characters to seek justification in the field of typology, Milton tests the very nature of typological thought.

## III

When the Chorus tells Samson to fear no more "the bait of honied words," they indicate in part that the situation is changing, and a new situation requires a new proverb. As we have already noted, the phrase "honied words" classifies Dalila in terms of the dichotomous personification of the feminine which informs the text of Proverbs. One part of the dichotomy is the personification of wisdom as a woman of honor and integrity; the other part involves the figure of the stranger or foreign woman whose acquaintance brings folly and disaster. It is one thing to identify the source of the allusion, profiting, as critics do, from the anagnorisis of hindsight. What also matters are the consequences and implications of the act of classification, which is the event of naming or recognizing Dalila as the foreign woman of Proverbs by the Chorus, and potentially by literary critics.

Generally speaking, the classifying or naming of a particular character or individual provides a means of neutralizing the threat that that character poses to a particular group. Samson, who appears to have been neutralized as a military threat to the Philistines, feels the sting of words—"Am I not sung and proverb'd for a Fool / In every street" (203–04)—and the sting of sight: "Perhaps my enemies . . . come to stare / At my affliction" (113–14). The relevant biblical illustration is found in Hebrews, chapter x:

But call to remembrance the former days, in which, after ye were *illumi-nated*, ye endured a great fight of afflictions;

Partly, whilst ye were made a *gazingstock* both by reproaches and afflictions; and partly, whilst ye became companions of them that were so used. (32–33, emphasis mine).

.Two kinds of recognition are distinguished in this passage: the spiritual and the corporeal. The ensuing Hebrews, chapter xi, enshrines Samson as a hero of faith after defining faith as the object of spiritual recognition, "the evidence of things not seen."

Like Samson, Dalila is subjected to the judgmental gaze of others. Her defense, interpreted as defection from the law of marriage by Samson, is, in her own view, revolutionary. It takes the form of her bold comparison of herself to the heroines of Israel as she convincingly approxi-mates the narrative of Jael and Sisera to her own experience. The compari-son begins, interestingly, with a proverb:

> Fame if not double-fac't is double-mouth'd,
> And with contrary blast proclaims most deeds;
> On both his wings, one black, the other white,
> Bears greatest names in his wild aery flight.           (971–74)

Her maxim on fame argues that history is purely a matter of how one looks at it. She then elaborates the particulars of her "contrary blast" from the generalities of her proverb:

> My name perhaps among the Circumcis'd
> In *Dan*, in *Judah*, and the bordering Tribes,
> To all posterity may stand defam'd,
> With malediction mention'd, and the blot
> Of falsehood most unconjugal traduc't.
> But in my country where I most desire,
> In *Ekron, Gaza, Asdod*, and in *Gath*
> I shall be nam'd among the famousest
> Of Women, sung at solemn festivals,
> Living and dead recorded, who to save
> Her country from a fierce destroyer, chose
> Above the faith of wedlock bands, my tomb
> With odors visited and annual flowers.
> Not less renown'd than in Mount *Ephraim*,
> *Jael*, who with inhospitable guile
> Smote *Sisera* sleeping through the Temples nail'd.
> Nor shall I count it heinous to enjoy
> The public marks of honor and reward
> Conferr'd upon me, for the piety
> Which to my country I was judg'd to have shown.[15]      (975–94)

Stanley Fish examines the act of interpretation in the motif of marking or writing upon a blank surface.[16] The motif Fish observes functions significantly in Dalila's comparison of herself to Jael. Dalila concedes that she will be considered a blot or stigma in the written records of Israel, even as writing itself is a stigma upon a blank page. In the unwritten records of her own country, however, the public marks of honor are still possible. The page is still clean. By comparing herself to Jael, Dalila appropriates, if only temporarily, the narrative in which Samson has been trying to find his place: a narrative of national deliverance. The Chorus's reference to Dalila's "honied words" attempts to repudiate her comparison with Jael and seeks to neutralize her claim by identifying her with a different, less honorable aspect of the feminine within their own traditions.

The allusion appears to mediate our understanding of the middle episode of *Samson Agonistes* by inviting us to read the text of Judges, the source of the dramatic action, in terms of the text of Proverbs, the source of the allusion. The episode provides a particular kind of temporal experience; the proverb, being by nature an attempt to comprehend a particular kind of experience, seeks to view or recognize the episode as if under the aspect of eternity. Coupled with this notion of transcendence is the notion of authority, which is essential to the meaning of the Hebrew word for proverb, *mashal*. According to Carole Fontaine, the "citation of a proverb or saying to analyze a situation (whether social or literary) may be termed a 'proverb performance.' " Fontaine points out that *mashal*, or "saying," has two senses: one of similarity and one of authority. The proverb, she argues, "expresses a connection between a psychological attitude and the subsequent effects of that orientation. Once this 'similitude' is understood, the proverb then allows people to 'rule over' such situations wherever they are encountered. . . . Proverbs are not simply 'observational,' but, rather, persuasive sayings that exert social control." Fontaine's theory is supported by the seventeenth-century commentary of Robert Allen:

*King Salomons Proverbs* or *Parables* onely, are worthy to be called (as they are in the Hebrew tongue) *Meshalim* of the verbe *Mashal*, which signifieth *to beare a chief rule*, or *to have a singular dominion and soveraignty above other*. For these *sentences* of this most wise *King*, are of like excellency, with the *King* himselfe: they are of special dignity and preheminence, even predominant, and of very rare excellency, as it were bright shining Diamonds, or glistering Starres, to adorne and beautify speeches of more large discourse.

Allen's metaphor of the "glistering Starres" is particularly apt to the general role of the proverb or proverb allusion, suggesting as it does the functions of elevation and watchfulness, transcendence and vision, within the progress of a "more large discourse."[17]

Proverbs are often delivered by characters immersed in the very circumstances they seek to understand. It is wise to search for understanding but folly to presume one possesses it totally. Samson learns this distinction; so too does the Chorus over the course of the poem. In order to account thoroughly for the function of wisdom allusions in *Samson Agonistes*, we must, as critics of the poem have always done, evaluate the fallibility of the Chorus. Let us therefore consider a second, misogynistic edict delivered by the Chorus:

> Favor'd of Heav'n who finds
> One virtuous, rarely found,
> That in domestic good combines:
> Happy that house! his way to peace is smooth:
> But virtue which breaks through all opposition,
> And all temptation can remove,
> Most shines and most acceptable is above.
> Therefore God's universal Law
> Gave to the man despotic power
> Over his female in due awe,
> Nor from that right to part an hour,
> Smile she or lour:
> So shall he least confusion draw
> On his whole life, not sway'd
> By female usurpation, nor dismay'd.          (1046–60)

This edict follows the traditional formula of wisdom by offering advice in a specific, experiential context. In this case the context is marriage. The statement concerning "God's universal Law" is offered with the force of a general, timeless truth. While some readers may still attribute its misogyny directly to Milton, it is really a provisional interpretation of the law in a tragic, and therefore limited, context. Indeed, the tragic element is made more acute by the paraphrase of Proverbs xxi, 10–11, the portrait of the woman of worth, which precedes the maxim of "despotic power," and which establishes the dichotomous personification of the feminine completed by the phrase "honied words," which appears just seven lines later. There can be no timeless quality to this edict because the events which the Chorus interprets have not yet reached their conclusion. In fact, the rigidity of the Chorus's law is about to be destabilized by the motions of grace. A hint of this irony is conveyed even in the structure of the Chorus's statement since the verb "Gave" and its object, "power," connote grace and law, respectively.

Instead of attributing the Chorus's misogyny to Milton, we must bear in mind how Milton characterizes the Chorus in terms of the social motivation of wisdom. In the case of *Samson Agonistes,* the proverbs delivered by the Chorus represent attempts to bring the obviously dissonant and disorderly facts of Samson's career, and particularly his experience with Dalila, into some form of interpretive coherence. The interpretive process characterizes the Chorus as fallible. The use of proverbs by the Chorus in the wake of Samson's exchange with Dalila reflects their anxieties for continuity and interpretation, two anxieties which are, perhaps, ultimately inseparable. The "anxiety of continuity," let us recall, is Frye's term for one of the central characteristics of wisdom literature. According to Frye, if prophecy is the individualizing of the revolutionary impulse in biblical history, then wisdom is the individualizing of the law: "Law is general: wisdom begins in interpreting and commenting on law, and applying it to specific and variable situations" (p. 121). Ideally, this means allowing the morality of the law to govern and inform our thoughts, actions, and perceptions. Samson's career falls short of the ideals of the revolutionary role which was prophesied for him while many of the proverbs of the Chorus, particularly its assertion of despotic male authority, fall short of the ideal of the law. What we discover in those choral proverbs, which presume, in their rhetorical nature as generalized truths, to transcend the temporal movement of the drama, is the verbal counterpart, in the sphere of the law, of Samson's failed efforts as a revolutionary in the sphere of prophecy: both presume a degree of divine authority which they perhaps have not been granted. Only the Semichorus portrays an authority equal to the inward illumination which causes Samson, after the recognition of the "rousing motions," and with the caution rather than the reckless presumption of genuine liberty, to proceed to the temple.

## IV

When the Chorus labels Dalila as the foreign woman of Proverbs, they react against her claim to have fulfilled for the Philistines the very offices to which Samson was appointed for Israel: deliverer, prophet, and giver of wisdom. Deborah was all of these things, and Dalila emulates Deborah by predicting the sweetness of her own future reputation. Deborah was a popular first name in the seventeenth century; Milton gave the name to his third and perhaps favorite daughter. The notion that the biblical Deborah was a speaker of "honied words" is played upon by a number of Renaissance poets and theologians, including Thomas Heywood:

The name *Deborah,* in the originall, implyeth a *Word,* or a *Bee;* neither was her name any way averse to her nature, for as she was mellifluous in her tongue, when she either pronounced the sacred oracles of God, or sat upon any judicatory causes, amongst his people: so she had also a sting at all times, upon any just occasion to wound and be avenged on his enemies the *Canaanites,* who then most barbarously and cruelly oppressed his owne chosen nation.[18]

The sixteenth-century theologian Peter Martyr also speaks of Deborah as fulfilling the meaning of her name: "And if we should look upon the Etimology of her name, we shall thinke that her orations were verye sweete. For Deborah with the Hebrues is a bee, which beast we know is a diligent artificer in makyng of hony."[19] For both writers, the exception of Deborah as woman judge is made to reinforce the rule of a male-dominated hierarchy of the sexes. For Heywood, the judgeship of Deborah is a necessary scourge to male pride; for Martyr it is evidence that God's power "is not bounde unto noble men and strong men, but he can easilye use the weake and feable ones" (cap. 4, fol. 93). Spenser cites Deborah in *The Faerie Queene* (III, iv, 2) as part of his homage to Elizabeth I. As with Peter Martyr's opinion of Deborah's judgeship, the implication in Spenser's comparison is that Elizabeth's reign was an act of exceptional providence. But to marvel at exceptions is to strengthen the rule: in Book V of *The Faerie Queene,* Britomart ascends the throne of wisdom after restoring the hierarchy violated by her adversaries:

> And changing all that forme of common weale,
> The liberty of women did repeale,
> Which they had long usurpt; and them restoring
> To mens subjection, did true Justice deal:
> That all they as a Goddesse her adoring.
> Her wisedome did admire, and hearkned to her loring.    (vii, 42)

Milton presents a wise and spiritually warfaring Lady in *Comus,* but disparages the historical figure of the woman warrior in his treatment of Boadicea in the *History of Britain.* He dismisses antique historians who suppose that "with the Britans it was usual for Woemen to be thir Leaders" (YP V, p. 79). In *Samson Agonistes,* the propriety of roles in relation to gender corresponds to distinction between public and private responsibilities. Both Jael and Dalila take action in private, domestic settings, offending against the laws of hospitality and matrimony for the sake of public or national interests. Samson sets up a double standard in his condemnation of Dalila: public and private interests were joined in his proposed first marriage to the Woman of Timna since the marriage was supposed to have provided some means or "occasion" to advance the public cause of Israel's deliverance, though it is hard to see how. We can say, at least, that the condition of double standards and the necessity of divided loyalties justify Milton's choice of the tragic form. Perhaps Milton saw in Judges, with its sense of historical crisis, its questioning of charismatic leadership, and its close interconnection of sexual and political violence the disturbed and disorderly reflection of his era.

In the framework of the entire Bible, both Old and New Testaments, Samson is established as a type of Christ when he is named a hero of faith in Hebrews xi, 32. The same verse, incidentally, omits Deborah in favor of Barak, the ineffectual, doubt-ridden Hebrew general who turned to Deborah for inspiration. In the local context of Judges, Samson can be linked typologically to Deborah through the honey he gathered from the body of the lion he killed on his way to Timna, as well as through the riddle he invented afterwards: "Out of the eater came forth meat, and out of the strong came forth sweetness" (Judg. xiv, 14). The riddle is a device of wisdom literature. Milton's Samson poses a riddle when he asks, "what is strength without a double share / Of wisdom?" Within Judges, the link between honey (Samson's lion) and the honey bee (Deborah) serves to contrast the wise prophetess from the errant, aimless, practical joker the biblical Samson so often is. The difference between Deborah's success and Samson's failures implies a gradual falling away from the ideals of the divine summons or charisma of judgeship. Judges therefore gives us, as Gerhard von Rad argues, a pessimistic view of charismatic political leadership. In the larger context of Christian typological exegesis, however, we find that Samson's failures do not necessarily threaten his status as a type, for typology depends to some extent, as Patricia Parker has suggested, upon a dialectic of approximation and difference, and even upon a "crucial element of failure and destruction" which allows the type to be superseded by the figure of Christ.[20]

## V

The dialectic of approximation and difference in typological relations is a crucial element in the encounter between Samson and Dalila. Judges provides both heroes and heroines to identify with. Perhaps what embitters Samson most is his sense of similarity to Dalila when she claims the "masculine" office of deliverer while reminding him of his "effeminate" weakness. I have called typology a theory of history. When the nature of political power and the persistence of violent political change are connected to issues of gender, the meaning of history as a term in critical discourse is open to question.

Mieke Bal's major studies of Judges pursue this connection to its fullest extent.[21] Jacqueline DiSalvo examines similar connections in her recent statements on *Samson Agonistes*. Both scholars pursue the parallels between Dalila and Jael and Deborah. For Bal, literary representation is an integral part of the record of history. If the record is constituted in the interests of certain versions of political coherence, then its status as representation makes it both "a meaningful act of cultural expression as well as an instrument of political and social repression" (*Death and Dissymmetry*, p. 18). What Bal terms "counter-coherence," really a strategy of reading, makes it possible to "glimpse a possible alternative main line that changes the entire status of the book as document" (p. 7). One feature of this alternative is the positive comparison of Dalila and Jael, a comparison that opens the relations between gender and political violence to new scrutiny. DiSalvo is equally concerned with *Samson Agonistes* as representation. In comparing Milton and Brecht, she seeks to "see what is historically specific in Milton's representation" and to "reveal the issues involved in the construction of Milton's discourse" (p. 204). The equation of Dalila and Jael in *Samson Agonistes* becomes, as it does for Bal in Judges, an "alternative reconstruction of the text" (p. 225). Both scholars are concerned with the nexus of sexual and political authority. For Bal, the story of Dalila, which has been traditionally used to illustrate "an 'eternal' truth: women are treacherous, especially in love" (p. 24), can be reversed. She argues that since "the identity of men depends heavily on their control over women as sexual beings, this reversal of power is what threatens them most. This is the strongest motivation for the survival of these stories [of Dalila and Jael] as ideostories" (p. 27).

The aspect of this discussion which I will pursue concerns the positive comparison of Dalila and Jael, which occurs in a moment of recognition at the end of the middle episode of *Samson Agonistes*, to the overall structure of the poem, particularly as it is defined by the pivotal anagnorisis of Samson's "rousing motions." This means treating the poem, as both DiSalvo and Bal insist, as the literary representation, and therefore interpretation, of historic events. Two aspects of representation are relevant. The first considers a representation of events as one of a number of possible, alternative representations. The second concerns the relationship between the form of representation, or genre, and issues of gender.

Choice of genre is, of course, important to the poet's approach to the story. Choices signal the poet's commitment to the issues of what happened, how it happened, and how it might be mediated for a particular audience. *Samson Agonistes* is a tragic poem modeled on the greatest classical examples as well as, although to a lesser extent, the critical precepts of Aristotle. As such, its central anagnorisis or moment of recognition defines, to a large extent, the structure of the entire poem. Dalila's identification with Jael and Samson's "rousing motions" are structurally parallel: both consist of moments of recognition followed by departures. What distinguishes the two recognitions is that Samson's recognition defines the overall structure of Milton's representation of the Judges narrative. Dalila's does not.

*Samson Agonistes* is a tragic poem which is concerned with the history of a people. The premise that history is a male province defined by masculine acts of war and violence is exposed and criticized by both Bal and DiSalvo. An important parallel emerges between the poem and its biblical source at this point. While Judges, chapter v, the Song of Deborah, is poetry, Judges, chapter iv, the prose narrative which records the same events, and which precedes the Song of Deborah in the Bible, was, in fact, written at a later date. The prose version appears to offer, as Frye describes it, "one of many possible ways of explaining what happened" (p. 215). Bal argues, however, that in the culture in which the story of Jael was recorded, lyric and epic were considered feminine and masculine forms, respectively (*Murder*, p. 124). In the culture in which Judges is recreated as *Samson Agonistes*, we may further observe what Joseph Wittreich terms the "genderfication of genre," whereby epic and prophecy especially, but also tragedy, were considered male domains (*Feminist Milton*, p. 73). The presiding criterion for the masculinity of these genres is overt concern with history.

Milton understood genre as a hierarchy. Samson's "rousing motions" provide the structural hinge of a tragic poem. These motions signal Samson's return to the sphere of history from which he has been exiled and determine the outcome of the poem. Dalila's identification with Jael is lyrical: a highly charged poetic flight which resides within a larger poem without really defining or determining its overall structure. Both recognitions are prophetic. Dalila predicts she will acquire the "marks of public honour"; Samson says "This day shall be remarkable in my life," that is, re-*mark*-ed, re-written, re-interpreted, re-deemed. The sense of the "remarkable" becomes a nexus of literary form and the interpretation of history. The structure of the poem does subordinate Dalila's recognition to Samson's; this subordination does not, however, endorse the conception of a preeminently male history disrupted by female treachery that Samson offers in the middle episodes. The exploits Samson recounts are, for the most part, pointless, time-wasting pseudoactions which confuse thoughtless and even subhuman male license with genuine human liberty. Dalila's "honied words" become an attack on the confusion of license and liberty in Samson's thinking. History, the poem argues, consists only of those moments in which God, not Samson, freely acts. This vision of history is the inheritance of genuine liberty.

## VI

In his challenging analysis of *Samson Agonistes*, Stanley Fish draws attention to the motif of the marking or inscribing of interpretations upon blank surfaces. When Manoa and the Chorus decide to cleanse Samson's body after his death, for example, Fish paraphrases their intention: "Let us erase from the body what time and history have inscribed on it, and when it is once again a smooth blank surface, let us inscribe on it those significances that support the story we wish to tell ourselves" (p. 563). Dalila, Fish contends, compares herself to Jael because she is anxious to be "proverbed": "She assimilates herself to a narrative type (the woman who chooses patriotism before love) even before the story is written. She cannot conceive of herself apart from some conventional category, and it really doesn't matter to her which category it is" (p. 584). Fish argues that the activities of narration and interpretation, which are indeed what *Samson Agonistes* is all about, represent failed attempts to achieve illusory, self-deceiving versions of coherence and consistency: "The only wisdom to be carried away from the play is that there is no wisdom to be carried away, and that we are alone, like Samson, and like the children of Israel of whom it is said in the last verse of Judges: 'and every man did that which was right in his own eyes' " (p. 586).

Fish's argument can be aligned with the recent interpretation advanced by Joseph Wittreich: if Wittreich views the poem as a tragedy of false prophecy, then Fish views the poem as a tragedy of false wisdom.[22] Fish's conclusion—that "the only wisdom to be carried away from the play is that there is no wisdom to be carried away"—offers (as does Wittreich's) a rigid and reductive summation after an analysis as subtle and complex as the poem itself. In countering the assertion that "there is no wisdom," let us consider the quotation from Judges which concludes Fish's study— "and every man did that which was right in his own eyes" (Judg. xxi, 25). The quotation establishes, if read in its context at the end of Judges, a note of anticipation and deferral that suggests that the redactor of Judges was conscious of the position of the narrative between two relatively idealized periods of charismatic military leadership, the periods of Joshua and David. As Gerhard von Rad has suggested, "Behind these narratives lies, it would seem, the unspoken question, where is the one who serves his people as deliverer not merely on one occasion alone?" (p. 329). I contend that this question, especially since it is "unspoken," presents the essential tension in biblical narrative as Milton read it. The same essential tension is recreated in *Samson Agonistes*.

*Samson Agonistes* is largely about the act of interpretation, and the Chorus, with its fixed, provisional interpretations of events, portrays the anxiety for coherence and continuity in its most acute and, in places, fallible form. But this is not the measure of *Samson Agonistes*. The tensions between prophecy and wisdom which are established in the fabric of biblical allusion in the poem; the modeling of characters' speeches on different biblical modes such as psalmody, prophecy, and wisdom; and the manner in which allusions extend their scopes of reference outward through the biblical canon from the moment in biblical history which Milton recreates, combine to engage the "fit" reader in the tensions and paradoxes that inform the Bible. The phrase "honied words" is only one example of this kind of engagement. As the central example in this study, "honied words," which refers simultaneously to prophecy in Deborah and to wisdom in Proverbs, as well as to Psalm xix, 8–9, is perhaps a minimal entity in the complex, allusive network which confronts us in this poem. What is more, the dialectical relation between prophecy and wisdom which this particular allusion develops energizes the enterprise of critical reading by engaging a range of other biblical texts besides the local Judges narrative within the historically comprehensive framework of typology. For Milton, this framework offers the answers to what von Rad calls the "unspoken" question in the Judges narrative: the Old Testament's answer is David; the New Testament's answer is Christ.

## VII

Proverbs viii, 30 says that God made the world by wisdom, and that wisdom played before the throne of God before the world was made: "I was daily his delight, rejoicing always before him." *Samson Agonistes* presents an analogy of the playfulness of wisdom when Samson is invited to play and sport before the Philistine lords in their temple. In the same manner, the soldiers who mock Christ during his Passion enact a cruel sport in the presence of a royal figure. Both actions represent demonic analogies of divine creation since they transpire in the fallen world. At the same time, for both Samson in the temple and Christ in his Passion, there is the sense in which submission to human authority coincides perfectly with obedience to the divine will. The authenticity of the "rousing motions" which direct Samson to the temple remains, of course, a contentious issue in Milton criticism. What is impressive about the climax of

*Samson Agonistes,* however, is the manner in which outward circumstance, particularly in the summons of the Officer, and free, inward promptings, or the "rousing motions," converge into a unity of purpose and occasion. In spite of this, the condition of divisive uncertainty is maintained in the Messenger's description of Samson's final moment: "he stood, as one who pray'd / or some great matter in his mind revolv'd" (1637–38). The emphasis on image or similitude in the observation rather than the confirmation of Samson's inner condition admittedly retains the minimal possibility of disjunction between Samson's will and God's. It is precisely in this respect that Dalila bears a fleeting resemblance to Samson, for while her comparison of herself to Jael is rejected out of hand by the reactionary Chorus, it persists as a tangible possibility from her perspective, as well, perhaps, as from the perspective of many readers. Dalila's comparison of herself to Jael is perhaps an important corollary to Samson's position at the climax: it is either an imposture or a possibility, two alternatives which the poem never entirely relinquishes.

The differences and similarities between Samson's actions and Dalila's, and the perspectives from which they are viewed and judged, are part of the debate on authority and liberty which is developed throughout the poem and which governs its climax. Part of this debate is conveyed in the symbol of the temple, primarily a pagan symbol in the poem, but implicitly a symbol of the divinely created human form when we recall Christ's prediction of his Resurrection: "Destroy this temple, and in three days I will raise it up" (John ii, 19). In Proverbs ix, 1–5, wisdom builds a seven-pillared temple and therein offers a banquet of bread and wine. Christian typology in the Augustinian tradition equates her temple with the church and subsumes the feminine figure of wisdom in the logos, the Christ who is, as Milton says in *Paradise Lost,* the wisdom of God. As Denise Lynch has shown, this typology is central to George Herbert, whose masterpiece *The Temple* found in the liturgy of the Eucharist a vocabulary of poetic symbols.[23] Milton's temple was the "upright heart and pure," and its central ritual was the unforced, conscientious expression of the Word of God written on the individual heart. Stated broadly, all of his poems and prose treatises consider various assaults upon this inner temple by external structures of authority. In the *Treatise of Civil Power,* for example, Milton argues that God works only from within: "But how compells he? doubtless no otherwise than he draws, without which no man can come to him, *John vi, 44;* and that is by the inward perswasive motions of his spirit and by his ministers; not by the outward compulsions of a magistrate or his officers" (YP VII, p. 262). This is certainly an important gloss on the "rousing motions" Samson finds within himself. He is,

Milton suggests, "persuaded inwardly that this was from God" ("The Argument"). Dalila, in contrast, is continually pressured by voices outside of her—"the Priest / Was not behind, but ever at my ear" (857–58). She was finally persuaded, she concedes, by

> that grounded maxim
> So rife and celebrated in the mouths
> Of wisest men, that to the public good
> Private respects must yield.                    (865–68)

Samson's moment of insight defines the overall structure of the poem by providing its peripeteia or reversal as well as its anagnorisis or recognition. As the passage from the *Treatise of Civil Power* suggests, reversal in Milton invariably focuses on authority, including the kind of authority Dalila confronts. Reversal of authority in *Samson Agonistes* is signaled when Samson resumes the discourse of wisdom and proceeds to instruct his elders. His speech is suddenly rich in sayings and aphorisms: "Commands are no constraints" (1372), "Masters' commands come with a power resistless" (1404), "So mutable are all the ways of men" (1407), "Lords are lordliest in thir wine" (1418). This point of reversal in *Samson Agonistes* offers the proverb as prophecy: the formula of hindsight presents the prospect of a suddenly open future; the enormous divisions between law and grace, wisdom and prophecy, past and future—divisions which are, as the Chorus observes "strain'd / Up to the height, whether to hold or break"—are finally to be calmed and spent. (1348–49).[24]

The scattering of aphorisms in Samson's final speeches may offer a perspective on the structure of biblical tragedy as Milton conceived it. Aphoristic discourse is, by nature, broken, disjoined, and divided. So too, perhaps, are the episodes of *Samson Agonistes* disjoined from the moment of reversal and recognition. Illumination need not be the logical culmination of a causal sequence. It may simply be granted, as wisdom is, from father to son at the correct moment. Metaphors for this kind of disjunctive unity are common in the biblical commentaries of the period. To John Diodati, proverbs are "Jewels, not tyed or linked together in any chain, or connection, but scattered here and there without *Method.*" To Allen they are "glistering Starres." George Herbert called the entire Bible the "book of stars" and asked "how all [its] lights combine" in the "constellation" of a story.[25] These metaphors help to illustrate the role of proverbial discourse in *Samson Agonistes:* the contexts, situations, and events that proverbs address are various, their points of reference in the biblical canon extensive. Yet they illuminate.

By identifying recognition, or the passage from ignorance to knowledge, with wisdom, as the gracious illumination of the divine will, Milton adapts the structure of the poem to his argument by indicating a central premise in his interpretation of the Judges narrative: providential history consists of those moments in which God acts. The form of this history is only recognizable when license and presumption are distinguished from liberty and patience in the mind of the reader. The distinction is apparent in the motions of divine grace; the structure of *Samson Agonistes* gives priority to Samson's experience of these motions. In drawing this conclusion, I do not expect to step beyond the domain of critical conflict, like Samson bidding farewell to the Chorus. This conclusion has been strongly tested in recent criticism. I am not, however, concerned with the "canonization" of Samson. I am concerned with the possibility that *Samson Agonistes* is a "faithful" interpretation of Judges. If that is a worthy premise, it requires fidelity to the genuine complexity of Milton's poem through the maintenance of the different perspectives it creates. By considering the contrasting perspective which Dalila presents when she compares herself to Jael and Deborah, Milton clearly recognizes the possibility of alternative perspectives even as he proceeds with his own. The critical challenge Milton embodies in Dalila is therefore integral to his idea of a faithful interpretation. If her "honied words" recede in the dark confines of the middle episodes, they also combine, significantly, provocatively, and to the great enrichment of the poem, with other scriptural "lights."

University of Alberta

## NOTES

1. John Milton, *Samson Agonistes*, 85, in *Complete Poems and Major Prose* ed. Merritt Y. Hughes (Indianapolis, 1984).

2. Milton is often characterized as struggling with this uneasy tension in his own thought. As Douglas Bush, "Milton," in *The Renaissance and English Humanism* (1939; rpt Toronto, 1972), p. 125, eloquently puts it, "If he, a warfaring Christian, must choose between the classical light of nature and the Hebrew light of revelation, he cannot hesitate, whatever the cost."

3. Eugene Rice, *The Renaissance Idea of Wisdom* (Cambridge, 1958), p. 142.

4. John Milton, *Christian Doctrine*, in *Complete Prose Works of John Milton*, 8 vols., ed. Don Wolfe et al. (New Haven, 1953–82), vol. VI, p. 647. All citations of Milton's prose works are to this edition and are denoted in the text by YP, with volume and page numbers following.

5. Carole Fontaine, "Proverbs: Introduction," in *Harper's Bible Commentary*, ed. James L. Mays et al. (San Francisco, 1988), p. 496.

6. Aristotle, *Poetics*, in *Literary Criticism from Plato to Dryden*, ed. Alan H. Gilbert (Detroit, 1984), p. 84.

7. Jacqueline DiSalvo, "Make War Not Love: On *Samson Agonistes* and *The Caucasian Chalk Circle*," in *Milton Studies* XXIV, ed. James D. Simmonds (Pittsburgh, 1988), pp. 203–31. See also DiSalvo's "Milton and Shaw Once More: *Samson Agonistes* and *Saint Joan*," *MQ* XXII (1988), 115–20. The figure of Deborah in Milton's work is also discussed by Stevie Davies in *The Feminine Reclaimed: The Idea of Woman in Spenser, Shakespeare and Milton* (Brighton, 1986). Joseph Wittreich discusses Dalila, Jael, and Deborah in *Feminist Milton* (Ithaca, 1987), pp. 126–27. Stella Revard comments on the relation between Dalila and Jael, the heroine of the Song of Deborah, in "Dalila as Euripidean Heroine," *Papers on Language and Literature* XXII (1987), 291–302. Mieke Bal's comparison of Dalila and Jael is found in *Death and Dissymmetry* (Chicago, 1988), pp. 14–15, 65.

8. Heather Asals, "In Defense of Dalila: *Samson Agonistes* and the Reformation Theology of the Word," *JEGP* LXXIV (1975), 184. The metaphor of scripture as honey was commonplace since the Middle Ages. In "The H. Scripture I," Herbert, *George Herbert and the Seventeenth Century Religious Poets*, ed. Mario Di Cesare (New York, 1978), p. 27, writes: "Oh Book! infinite sweetness! let my heart / Suck ev'ry letter, and a honey gain." Asals's reading can be compared with "regenerationist" readings of *Samson Agonistes*. According to the regenerationist position, the middle episodes are related to the climax because each episode prepares Samson for the climax and shows his progress toward it. The regenerationist position has been strongly challenged by Joseph Wittreich, *Interpreting "Samson Agonistes"* (Princeton, 1986). While the regenerationist position stresses the continuity of the episodes, my reading stresses discontinuity: Samson receives wisdom in an event which makes him finally "separate to God" (31). Taking Samson's cultic and messianic "separateness" as a premise, Milton devises a structure which distinguishes, indeed separates, the union of God's will and Samson's at the point of recognition from previous, reckless presumptions of this union.

9. *Harper's Bible Dictionary*, ed. Paul J. Achtemeier et al. (San Francisco, 1985), p. 214. See also Renaissance commentators noted later in the text.

10. James G. Williams, *Those Who Pondered Proverbs: Aphoristic Thinking and Biblical Literature* (Sheffield, 1981) p. 25. In support of his observation, Williams cites S. Amsler, "La Sagesse de la Femme," in *La Sagesse de l'Ancien Testament*, ed. M. Gilbert (Gembloux, Belgium, 1979). See also Claudia Camp, *Wisdom and the Feminine in the Book of Proverbs* (Sheffield, 1985), pp. 115–20, as well as James G. Williams, *Women Recounted: Narrative Thinking and the God of Israel* (Sheffield, 1982). Citations which illustrate the primacy of seductive language include Proverbs ii, 16; vi, 24; vii, 5, 21, and xxii, 14, in addition to Proverbs v, 3 (Williams, p. 25).

11. Northrop Frye, *The Great Code: The Bible and Literature* (Toronto, 1982), p. 121. The same ideas are treated in Frye's *The Critical Path* (Bloomington, 1973), pp. 37–38. *The Rhetoric of Aristotle*, trans. Lane Cooper (New York, 1932), p. 152. Aristotle defines the maxim as a statement "not about a particular fact . . . but of a general nature," especially "statement about those things which concern human action, about what is to be chosen or avoided in human conduct" (p. 150). The definition is clearly relevant to the function of the biblical proverb. Aristotle distinguishes the proverb from the maxim, as rhetorical devices, by noting that some proverbs are also maxims (p. 153), and that proverbs are always metaphors (p. 215).

12. William Camden, *Remains Concerning Britain*, ed. R. D. Dunn (Toronto, 1984), p. 270. John Clarke, "Epistle to the Reader," *Paroemiologioa Anglo-Latina* (London, 1639), n.p.

13. Thomas Wilson, *The Arte of Rhetorique*, ed. Thomas J. Derrick (New York, 1982), p. 20.

14. Henry Delaune, *Patrikon Doron or A Legacy to His Sons, Being a Miscellany of Precepts; Theological, Moral, Political, Oeconomical, Digested Into Seven Centuries of Quadrins*, 2nd ed. (London, 1657), cent. I, quat. 78, p. 20.

15. Her prediction can be compared with the following passage from the Song of Deborah:

> Blessed above women shall Jael the wife of Heber the Kenite be; blessed shall she be above women in the tent.
> He asked water, and she gave him milk; she brought forth butter in a lordly dish.
> She put her hand to the nail, and her right hand to the workmen's hammer; and with the hammer she smote Sisera, she smote off his head, when she had pierced and stricken through his temples. (Judg. v, 24–26)

16. Stanley Fish, "Spectacle and Evidence in *Samson Agonistes*," *Critical Inquiry* XV (1989), 563.

17. Carole R. Fontaine, "Proverbs: Introduction," in *Harper's Bible Commentary*, ed. James L. Mays et al. (San Francisco, 1988), p. 496. See also Carole R. Fontaine, *Traditional Sayings in the Old Testament: A Contextual Study* (Sheffield, 1982). Robert Allen, "Epistle to the Reader," in *Concordances of the Holy Proverbs of King Salomon* (London, 1612), p. b2.

18. *Milton: A Biography*, p. 411. Parker states that the name *Deborah* means "a word." Deborah is "a prophetess, a bringer of glad tidings" (p. 411). Both etymologies are correct, but the significance of the "honey bee" is well developed in a number of Renaissance commentaries on Judges. Thomas Heywood, *Exemplary Lives and Memorable Acts of Nine of the Most Worthy Women of the World* (London, 1640), p. 6.

19. Peter Martyr, *Most Fruitful and Learned Comentaries of Doctor Peter Martir* (London, 1654), cap. 4, fol 97.

20. Gerhard von Rad, *Old Testament Theology* (New York, 1957), vol. I, pp. 327–34. Patricia Parker, *Inescapable Romance: Studies in the Poetics of a Mode* (Princeton, 1979), pp. 125–26.

21. See also Mieke Bal, *Murder and Difference: Gender, Genre and Scholarship on Sisera's Death*, trans. Matthew Gumpert (Bloomington, Ind., 1988).

22. Fish rightly observes that Wittreich's analysis hinges on Samson's speech to the Philistine Lords ("Spectacle and Evidence," 580). The disjunction between the divine and the human wills is a crucial phase in Wittreich's interpretation of Samson as a self-seeking, false prophet in *Interpreting Samson Agonistes*. Wittreich bases his case on Samson's claim to act of his "own accord" in his speech to the Lords before the destruction of the temple (pp. 110–13). I have argued against Wittreich's analysis of this pivotal passage in "John 10:18 and the Typology of *Samson Agonistes*," *ELN* XXVII (December 1989), 49–52.

23. Denise Lynch, "Herbert's Love (III) and Augustine on Wisdom," *ELN* XXVII (September 1989), 40–41.

24. In a similar way, in *Paradise Regained*, Jesus dismisses Satan with proverbs such as "Man lives not by Bread only" (I, 349) and "Tempt not the Lord thy God" (IV, 561). The literary devices of wisdom, which include the parable, are a distinctive feature of the Gospels.

25. John Diodati, "Analysis of Proverbs," in *Pious and Learned Annotations Upon the Holy Bible* (London, 1651); "The H. Scriptures II." Qtd. from *George Herbert and the Seventeenth Century Religious Poets*, ed. Mario Di Cesare (New York, 1978), p. 27.

# "CHRISTS VICTORIE OVER THE DRAGON": THE APOCALYPSE IN *PARADISE REGAINED*

## Samuel Smith

WHEN NORTHROP FRYE remarked that the theme of *Paradise Regained* is "a parody of a dragon-killing romance, or more accurately, it presents the reality of which the dragon-killing romance is a parody," he obliquely pinpointed one of the most engaging actions in Milton's brief epic. Milton's poem does indeed present a dragon-killing, but, as Frye observed, it is a dragon-killing on a level of reality which transcends that of romance. The dragon-killing presented in *Paradise Regained* occurs on the most transcendent level possible: that of prophecy, particularly the apocalyptic prefiguring of the final conflict between Christ and the dragon as that conflict is described in the Book of Revelation. An examination of seventeenth-century commentary on the gospel accounts of the temptation in the wilderness and on St. John's description in Revelation of the cosmic battle between Christ and Satan, especially in the light of the typological identities perceived between the two accounts, reveals an apocalypse concealed in *Paradise Regained* that anticipates and informs the "sudden" profusion of allusions to Revelation readers have noted at the end of the poem.[1]

More than fifty years ago William Haller identified as one of the most significant expressions of Puritan typology the threefold conflict between Christ and Satan. Haller observed that the encounters between Adam and Satan in the Garden of Eden, between Jesus and Satan in the wilderness of Judea, and between Christ as Michael and Satan as dragon in the final apocalyptic battle prophesied in Revelation demonstrated for Puritans that "all existence and very human life" was a "phase of conflict between Christ and Satan." In a penetrating look at the angelic hymn sung at the very end of Milton's poem, Barbara Lewalski asserts the crucial role of the middle phase of the threefold conflict:

He [Jesus] has now conquered Satan, but that conquest only foreshadows Satan's forthcoming fall like an autumnal star or lightning at Christ's crucifixion, as well as his last and deadliest wound at the end of time. The angelic hymn hereby confirms the Father's earlier designation of the temptation episode as the epitome of human history; in it Christ has subsumed the past and by working out the rudiments of his great warfare has released all the potentialities which the future may hold.

I wish to extend this insight and demonstrate that in Milton's retelling of the Temptation episode—"the epitome of human history," Christ's final victory over the dragon is typologically and prophetically present.[2]

   The typological presence of the apocalyptic dragon in a poetic narrative about the temptation of Jesus would certainly have been no great surprise to Milton's contemporaries. Popular seventeenth-century protestant exegetes like William Perkins, Thomas Taylor, and David Pareus connect the devil who tempts Jesus in the desert with the great red dragon who wars against God's chosen in Revelation.[3] In the process of scoring a telling point about tyrannous temporal authority in *The Tenure of Kings and Magistrates*, Milton himself follows this lead for his own purpose:

[God-ordained government] must be also understood of lawfull and just power, els we read of great power in the affaires and Kingdoms of the World permitted to the Devil: for saith he to Christ, *Luke* 4.6. *All this power will I give thee and the glory of them, for it is deliver'd to me, & to whomsoever I will, I give it:* neither did he ly, or Christ gainsay what he affirm'd; for in the thirteenth of the *Revelation* wee read how the Dragon gave to the beast *his power, his seate, and great authority:* which beast so autoriz'd most expound to be the tyrannical powers and Kingdoms of the earth.[4]

Of those many expositions of the nature of the great red dragon of the apocalypse, the one with important implications for what Milton presents in *Paradise Regained* is Thomas Taylor's *Christs Victorie Over the Dragon or Satans Downfall* (1633)—a title which could function as the title of Milton's poem, especially in light of the end. Taylor's *Christs Victorie* is a unique volume among the plethora of seventeenth-century commentaries on the Book of Revelation: his book is a massive 855-page exposition of a single chapter—Revelation, Chapter xii. In this long, discursive effort Taylor delineates with great detail, among other things, the nature of the dragon, outlining and exposing the dragon's strategies for effecting the fall of God's prophets and ministers. The dragon's malicious strategies are symbolized by his ability to sweep the stars (symbolizing God's ministers) out of the sky by swinging his awe-ful tail at them. The remarkable correlations between Taylor's apocalyptic dragon and Milton's Satan as he attempts to effect the fall of Jesus—"our Morning Star then in his rise" (*PR* I, 294)—suggests a conscious effort on Milton's part to infuse his poem with the highest cosmic and eternal import by imbuing *Paradise Regained* with the prophetic presence of the Revelation text and its typology of the dragon in conflict with Christ as that presence was perceived by his contemporaries.[5]

Taylor identifies three primary means of attack represented by the dragon's tail: the violent strength of the tail signifies physical persecution ("force and tyranny"), its marvelous aspect suggests "flattery and faire persuasions," and the stinging poison supposed to be in the tail symbolizes heresies taught by false prophets and teachers (*Christs Victorie*, pp. 229–30). Milton's use of Luke's sequence in *Paradise Regained* results in three temptations in three successive days, with each day's temptation emphasizing—but not to the point of exclusion—these three strategies in the reverse order of Taylor's listing. Thus the first day's temptation, centered on the stones-to-bread temptation, reveals the dragon's attempt to lure Jesus into assuming a false prophethood and Jesus' counterthrusting exposure of Satan's role as false prophet and heretic. The second day, focused on the offer of an earthly kingdom provided by the dragon, witnesses Satan's repeated attempts to bring Jesus' messiahship under his own draconic authority by flattering and enticing him, offering "faire persuasions" to the young prophet who would be king. The third and final day, climaxed with the malevolent propping of Jesus upon the temple pinnacle shortly after a violent night of apocalyptic storm, presents the dragon's desperate attempt to force the fall of Jesus by subjecting him to physical persecution.[6]

Milton uses many devices to establish and maintain the apocalyptic context before the main action of the actual temptations begins. The coming of God's kingdom has been announced by John the Baptist, whose voice is "More awful than the sound of Trumpet" (*PR* I, 19). Walter MacKellar associates John the Baptist's declaration with the trumpet voice of Christ in the prologue of the Book of Revelation and the trumpet opening the vision of God's throne, his heavenly attendants, and the appearance of the Lamb slain for the sins of the world—the dragon's counterpart—in Revelation, chapters iv and v (*A Variorum Commentary*, p. 53). It is worth remembering that, in St. John's gospel, John the Baptist is the first to identify Jesus as "the Lamb of God, which taketh away the sin of the world" (i, 29). The image of Jesus as the sacrificial Lamb dominates his appearances in Revelation, which primarily derive from the type of the Passover Lamb and the suffering servant who is metaphorically presented as a sheep led to the slaughter in Isaiah, chapter liii. In *Paradise Regained*, Jesus' own realization that he will fulfill this figure comes first in his initial meditation before the Temptation begins, where he remarks

                    that my way must lie
        Through many a hard assay even to the death,
        Ere I the promis'd Kingdom can attain,
        Or work Redemption for mankind, whose sins'
        Full weight must be transposed upon my head.    (*PR* I, 263–67)

This echoes the Father's earlier announcement to Gabriel and those
present in heaven that Jesus is destined "To conquer Sin and Death the
two grand foes, / By humiliation and strong sufferance" (*PR* I, 159–60).
This typological figure of Jesus as the Lamb in the apocalypse is further
suggested by the heavenly scene following the Father's announcement,
a scene which closely parallels St. John's apocalyptic portrayal of the
worship ceremonies in heaven with the angels' and elders' songs of
praise:

                        and all Heaven
        Admiring stood a space, then into Hymns
        Burst forth, and in Celestial measures mov'd,
        Circling the throne and singing, while the hand
        Sung with the voice.                    (*PR* I, 168–72)

—the "Victory and triumph" prophesied of God's Son. Here Milton explicitly remembers the heavenly spectacle in Revelation, chapter v, where all
heaven stands waiting—"a space"—to see who will prove worthy to open
the seven-sealed scroll. When the Lamb who is also the Lion of the tribe
of Judah finally relieves the tension by taking the book, all in heaven burst
into a song praising the slain Lamb for obtaining redemption for mankind
(Revelation v, 9–10). In this way Milton creates for his theater of earthly
events (which largely present the redemption obtained for fallen mankind
by God's Christ) the celestial audience of the apocalypse. He has also
anticipated the arrival of the apocalypse's dragon by suggesting in Jesus
the dragon's chief foil, the Lamb.

    A second more direct apocalyptic image of Jesus occurs at the end of
his long, initial meditation on his messianic mission. The narrator identifies Jesus as "our Morning Star then in his rise," echoing Christ's self-
revelation in Revelation xxii, 16. But this metaphorical title also links
Jesus with the stars of Revelation, chapter xii, marking Jesus as the object
of the great red dragon's malicious destroying intent. Fittingly then, Satan's appearance at the baptism of Jesus and his decision to attack Jesus
immediately after that sign of God's high favor signal the possibilities for
his role as the dragon. Like most seventeenth-century commentators,
William Perkins begins his exposition of Matthew's temptation narrative
with a discussion of Jesus' baptism as a symbolic act designating his role as
God's chosen prophet. He concludes his observations by remarking that

Satan delights in attacking God's appointed prophet or minister (the two are the same for Perkins and Taylor) immediately after his public calling, and he indicates that Satan's immediate assault on Jesus after the sign of his baptism typifies a similar event in Revelation, chapter xii, revealing Satan as "that *great red dragon, that with his taile drew downe the third part of the starres of heaven*, that is, of the ministers and preachers of the word, and cast them to the earth, Revel. 12.3.4" (*The Combate Betweene Christ and the Devill*, p. 372). Thomas Taylor follows Perkins's lead when handling the baptism in his own commentary on Matthew's account by linking baptism as a symbol of birth/rebirth to a similarly functioning image at the beginning of Revelation, chapter xii: "Christ was no sooner baptized, but he must go forth to be exercised with Satan: and his members also, who not onely by outward profession, but inward sincerety also make a league with God to renounce Satan, sinne, and this evill world, shall not want all the molestation that Satan can create them. Rev. 12. the red dragon watcheth for the child to be born, to devoure it" (*Christs Combate*, p. 4). This parallel between Satan's attack on Jesus in the wilderness and the dragon waiting to devour the woman's man-child the moment it is born (Revelation xii, 4) is sustained by baptism's recognized symbolic value as a type of spiritual birth, renewal, and identification with the way of Christ. In the case of Jesus it marks the anointing or "begetting" of God's Messiah. Milton's Satan suspects that this unusual baptism signals the birth of the Messiah, and he comes like the dragon to devour the Son at the birth of his ministry of redemption and restoration for man, and destruction and doom for Satan and the fallen angels. Combining this recognized apocalyptic context for the Temptation story with Milton's own poignant allusions to Revelation early in *Paradise Regained*, the contemporary readers of Milton's poem were prepared, like Jesus, to penetrate Satan's disguises and know the horrible dragon by his actions and words. The aim of this essay is to discern apocalyptic content and discover the red dragon in Milton's brief epic.

Although Satan first appears as "an aged man in Rural weeds" (*PR* I, 314), the ensuing dialogic encounter with Jesus clearly reveals him as the great red dragon exposed by Taylor in *Christs Victorie Over the Dragon*. First, the dragon takes advantage of God's prophet by attacking him at his weakest moment, in his "solitariness" and in his "soreness," a result of the forty days' fast. Second, the dragon comes "under pretence of peace, and cloake of friendship, that hee may slay and devour" (*Christs Victorie*, p. 155). But the dragon beneath the old man is most clearly evident in his means of attack: heresy and false prophecy, the essence of the poison in the dragon's tail. Taylor asserts that the dragon brings down the stars which symbolize God's prophets by poyson and infection: much poyson lieth in the taile of a serpent, the dragon poysoned a great number more with heresie, and poysoned opinions, against the truth of the Christian religion, for which end he daily stirreth up hereticks, and false apostles, and false teachers, who being furnished with all arts to deceive, draw a number of the starres away, from sound and heavenly truth, into the apostasie of earthly and impious doctrines, cleane contrary to Scripture, and to the person, natures, and offices of Jesus Christ. Thus the Prophet *Isay* 9. 15 saith, The false prophet which teacheth lies, is the taile.[7]

Satan's first speech to Jesus begins with the damnable heresy of a fatalism which implicitly denies God's providence: "What ill chance hath brought thee to this place" (*PR* I, 321). The actual rhetorical phrasing of the temptation to turn stones into bread includes not only the intimation of doubt concerning Jesus's Sonship, but also what Edward LeComte labels the "sinful-means-to-good-end heresy" evident in the appeal to charity toward the poor, hungry inhabitants of the desert.[8]

> But if thou be the Son of God, command
> That out of these hard stones be made thee bread;
> So shalt thou save thyself and us relieve
> With food, whereof we wretched seldom taste.        (*PR* I, 342–45)

Jesus' biblical response to this temptation, "Man lives not by bread only, but each Word / Proceeding from the mouth of God" (*PR* I, 349–50), cuts like a sword into the envenomed tail of the dragon. Jesus' response also characterizes the communion of saints on earth symbolized by the battle-field of "heaven" in Revelation xii, 9, saints of the church militant who are objects of the dragon's ire. These saints reject the world in order to experience the kingdom of God, patterning their lives on the holy example of the Lamb. Remarkably, these saints "live not by bread, but by every word of God" (*Christs Victorie*, p. 232).

His innocuous disguise now penetrated by Jesus, and his poison tail of heresy wounded by the two-edged sword of God's Word, the dragon Satan attempts to identify himself as God's servant and prophet:

> I came among the Sons of God when he
> Gave up into my hands *Uzzean Job*
> To prove him and illustrate his high worth;
> And when to all his Angels he propos'd
> To draw the proud King *Ahab* into fraud.
> That he might fall in Ramoth, they demurring,
> I undertook that office, and the tongues
> Of all his flattering Prophets glibb'd with lies
> To his destruction, as I had in charge;
> For what he bids I do.                         (*PR* I, 368–77)

Jesus incisively qualifies this sophistical argument by identifying Satan's true motivation and nature:

> Wilt thou impute to obedience what thy fear
> Extorts, or pleasure to do ill excites?
> What but thy malice mov'd thee to misdeem
> Of righteous *Job,* then cruelly to afflict him
> With all inflictions? But his patientce won.
> The other service was thy chosen task,
> To be a liar in four hundred mouths;
> *For lying is thy sustenance, thy food.*
>
> (*PR* I, 422–29, my emphasis)

While Satan is effectively distanced from the true prophet who "lives not by bread, but by the Word of God [truth]," the allusion to Ahab's four hundred lying prophets (1 Kings xxii) negatively defines Satan as a false prophetic inspiration and clearly designates him as the dragon of the apocalypse once more. The earlier allusion to Satan's dealings with Job has received considerable critical attention, but the purpose and meaning of the allusion to Ahab's false prophets have not been sufficiently explained in context.9 This biblical incident finds its typological meaning in the context of the final struggle between Christ and the dragon. Indeed, Taylor's prime example of the dragon's past success in using his tail envenomed with the poison of heresy and false prophecy is "I Kings 22.21. He [the Dragon] offereth himselfe to be a lying spirit in the mouth of Ahabs Prophets; and striketh down with his taile 400 [prophets=stars] at once" (*Christs Victorie,* p. 232). Taylor's application has support from Perkins in his exposition of the temptation narrative: "And when *Ahab* went to fight against the King of Syriah, Satan became a lying spirit in the mouth of 400 Prophets & moe [sic], I King. 22.22. This is that *great red dragon, that with his taile drew downe the third part of the starres of heaven* . . . Revel. 12.3.4" (p. 384). Ironically, by offering this particular illustration of his past prophetic "service" to God in an attempt to defend himself, Satan inadvertently but typically undercuts himself, revealing his true nature as the dragon who brings down God's prophets by seducing them with heresies and false prophecies. It is a mistake that will be repeated again, suggesting for the initiated reader the image of Satan as dragon continually wielding his tail in such a way as to overreach his strength and expose his vulnerable underbelly to the sharp thrusts of Jesus' Word.

The sustained presence of the apocalyptic context intensifies the issue of Satan's draconic pretense to be the friend and counselor of man:

Men generally think me much a foe
To all mankind: why should I? They to me
Never did wrong or violence; by them
I lost not what I lost, rather by them
I gain'd what I have gain'd, and with them dwell
Copartner in these Regions of the World,
If not disposer; lend them oft my aid,
Oft my advice by presages and signs,
And answers, oracles, portents and dreams,
Whereby they may direct their future life.          (PR I, 387–96)

Jesus' equally cutting response to this claim again reveals what Taylor calls "the deeper plot of the dragon," which is to "pretend peace, friendship, [and] amitie" with men in order to "slay and devour" them (*Christs Victorie*, p. 155):

Thou pretend'st to truth; all Oracles
By thee are giv'n, and what confest more true
Among the Nations? That hath been thy craft,
By mixing somewhat true to vent more lies.
But what have been thy answers, what but dark,
Ambiguous and with doubt sense deluding,
Which they who aks'd have seldom understood,
And not well understood, as good not known?
Who ever by consulting at thy shrine
Return'd the wiser, or the more instruct
To fly or follow what concern'd him most
And run not sooner to his fatal snare?          (PR I, 430–41)

This strong denunciation and Jesus' subsequent self-identification as God's "living Oracle" (*PR* I, 460) leave Satan "inly stung with anger and disdain" (*PR* I, 466), and as dragon he retreats from his first attack on Jesus with a desperate appeal to a sense of fairness: God has, after all, allowed divine inspiration to the false prophet Balaam. But Satan's hand is not strengthened by another ironically undercutting allusion to the prophet who became the New Testament prototype of the false prophet of apostasy (2 Peter ii, 15, Jude xi, and Revelation ii, 14).

Jesus simply waves him off, neither bidding nor forbidding his return, since the dragon can do no more than God allows. The completeness of Jesus' victory over the dragon and his stinging tail of poison at this point in the narrative are aptly highlighted by Perkins's use of Revelation, chapter xii, as a text which instructs readers' response to Jesus' refusal to turn the stones into bread: "We therefore may now say with *that loud voice*; Now is salvation in heaven, and strength, and power, and the kingdome of our God, and the power of his Christ: for the accuser of the brethren is cast down" (p. 372, with a marginal note marking Revelation, xii, 10, as the quoted text). Perkin's use of Revelation, chapter xii, here suggests that anyone who desires to understand fully the meaning of Jesus' temptation and victory in the wilderness must examine that event under the revealing lens of the apocalypse, a suggestion which Milton appears to have taken seriously. And the declaration that the successful rejection of the first temptation means "Now is salvation . . . and the kingdome of our God" has important ramifications for Milton's lengthy look at the nature of God's kingdom and salvation during the second day's temptation.

The interlude between the first and second days of temptation includes the disciples' plaintive cry to God for the missing Jesus, Mary's meditation, and Satan's demonic council in middle air. Milton uses both typological allusion and direct verbal phrasing to sustain the apocalyptic context established in Book I. The disciples, after having witnessed the Father's audible approbation of his Son at his baptism, begin to doubt when they cannot find the newly announced Messiah:

> And as the days increas'd, increas'd their doubt:
> Sometimes they thought he might be only shown,
> And for a time caught up to God, as once
> *Moses* was in the Mount, and missing long;
> And the great *Thisbite* who on fiery wheels
> Rode up to Heaven, yet once again to come.     (*PR* II, 12–17)

The phrasing of the disciples' doubt concerning Jesus, "Sometimes they thought he might be only shown, / And for a time *caught up to God*" (my emphasis), directly echoes Revelation xii, 5: "And she [the woman clothed with the sun] brought forth a man child, who was to rule all nations with a rod of iron: and her child was *caught up to God*, and to his throne" (my emphasis). At this point the dragon turns on the woman, but she escapes into the wilderness where she is miraculously sustained. Thomas Taylor supposes that the woman is nourished in the wilderness with the same manna provided for Moses and his people in Sinai and Elijah when he fled to the wilderness to escape Jezebel (*Christs Victorie*, pp. 317, 777). This intensifies the allusive function of Moses and Elijah in reference to the disciples' fear that Jesus has been "caught up to God," suggesting that in some way the apocalyptic struggle is now being acted out. The allusion also reflects back to Jesus' reliance on the examples of Moses and Elijah, along with the apocalyptic prophet Daniel, as chief sources of his own spiritual strength and sustenance during the first day's temptation.

Mary's thoughts about Jesus' disappearance offer a variation on the same theme within the same apocalyptic context. Unlike the disciples, who desire Jesus' temporal kingship over Israel, Mary fears his potential rise to political power—and for good reasons. Her past experience of having to flee in terror from the inhumanly jealous Herod, along with her memory of Simeon's prophecy that her son would cause the "fall and rising . . . / of many in Israel" (*PR* II, 89–90), creates in her misgivings about Jesus' kingship. She recalls the lowly circumstances of Jesus' birth and what followed soon after:

> yet soon enforc't to fly
> Then into Egypt, till the Murd'rous King
> Were dead, who sought his life, and missing fill'd
> With infant blood the streets of *Bethlehem*.          (*PR* II, 75–78)

This serves as a typological allusion to the action of Revelation, chapter xii. Herod, "the Murd'rous King," is a type of the dragon who stands "before the woman which was ready to be delivered, for to devour her child as soon as it was born" (Rev. xii, 4). In his discussion of this passage, Taylor identifies the type baldly: "How *Herod* the dragon stood before the woman seeking to slay the childe Jesus so soone as he was born, appeareth Mat. 2.16."[10] When the child is caught up to God, the dragon sends a flood forth to destroy the woman, a flood identified with the "infant blood" shed in Bethlehem in Herod's desperate attempt to annihilate the Messiah.

Provided with such clues to the typological, and thus prophetic, presence of Revelation, chapter xii, in the poem, I wish to emphasize that the Miltonic narrator's "So spake th'old Serpent" (*PR* II, 147) after Satan's first speech at the demonic council looks forward to the dragon as well as backward to the garden. MacKellar identifies the allusion to Revelation xii, 9: "And the great dragon cast out, that old serpent, called the Devil, and Satan."[11] This allusion sustains the apocalyptic context/intertext and foreshadows Satan's fall at the end of the poem and the end of time. But the allusion also suggests that the demonic council represents the dragon and his angels discussing strategies for the effective use of the dragon's tail in order to cast down this new man, this "Morning Star," before he can accomplish the great work which God has ordained him to perform. Thus Milton's interlude maintains his "concealed" apocalypse and alerts his readers to see in and through the battle at hand to the final conflict described in Revelation.

While alert readers might be mildly surprised to discover the kingdom temptation preceding that of the temple tower, they are not likely to be surprised at all by Satan's appearance. He comes "Not rustic as before, but seemlier clad, / As one in City, or Court, or Palace bred, / And with fair speech these words to him address'd" (*PR* II, 299–301). Satan arrives as from the palace court to be an advisor or mentor to the young prospective Messiah who needs guidance about how best to achieve his kingdom. His is clearly the guise of the dragon, approaching Jesus in the way Taylor describes the dragon's approach to the young prophet he wishes to ensnare with his tail and cast down like a falling star: "Although he be a dragon . . . he commeth commonly as a friend, and in the habit of a good counseller, and though he be a prince of darknesse, he transforms himselfe into an Angell of light. 2 Cor. 11.14. that where he cannot force, he may allure."[12] Thus the dragon's speech is "fair," and he will offer Jesus means to a kingdom as if he were but a friend and counselor with Jesus' own best interests at heart. But William Perkins's observation about Satan's offer of the kingdoms of the world also applies to Milton's second day of temptation: "Satan's drift is to cause Christ to take him for his lord, to depend and wait on him for his kingdome, and to acknowledge him to be the giver thereof" (*The Combate Betweene Christ and the Devill*, p. 399). I will also argue that on this second day Satan as the dragon attempts to coerce Jesus into becoming a beast, that is a monarch empowered by the dragon, in the way described in Revelation, chapter xiii. It is an admirable strategy on Satan's part: to seduce Jesus into becoming an Antichrist holding temporal power in order to prevent the eternal kingdom of God, which has been ordained to be obtainable only by suffering.

Having failed to poison Jesus with the venom of heresy and false prophecy during the first day, Satan now swings his dragon tail in a more alluring manner, hoping to "wile" his way into Jesus' heart as he did Eve's. His method of temptation on this second day accords with Taylor's description of the second way the dragon wields his tail against the stars of heaven.

By flattery and insinuations, by which, as by a dragons tayle the Pastors were beaten down: for as dogs do use to fawne and flatter their masters with their taile; so the dragon not by open force onely, but by secret fraud and insinuation assaileth the stars; namely by many faire promises, and sugred perswasions, making offers of wealth and preferment, favor, and whatever else the world can bestow on her favorites. (*Christs Victorie*, p. 228)

Milton's dragon is full of "flattery, faire promises, and sugred perswasions" on this second day. The sugared persuasion of the banquet spread "in *regal* mode" (*PR* II, 340, my emphasis) is followed by a blatant offer of "wealth and preferment" if only Jesus will take his kingdom upon Satan's authority:

> Money brings Honor, Friends, Conquest, and Realms;
> What rais'd *Antipater* the *Edomite,*
> And his Son *Herod* plac'd on *Judah's* Throne
> (Thy throne) but gold that got him puissant friends?
> Therefore, if at great things thou wouldst arrive,
> Get riches first, get Wealth, and Treasure heep,
> Not difficult, if thou hearken to me,
> Riches are mine, Fortune is in my hand,
> They whom I favor thrive in wealth amain,
> While Virtue, Valor, Wisdom sit in want.          (*PR* II, 422–31)

Satan's illustration of his success in this vein—Herod—is ironically devastating, revealing, and affirming his true nature as the great red dragon, especially for readers alert to the apocalyptic context and only recently having come from overhearing Mary's meditations on the same "Murd'rous King!" Here the dragon overreaches himself again, exposing his vulnerable underbelly not only to Jesus, but to the reader as well.

Confounded by Jesus' refusal of the royal banquet and his scathing rejection of a kingdom through riches, Satan's third attempt to seduce Jesus into taking the kingdom at his hand offers glory. Dragonlike, he flatters Jesus to draw him in:

> I see thou know'st what is of use to know,
> What best to say canst say, to do canst do;
> Thy actions to thy words accord, thy words
> To thy large heart give utterance due, thy heart
> Contains of good, wise, just, the perfect shape.
> Should Kings and Nations from thy mouth consult,
> Thy Counsel would be as the Oracle
> *Urim* and *Thummin,* those oraculous gems
> On *Aaron's* breast, or tongue of seers old
> Infallible; or wert thou sought to deeds
> That might require th' array of war, thy skill
> Of conduct would be such, that all the world
> Could not sustain thy Prowess, or subsist
> In battle, though against thy few in arms.
> These Godlike Virtues wherefore dost thou hide?    (*PR* III, 7–21)

The syntax of the first five lines of this passage and the rhetoric of the entire speech demonstrate Satan's attempt to wile his way into the heart of Jesus through flattery, hoping to succeed as he did with Eve. But the oracular Jesus responds that the glory of princes often amounts to no more than the very flattery Satan has lavishly bestowed on him: he desires no "praise unmixt" from those who "extol things vulgar" (*PR* III, 48, 50–51). More to the point, conquerors seduced by the lure of glory "swell with pride, and must be titl'd Gods . . . Worship't with Temple, Priest, and Sacrifice" (*PR* III, 81, 83). These lines indict the traditional deification of Roman emperors, anticipating Satan's offer of Rome later in the day. But they also evoke the evil tyrant of Revelation, chapter xiii, the blasphemous beast who requires the worship of all the inhabitants of the earth and receives his power from the dragon, which—as I have demonstrated—Milton connected with Satan's offer of the kingdoms of the world during the temptation in the wilderness. Even Satan's flattery reveals his attempt to make Jesus his beast. His remarks that no army could withstand Jesus' warrior prowess recalls the wonder of the people who worship the beast, saying "Who is like unto the beast? who is able to make war with him?" (Revelation xiii, 4).

The dragon's beast appears in a more typological fashion in Satan's fourth try at the kingdom temptation, when he tests Jesus' patience by presenting the oppression of Israel by foreign conquerors in a way that gives a strong sense of urgency to the need for a messiah. He appeals to Jesus' sense of duty, taking his cue from Jesus' response to the previous attempt, portraying the Roman emperor Tiberius as a kind of Antiochus Epiphanes, or a ruler who in his pride usurps the place of Israel's God. The choice of Antiochus is prophetically and typologically significant. Antiochus Epiphanes's blasphemous desecration of the Jewish temple in the second century B.C.E. led commentators in a long tradition to identify him with the sacrilegious king responsible for "the abomination that maketh desolate" in the apocalyptic prophecy of Daniel (xi, 31). This king demonstrates satanic pride: "And the king shall do according to his will; and he shall exalt himself, and magnify himself above every god, and shall speak marvellous things against the God of gods, and shall prosper till the indignation be accomplished: for that what is determined shall be done" (Dan. xi, 36). Identified with this king, Antiochus becomes a type of the blaspheming beast who receives his power from the dragon:[13]

And they worshipped the dragon which gave power unto the beast: and they worshipped the beast, saying, Who is like unto the beast? who is able to make war with him? And there was given unto him a mouth speaking great blasphemies; and power was given unto him . . . And he opened his mouth in blasphemy against God, to blaspheme his name, and his tabernacle, and them that dwell in heaven. (Rev. xiii, 4–6)

The apocalyptic context evoked by Antiochus as a type of Antichrist aids the reader's recognition that the kings whom Satan sets up for Jesus to topple and replace are the dragon's own beasts and puppets, and the fiend's ploy is to make a beast and puppet of Jesus as well.

Jesus' answer to this stresses his contrary role as the Lamb slain for the sins of the world. Emphasizing the prophecies of God which Satan conveniently overlooks, he states:

> What if he hath decreed that I shall first
> Be tried in humble state, and things adverse,
> By tribulations, injuries, insults,
> Contempts, and scorns, and snares, and violence,
> Suffering, abstaining, quietly expecting
> Without distrust or doubt, that he may know
> What I can suffer, how obey? who best
> Can suffer, best can do; best reign, who first
> Well hath obey'd.                          (PR III, 188–96)

The Lamb of Revelation, "worthy . . . to receive power, and riches, and wisdom, and strength, and honour, and glory, and blessing" (Rev. v, 12), provides the best illustration of the truth of Jesus' words.[14] But he probably learned them from the "Prophetic writ" with its type of the Passover lamb and its portrayal of the suffering servant in Isaiah liii, 7: "He was oppressed, and he was afflicted, yet he opened not his mouth: he is brought as a lamb to the slaughter, and as a sheep before her shearers is dumb, so he openeth not his mouth." Here is obedience with "quiet expectation."

Unable to fathom the Messiah as Lamb, Satan remarks Jesus' worldly naiveté and takes him up to a mountain to show him "the Monarchies of th' Earth, thir pomp and state" (PR III, 246). His offer of the military power of Parthia marks his fifth attempt to bring Jesus' kingdom under his own authority, but the description of the violent, conquering force of the Parthian army identifies it with the military might of the dragon's beast. In the preface to Samuel Hartlib's edition of The Revelation Reveled, John Dury asserts that the government of the beast will "do all things by a Brutish and bodilie violence and force, rather than in a friendlie and amiable waie."[15] In fact, the vision of Parthian destruction presented by Satan corresponds to the character of the beastly government described by Dury: it will "destroie without mercie all that stands in the waie of [its] will." The offer of Parthia has no chance with a Messiah who has determined beforehand that it is "more humane, more heavenly" to "conquer willing hearts" with "winning words," making "persuasion do the work of fear" (PR I, 221–23). But when Jesus refuses the kingdom from Satan's hand in this new form, prophetically judging

Parthia for its violence, he in effect refuses to become the beast who receives power from the dragon.

Satan's bold presentation of the Roman empire subsumes all of the means he has used to lure Jesus to accept his kingdom at Satan's authority on this second day. It also enhances the apocalyptic context. Rome was categorically identified by nearly all seventeenth-century Protestant theologians with Antichrist, and the initial description of that city in Milton's poem suggests the whore of Babylon from Revelation, chapters xvii and xviii:[16] "The City which thou seest no other deem / Than great and glorious *Rome*, Queen of the Earth / So far renown'd, and with the spoils enricht / Of Nations" (*PR* IV, 44–47). Here is the great harlot who considers herself "a queen" to all the "kings of the earth" (Rev. xviii, 7–9), who "reigneth over the kings of the earth" (Revelation xvii, 18), and who enriches and is enriched by "the merchants of the earth" (Rev. xviii, 11). Seductive as this whore, Milton's Satan again swings his alluring dragon tail of fair promises and sugared persuasions, flattering Jesus and putting the offer in terms of achieving a good and desirable end: Jesus can demonstrate his own virtue and supplant the evil tyrant Tiberius at the same time:

> With what ease,
> Endu'd with Regal Virtues as thou art,
> Appearing, and beginning noble deeds,
> Might'st thou expel this monster from his Throne
> Now made a sty, and in his place ascending
> A victor people free from servile yoke?
> And with my help thou mayst; to me the power
> Is given, and by that right I give it thee.
> Aim therefore at no less than all the world.     (*PR* IV, 97–105)

Satan's claim to have the power and right to give Jesus the empire that rules the entire world echoes his initial "I have also power to give" (*PR* II, 393) when he offers Jesus the royal banquet at the beginning of this day. He makes it clear that he would be the dragon authority behind Jesus' beastly kingship.

Jesus' reply exposes the dragon's game. He sees what Tiberius is, who made him what he is, and what he himself would become if he accepted Satan's draconic offer:

> [thou] proceed'st to talk
> Of the Emperor, how easily subdu'd,
> How gloriously; I shall, thou say'st, expel
> A brutish monster; what if I withal
> Expel a Devil who first made him such?     (*PR* IV, 125–29)

"A brutish monster" fits the apocalyptic beast and the word *devil* could be functionally replaced by *dragon* if it would not counter the apocalyptic method of revealing truth by concealing it under images and words that can be penetrated only by the initiated.

Despite Jesus' pointed allusion to the apocalyptic image of Daniel's "stone that shall to pieces dash / All monarchies besides throughout the world" (*PR* IV, 149–50), prophesying Jesus' destruction of all beasts empowered by the dragon, Satan still pushes brutishly forward with the blatant offer that most clearly marks him as that dragon:[17]

> The Kingdoms of the world to thee I give;
> For giv'n to me, I give to whom I please,
> No trifle; yet with this reserve, not else,
> On this condition, if thou wilt fall down,
> And worship me as thy superior Lord,
> Easily done, and hold them all of me;
> For what can less so great a gift deserve?          (*PR* IV, 163–69)

Many seventeenth-century divines, and Milton in *The Tenure of Kings and Magistrates*, identify this act with the dragon of Revelation. In the poem it is a desperate maneuver, revealing the dragon's utter inability to penetrate the truth of the Lamb. Jesus supplies the oracular utterance from Deuteronomy—"Thou shalt worhip / The Lord thy God, and only him shalt serve" (*PR* IV, 176–77)—that makes his dependence on God as the giver of his kingdom evident: "If given, by whom but by the King of Kings, / God over all supreme?" (*PR* IV, 185–86). Editors of *Paradise Regained* have noted the reference to John's title for Jesus in the Book of Revelation: "King of Kings." Milton's use of that title at precisely this juncture in the poem is strategic. The title "King of Kings" is given directly to the Lamb (Rev. xvii, 14), and he consequently exercises the judgment of God against the whore of Babylon, the beast, and the dragon, overcoming the dragon-empowered beast and the kings of the earth with the sharp two-edged sword which comes out of his mouth (Rev. xix, 15–21). The Lamb effectually becomes the stone that smashes all the kingdoms of the earth represented by Nebuchadnezzar's image in the Book of Daniel. Everything in his poem works together to make this future final conquest typologically and prophetically present in Jesus' current victory over the dragon in the wilderness. Milton poetically and prophetically transcends temporal restrictions to highlight the eternal and spiritual nature of Jesus' kingdom, and the way in which that kingdom is achieved.

It may be that Satan's desperate repetition of his kingdom offer signifies a nascent or perhaps unconscious apprehension of the spiritual nature of the Messiah's kingdom. Satan's demand that Jesus bow down and worship him in return for the kingdoms of the world can be interpreted as a request for spiritual worship. Taylor marks this as another indication of the dragon: "If Christ require spirituall worship, being a spiritual king, the dragon will require the same, Math. 4, If thou fall downe and worship me; And that which he could not obtaine of Christ he winneth of all the wicked in the world, who worship the beast and the dragon, Rev. 14.3" (*Christs Victorie*, p. 203). Satan's desperate request may also spring from his enmity toward Jesus: "Satan's malice and contrariety to Christ and Kingdome, and all he claimeth" means that "If Christ be Lord of all, the dragon will claim all. Math. 4. All these things will I give thee, for they are mine" (*Christs Victorie*, p. 203). Viewing Satan's uncloaked offer as the malicious act of the child-devouring, star-felling dragon would both explain and justify (if justification is needed) Jesus' particularly scathing response to Satan. His apocalyptic judgment of Satan as "That Evil one, Satan for ever damn'd" (*PR* IV, 194) is singularly appropriate. The Lamb is not about to bow down, either physically or spiritually, and worship the dragon.

At this point, given this rather climactic action in the context of the apocalyptic typology of Revelation enacted here, the inclusion of a temptation to kingdom through pagan knowledge and wisdom—a temptation which has puzzled more than one generation of *Paradise Regained* readers—may seem anticlimactic and unnecessary.[18] Why include it then? This is not a simple case of Milton's presenting last and so climactically what would have been the greatest temptation for him personally. It is, after all, the *use* of learning that is at issue, not its acquisition. Satan's nascent recognition of the true nature of Jesus' kingdom as a spiritual one could be one reason for this surprising maneuver. From Satan's perspective, it is a logical retreat, considering that Jesus has rejected Rome because no "*wise* and valiant man" (*PR* IV, 143, my emphasis) would seek to free the inwardly enslaved Romans.

But this form of the kingdom temptation also rounds out the tradition evident in William Perkins and Thomas Taylor. Perkins, taking some liberty with the text on Satan's offer of the kingdoms of the world to Jesus in an applicative (not interpretive) way, remarks that Satan's use of pagan wisdom as a means of redirecting the God-willed course of God's young prophets should be both expected and anticipated: "Even in Gods church the Devill workes mightily in this way, by stealing away the affections of yong students from the Bible, and ravishing them with delight in the writings of men; for thus he keeps them from the fountain of truth, that they either fall into error themselves, or be less able to discerne and confute it in others" (*The Combate Betweene Christ and the Devil*, p. 393). Milton's Jesus echoes this sentiment when he responds that the one who receives "light from above, from the fountain of light, / No other doctrine needs" (*PR* IV, 289–90), and then proceeds to expose the error of the ancient philosophers: "Much of the Soul they talk, but all awry" (*PR* IV, 313). Taylor directly links Perkins's observation to the dragon's "faire promises and sugred perswasions," and his tactic of promoting evil ends by good means and "handsomely apparrell[ing]" what is evil to make it seem good. Taylor's illustration of this tactic is a learning that would direct a man away from studying and relying on God's Word: "To neglect the study, & preaching of Gods word, and to carry men from the simple truth to toyes, and froth of human spirit and wit, is profoundness and depth of learning. Revel. 2.24. for how else came schoole-learning to banish the scriptures, for many hundred yeares, but under pretext of deeper learning?" (*Christs Victorie*, p. 160). The author who wrote *Of Education* could certainly accommodate these antischolasticism sentiments, and there seems to be an echo of Taylor in Jesus' denunciation of pagan wisdom in favor of the sufficiency of the scriptural tradition. His important qualification on the use of learning contains a use of the word *toys* in a way reminiscent of Taylor's remarks:

> who reads
> Incessantly, and to his reading brings not
> A spirit and judgment equal or superior
> (And what he brings, what needs he elsewhere seek)
> Uncertain and unsettl'd still remains,
> Deep verst in books and shallow in himself,
> Crude or intoxicate, collecting *toys*,
> And trifles for choice matters, worth a sponge.
>
> (PR IV, 322–29, my emphasis)

Jesus' response reveals that the dragon has spent the entire day wielding his alluring tail in vain.

The apparently anticlimactic offer may also serve another apocalyptic purpose. The temptation to learning represents the seventh form of the kingdom temptation. Satan as the dragon has completed a seven-phase offer of the kingdoms of the world in an attempt to usurp God's role as the giver of Jesus' kingdom. This represents a blasphemous parody of the sevenfold gift due to the Lamb because he has obeyed God and has been slain for the sins of the world: "Worthy is the Lamb that was slain to receive power, and riches, and *wisdom*, and strength, and honour, and glory, and blessing" (Rev. v, 12, my emphasis). But Jesus will not be deflected from a course that will carry him to the cross where he will win a victory that will earn him God's highest favor and humanity's redemption, and which will enable him to play the dragon-conquering role of the Lamb in the final apocalyptic conflict.

After remonstrating with Jesus for his rejection of his offer of the kingdom, and prognosticating a fate of suffering for Jesus which Jesus himself has already acknowledged twice, Satan returns Jesus to the desert wilderness and leaves him, "feigning to disappear" (*PR* IV, 397). But he returns to attack Jesus as he sleeps, fulfilling once again the paradigm of draconic behavior as Taylor delineates it. Taylor remarks that the dragon will "dissemble flight when he need not, when he doth not," departing "but for a season" only to "renew his forces and assaults" after the believer has fallen into a metaphorical sleep of security (*Christs Victorie*, p. 175). And the dragon also characteristically takes advantage of believers by attacking them in their literal sleep (*Christs Victorie*, p. 155). Thus Milton's Satan returns like Revelation's dragon, attacking Jesus as he sleeps, assaulting him with a frighteningly apocalyptic storm of cosmic disorder followed by a horrifying demonic assault. When Satan forces the winds to rush forward "From the four hinges of the world" (*PR* IV, 415), he counters the angel of God who holds back the four winds in Revelation vii, 1. Even the thunder, coming from "either Tropic" and "both ends of Heav'n" (*PR* IV, 409–10), suggests apocalyptic judgment from the four corners of the earth. The hideous demons tormenting Jesus in a dream can be compared to the hideous locusts which issue forth from the bottomless pit to torment men in Revelation, chapter ix. It is as if, recognizing he is losing the apocalyptic battle even now, Satan attempts to turn the Book of Revelation against the very one it reveals: Jesus Christ (Rev. i, 1).

The terrors of the storm and the dream also anticipate the final day of temptation and Satan's subsequent strategy of applying the strength of his sweeping tail to force Jesus to his will. Taylor indicates this as the dragon's preparation for combat: "The dragon gaineth no small advantage by spreading false fears and terror to dishearten us in our combat" (*Christs Victorie*, p. 177). But Jesus is not only *not* disheartened, he also penetrates Satan's ludicrous ploy of claiming the storm as a kind of fulfillment of his prophecy against Jesus for rejecting the kingdom at his hand. In doing so, Jesus pinpoints the crucial issue behind every aspect of the second day's temptation: "that I accepting [Satan's 'offer'd aid'] / At least might seem to hold all power of thee" (*PR* IV, 493–94)—a response which again suggests that Jesus is unwilling to become the beast who holds all power of the dragon.

"Swoln with rage" (*PR* IV, 499), Satan makes a last defense of all his previous actions; he then uses "Another method" (PR IV, 540) identifiable as the dragon's tail swung with "force and tyranny" (Christs Victorie, p. 227). In an act of tyrannic violence, Satan places Jesus on the pinnacle, in peril of his life. The image of Jesus and Satan high in the sky at the peak of the highest pinnacle's spire suggests the image of the war in heaven, and Satan's temptation correlates to the dragon discussed by Taylor. Satan's use of Psalm xci renders him a "preaching dragon," which is "the most dangerous" of false preachers, "who will winde us in by Scripture, and by that which is the only preservative against sinne, draw us into sinne" (Christs Victorie, p. 153). In this way the dragon attempts to turn the Christian's own weapon—God's Word—against him (Christs Victorie, p. 173). One of Taylor's many examples of this is the dragon's attempt to "bring Christ to presumption" by breaking off before quoting that part of Psalm xci that would enable Jesus to defeat him during the pinnacle temptation. That part of Psalm xci which Satan leaves unsaid is poignant: "Thou shalt tread upon the lion and the adder: the young lion and the *dragon* shalt thou trample under feet. Because he hath set his love upon me, therefore will I deliver him: I will set him on high, because he hath known my name" (Ps. xci, 13–14). Jesus has indeed set his love upon God and known his name: "King of Kings." Buttressed by his faith in God's providence and kingdom, Jesus defeats Satan with the "sharp sword" (Rev. xix, 15) that is the Word of God: "Also it is written, / Tempt not the Lord thy God" (PR IV, 560–61). As Jesus continues to stand by the grace and power of God, Satan is "smitten with amazement" (PR IV, 562) and falls, evoking the image of the fall of the dragon in Revelation, chapter xii.

At this point Milton's poetic power focuses on the theme of the eternal life depicted at the close of Revelation after Christ has overcome the dragon and his evil forces. Immediately after his victory, Jesus is presented with a celestial banquet from the true giver and an angelic hymn of praise, evoking the wedding feast of the Lamb in Revelation, chapter xix, and the Elysium of Revelation, chapter xxii.[19] Served by ministering angels, Jesus receives "Fruits fetched from the tree of life" (PR IV, 589) found on either side of the river of life in Revelation xxii, 2. More significantly, "to eat of the tree of life" is promised to "him that overcometh" Satan in Revelation ii, 7. Jesus *has* overcome Satan's temptations and in eating of the tree of life he establishes the type for his own promise since the glorified Jesus is the speaker in that verse. Jesus also drinks from the "fount of life Ambrosial" (PR IV, 590) promised "to him that is athirst" in Revelation xxi, 6.

The celestial banquet is appropriately accompanied by an angelic hymn of praise for the Son, a hymn which parallels the hymns of the martyred saints and the twenty-four elders in Revelation, chapter v. The angels echo John i, 14 ("And the Word was made flesh, and dwelt among us") when they speak of the Son as being "remote from Heaven, enshrin'd / In fleshly Tabernacle, and human form" (*PR* IV, 598–99). But they also evoke Revelation xxi, 3: "And I heard a great voice out of heaven saying, Behold, the tabernacle of God is with men, and he will dwell with them, and be their God." The angels also sing of Jesus' victory over Satan in apocalyptic terms: "him long of old / Thou didst rebel, and down from Heav'n cast / With all his army" (*PR* IV, 604–06). Elliot points out that this recalls both Revelation xii, 9, "And the great dragon was cast out, that old serpent, called the Devil, and Satan," and Revelation xx, 2–3, 10: "And he laid hold on the dragon, that old serpent, which is the Devil, and Satan, and bound him a thousand years, And cast him into the bottomless pit . . . And the devil that deceived them was cast into the lake of fire and brimstone."[20] The angels' warning to Satan, that "like an Autumnal Star / Or Lightning thou shalt fall from Heav'n trod down / Under his feet" (*PR* IV, 619–21), reinvokes the missing portion of Psalm xci which speaks of the dragon being trod under the feet of God's servant. The future tense of the warning reminds the reader that the final battle is yet to come, and its presence in this encounter is typological and prophetic. The hymn also provides the model response for saints: praise to God for the Lamb's victory over the dragon:

In that the Church rejoyceth, that now the Lord hath put forth his strength in the overthrow of the enemies, and set up his own kingdome where the dragon and his angels ruled in darknesse, Idolatry, cruelty, and tyranny, we learne, that *this Saints ought to rejoyce when they see Gods kingdome set up and prevaile against the dragon and his angels*. *Rev.* 11.15. (*Christs Victorie*, p. 510)

The angelic hymn makes Milton's typological and prophetic portrayal of the final phase of the conflict between Christ and Satan as it is described in Revelation complete.

Thus the Book of Revelation is poetically, prophetically, and typologically a key context for *Paradise Regained*, a context as important as the Book of Job (as demonstrated by Barbara Lewalski) and Ephesians, chapter vi, (as argued by Neil Forsyth). I suggest that the Christian soldier's manual of spiritual warfare is actually a quartet of manuals. As Taylor points out, the church is prepared for spiritual combat by the lessons of Ephesians, chapter vi, the example of Job, and the example of Jesus in Matthew, chapter iv, as well as Revelation (*Christs Victorie*, pp. 335–38, 343).[21] Milton too joins significant aspects of all four biblical texts, especially the Book of Revelation, in his own account of the temptation in the

wilderness. His "old experience" has once more enabled him to "attain /
To something like Prophetic strain" (*Il Penseroso*, 173–74) in a poetic
presentation of "Christs Victorie Over the Dragon."

Messiah College

NOTES

My most special thanks is to Elaine B. Safer for her always diligent and cogent aid
through every stage of this project. I also offer a special thanks to Mary Ann Radzinowicz for
her encouragement and caveats in the early stages. And I thank Arthur F. Kinney and Clyde
Ross for taking time to read and comment on a near final draft. I am grateful to Messiah
College for a very generous faculty scholarship grant which enabled me to finish this project.
I am also grateful to the very pleasant and helpful staff at the Folger Institute and Folger
Shakespeare Library, where two grants-in-aid for two seminars resulted in the beginning and
the end, the alpha and omega, of this work.

1. Northrop Frye, "Agon and Logos: Revolution and Revelation," in *The Prison and
the Pinnacle*, ed. Balachandra Rajan (Toronto, 1973), p. 136; Annabel Patterson has well
illustrated Milton's rejection of romance in the brief epic "*Paradise Regained:*" A Last
Chance At True Romance," in *Milton Studies*, XVII, ed. Richard S. Ide and Joseph Wittreich
(Pittsburgh, 1983), pp. 187–207; on allusions to Revelation, see Emory Elliot, "Milton's
Biblical Style in *Paradise Regained*," in *Milton Studies*, VI, ed. James D. Simmonds (Pitts-
burgh, 1974), pp. 227–41, 235–39; James H. Sims's list of Scripture allusions in *Paradise
Regained* in his *The Bible and Milton's Epics* (Gainesville, 1962), pp. 274–78; and Walter
MacKellar's *A Variorum Commentary on the Poems of John Milton, Volume Four: "Paradise
Regained*," with an essay on "Studies of Style and Verse Form" by Edward Weismiller (New
York, 1975), pp. 245–49. I hope to demonstrate that St. John's apocalypse is a more signifi-
cant intertext for *Paradise Regained*—at least as significant as the Book of Job—than has
previously been recognized.

2. William Haller, *The Rise of Puritanism* (New York, 1938), p. 151. The typological
mode of exegesis with regard to the second and third phases of the conflict between Christ
and Satan was so pervasive that Daniel Dike could entitle his commentary on Matthew iv, 1–
11 *Michael and the Dragon, or Christ Tempted and Satan Foyled* (London, 1635); Barbara
Lewalski, "Time and History in *Paradise Regained*," in *The Prison and the Pinnacle*, pp. 80–
81; *Paradise Regained*'s position as an apparent sequel to *Paradise Lost* and the prologue's
Pauline reference to the disobedience of Adam in Eden has clued many readers into the
typological relationship between the first and second phases of the threefold conflict. Unfortunately, the forward-looking nature of the brief epic—as a type of the final conflict—has not
been duly considered.

3. William Perkins, *The Combate Betweene Christ and the Devill Expounded*, in Vol.
3 of *Works* (Cambridge, 1609), esp. pp. 373, 384, 400; Thomas Taylor, *Christs Combate and
Conquest* (Cambridge, 1618), esp. pp. 4, 8, 310, 324–25, and *Christs Victorie Over the
Dragon or Satans Downfall* (London, 1633)—this work has crucial implications for *Paradise
Regained* and will be discussed at length; David Pareus, *A Commentary Upon the Divine
Revelation of the Apostle and Evangelist John*, trans. Elias Arnold (Amsterdam, 1644), p.

291. See also Dike, *Michael and the Dragon*, p. 223, and the marginal commentary in the 1607 Geneva New Testament (Beza/Tomsin/Junius), p. 130. As an example I offer Pareus, because he too is making a political point about tyranny with the typological connection:

> *And the Dragon gave him his power*] Here follows the *Beasts* power. But from whom hath he it? The *Dragon* gave it to him. Now there is no power but from God. And therefore the *Beasts power* is not lawfull: but a corruption of power and tyranny, having for its authour him, who said: *All these things will I give thee, if falling down thou wilt worship me.* viz. *the Devill that lying Sepent.* (P. 291)

Both Pareus and Milton are following a pattern established by Luther, who made the same textual connections between Matthew, chapter iv, and Revelation, chapter xiii, in a politicized attack on the pope as Antichrist. See Jaroslav Pelikan, "Some Uses of Apocalypse in the Magisterial Reformers," in *The Apocalypse in English Renaissance Thought and Literature*, ed. C. A. Patrides and Joseph Wittreich (Ithaca, 1984), pp. 85–86.

4. *Complete Prose Works of John Milton*, 8 vols., ed. Don M. Wolfe et al. (New Haven, 1953–82, vol. III, p. 210. All references to Milton's prose are taken from this edition and cited as *YP* unless noted otherwise.

5. Merritt Y. Hughes notes this line as an allusion to Revelation xxii, 16, where Christ says, "I am . . . the bright and morning star." All quotations from Milton's poetry are taken from *John Milton: Complete Poems and Major Prose*, ed. Merritt Y. Hughes (Indianapolis, 1957), unless notes otherwise.

6. Perhaps it is appropriate here to recollect Elizabeth Marie Pope, *"Paradise Regained": The Tradition and the Poem* (Baltimore, 1947), pp. xiii–xv. Pope observes two important things: First, Milton could trust his contemporary audience ("fit . . . though few") to be more aware of the important theological contexts for the Temptation narrative than are twentieth-century readers. Second, while no one commentator or theologian treats every aspect of the Temptation narrative, "commentators seldom or never stray outside the limits of established opinion, or offer purely personal or idiosyncratic views" (p. xv). Of course we might expect the case of the poet to be different. But I am attempting to provide twentieth-century readers with one of those significant theological contexts for *Paradise Regained* which has been neglected or, at best, underdeveloped.

7. Taylor, *Christs Victorie*, p. 228. It is pertinent to note that *Paradise Regained* has been recognized by many readers to be very concerned with "the person, nature, and offices of Jesus Christ." Barbara Lewalski, *Milton's Brief Epic* (Providence, 1966), argues convincingly that this first temptation is largely concerned with Jesus' office as prophet.

8. Edward LeComte, "Satan's Heresies in *Paradise Regained*," in *Milton Studies*, XII, ed. James D. Simmonds (Pittsburgh, 1979), p. 260. This is also characteristic of the way Taylor's dragon hinders good actions: "By thrusting them forward by evill meanes, and causing men to doe good things in an evill manner, and then all the grace of them is lost" (*Christs Victorie*, p. 161). This heresy is also embedded in the temptation of the kingdom.

9. Sister M. Christopher Pecheux, "The Council Scenes in *Paradise Lost*," in *Milton and Scriptural Tradition: The Bible Into Poetry*, ed. James H. Sims and Leland Ryken (Columbia, 1984), pp. 82–103, discusses this biblical event, but only as it relates to the nature of council scenes in *Paradise Lost*.

10. Taylor, *Christs Victorie*, p. 248. Pareus makes the same typological application in *A Commentary Upon the Divine Revelation*, p. 257.

11. *Variorum Commentary*, IV, p. 113. The double allusion to Revelation and Genesis recalls the typological trilogy of conflict between Christ and Satan for the salvation of mankind identified by Haller.

12. *Christs Victorie*, p. 152. The last phrase again presents Milton's interesting reversal of Taylor's order. Milton's Satan will attempt to force (day three on the pinnacle) where he has not been able to allure.

13. David Pareus pushes this common type a bit further, observing that in an historical interpretation of Revelation, chapter xii, the dragon with his swinging tail knocking ministers out of grace (stars out of heaven) alludes to Antiochus Epiphanes, who is a "type of Antichrist." See *A Commentary Upon the Divine Revelation*, p. 261.

14. MacKellar, *A Variorum Commentary*, p. 156, identifies Jesus' lines here with the "stoic" spirit of Revelation ii, 10: "Fear none of those things which thou shalt suffer: behold, the devil shall cast some of you into prison, that ye may be tried; and ye shall have tribulation ten days: be thou faithful unto death, and I will give thee a crown of life."

15. *The Revelation Reveled*, ed. Samuel Hartlib (London, 1651), p. 48. It is worth remembering that Hartlib was a friend of the young Milton, who dedicated *Of Education* to him.

16. Lewalski, *Milton's Brief Epic*, p. 275. See also Christopher Hill, *The Antichrist in the Seventeenth Century* (Oxford, 1971), for overwhelming detail on this point.

17. Taylor, *Christs Victorie*, p. 387, identifies the stone with Christ, who "breake[s] in pieces the power of the dragons."

18. Dick Taylor, "The Storm Scene in *Paradise Regained:* A Reinterpretation," *UTQ* XXIV (1955), p. 367, has argued cogently that the so-called "Athens" temptation is just one more form of the kingdom temptation.

19. See Edward Tayler, *Milton's Poetry: Its Development in Time* (Pittsburgh, 1979), p. 164. Tayler calls this banquet a reminder of the *eschaton*, or last things (Revelation).

20. Elliot, "Milton's Biblical Style," p. 238.

21. Lewalski, *Milton's Brief Epic* and Neil Forsyth, "Having Done All to Stand: Biblical and Classical Allusion in *Paradise Regained*," in *Milton Studies*, XXI, ed. James D. Simmonds (Pittsburgh, 1986), pp. 199–214; A much tighter and explicit presentation of this "quartet" of manuals is made by George Gyffard in his "Epistle Dedictore" to William Fulke's *Praelections upon the Sacred and Holy Revelation of S. John* (1573). Cf. John Bale's remarks: "He that will lyve godly in Christ, & be a pacient sufferer. He that wil stande in Gods feare, & prepare himself to temtacion. He that will be strong whan adversite shal come and avoyde all assaultes of antichrist, & the devil, let him geve him selfe whollye to the studye of this prophecye" (*The Image of Both Churches* [London, 1548], unpaginated preface).

# ARISTOTLE, THE ITALIAN COMMENTATORS, AND SOME ASPECTS OF MILTON'S CHRISTIAN TRAGEDY

## Derek N.C. Wood

MILTON'S REFERENCES to Aristotle's *Poetics* in the preface to *Samson Agonistes*, in *Of Education*, and elsewhere have invited analysis of his tragedy in the light of that philosopher's theory, or what has survived of it. Some of the commentary that has resulted has been disappointingly out of touch with Aristotle's argument and also with those versions of it that were current in Milton's day. Quite apart from this, it is clear that the results of such analysis must be affected by one's interpretation of the play: a reader who considers that Samson's morality is satanic will have an opinion about what constitutes the protagonist's hamartia that is different from that of a reader who thinks that Samson is the triumphant champion of God. And never have readings of the play been so full of contradictions and doubts as they are now. No longer is there disagreement merely over the spirit of the play or its structure. There is flat disagreement, quite simply, about what the play means: is Samson a sinner or a saint, a psychopath or a type of Christ; is the play a tragedy or a comedy? Barbara Lewalski, hearing a "cacophony of critical voices," begins her own reconsideration of the play by observing that "Whatever consensus once obtained about *Samson Agonistes* no longer exists."[1]

My own recent suggestion was that Samson is not satanic: he is a hero of faith, but he is an exemplum of a morality fashioned in the darkness under the Law and presented as ugly and un-Christian. He too is denied the promise, while suffering humanity awaits the incarnation of Christ. I suggested that the evidence of the text and context indicates that Milton is working with as much detachment as any Renaissance maker of fiction, the same dramatist's detachment that he himself criticized Salmasius for not appreciating. Salmasius assumed that a statement made by a character in a play represented the opinion of the dramatist—an error, according to Milton, a failure to understand that the voice of the fictional dramatic personage is not the voice of the author.[2]

However, few readers have resisted the understandable temptation to identify Milton to some extent with this "hero," who is himself a blind, stubborn, defeated revolutionary and clearly in favor of divorce. Jacqueline DiSalvo recently assumed that "Milton's and Samson's political goals" are identical, and this is the foundation for her argument that Milton "represents revolutionary virtues as a hypermasculinity" threatened by feminine and maternal principles.[3] I will try to show in this essay that Milton's presentation of Samson's violent Judaic ethic is Christian and unsympathetic, and that this sits more comfortably with Aristotle's conception of tragedy than do the traditional, orthodox readings. This avoids the strains we have been forced to accept in attempts to explain the causes of pity and fear in *Samson*, the nature of the tragic protagonist, the hamartia, the pathos, and the peripeteia. Milton scholars in the last half-century have done violence to the ideas put forward in the *Poetics*, not only as modern classical scholars understand them but also as Milton would have found them translated, analyzed, and discussed by the Italians he respected. This essay will begin by examining these misunderstandings, drawing attention in particular to a curious solecism about the nature of catharsis which has haunted even recent readings of the play. It will be suggested that the problems are caused partly by critics' determination to force onto the text their preferred readings. An alternative reading will reveal a Milton who is a sensitive but extremely inventive Aristotelian, and also a Christian syncretist.

We may consider first some simple problems that orthodox interpretations create for those who believe that Milton allowed himself to be influenced by Aristotle's theory of tragedy. Milton's preface records his agreement with Aristotle, that "raising pity and fear, or terror" is central to the function of tragedy, the *eleos* and *phobos* in the definition. In orthodox readings of Milton's play, Samson's final destructive action is more or less a triumphant Christian victory for the regenerate champion of God. Mary Ann Radzinowicz suggests that "in His free agent, Samson, He manifests the renewal of freedom to all men . . . the good mind and the good will issue into an exemplary act which teaches how God gives freedom."[4] For whom, then, are we to feel pity? For Samson, the short shock of death in the service of God is nothing fearful compared to the brooding terror of the outcast lying in the dust of Gaza, mangled in his "apprehensive tenderest parts" (624). Rather, it is an ecstasy of positive achievement after Dalila and Harapha, following his cruelly critical father and friends, had brought his hatred to the boil but stayed maddeningly out of reach. Less still can we feel pity if this is a divine reward for a process of penitent regeneration. If the play ends in triumph and success for Samson, it does not turn on that fall from good fortune to bad which

Aristotle considered an essential feature of the best constructed plot (53a15). Nor do we feel fear at the spectacle of someone like ourselves suffering undeservedly (53a4–8). If we locate Samson's fall in his capture, his loss of sight, and his enslavement at the mill, he evokes sympathy, in Aristotle's reasoning, but not pity and fear because he deserves to fall, having sinned through disobedience toward God, uxoriousness and garrulity (53a2–3).

Yet few readers are prepared to contemplate the possibility that Samson's end is not a triumph and most have accepted the consequences of their interpretations, some with considerable awkwardness. M. E. Grenander says of Samson's death, "There is nothing tragic in it, nor does it involve suffering . . . [it is] part of the emotional release of the play." Even the normally impressive W. R. Parker cannot give us a satisfactory Aristotelian solution, suggesting vaguely that we feel pity for Samson's "glorious past" and fear in "the last portion of the play." This is not how *eleos* and *phobos* work in the Aristotelian dynamics. Martin E. Mueller, recognizing that we cannot feel pity and terror for a champion who is rejoicing at being readmitted to God's service, takes the desperate step of treating Manoa as the tragic hero and heaping onto his shoulders the Aristotelian apparatus.[5] Even more desperate are the attempts to see the play as comedic and Samson as a comic hero. Boughner, having ingeniously discovered comedy in this tragedy, then criticizes Milton for failing to be very funny.[6] There is no reason at all to blame Milton because he does not do what he vehemently denounces in his prefatory remarks: the corrupt and absurd "error of intermixing comic stuff with tragic sadness and gravity." Only the determined predisposition to make the play fit certain theological principles, which the text nowhere points to, forces such contradictions on its readers.

A similar problem relates to the pathos which Aristotle defines in chapter 11 of the *Poetics* (52b11–13). Its importance is crucial, as B. R. Rees points out: the "action bringing pain or destruction, is essential to tragedy." In fact, as Else states, "the one thing absolutely essential to a tragedy was a *pathos* of heroic quality and scope." "The *pathos* is an act which is destructive to life or painful, such as killings, paroxysms of pain, woundings," in Else's translation. Although it seems clear that Samson's destruction of the Philistines satisfies Aristotle's requirements and should be considered the pathos, Milton scholars have retreated from conceding this. Grenander cannot admit that Samson's death is involved in the pathos and insists that his "internal suffering is the Tragic Incident" (p. 386). This is not Aristotelian. Oedipus's pathos was not his mental anguish but his killing of his father, Laius; in the case of Herakles, it was his killing of his wife and sons, not the misery that followed when his madness passed away. As the classical scholars remind us, it is something done, not a state (Rees, *AT*, p. 15). Incidentally, the intention to commit the act is sufficient, as Iphigeneia intends to kill Orestes in Euripides's play. As Rees insists, Samson's *"pathos* is his final, destructive action."[7]

The Christian regenerative reading makes it difficult for most scholars to accept the slaughter on Dagon's feast day as the pathos. Grenander cannot consider Samson's death a pathos since, supposedly, "there is nothing tragic in it, nor does it involve suffering" (p. 388), and Mueller concludes that this event is not tragic but is of the kind "which Aristotle expressly condemns as untragic" (p. 157). Mueller has in mind Aristotle's clear, unambiguous stipulation about the kind of act that can move audiences to pity and fear (53b14–22): if the destructive act is done by an enemy to an enemy there is nothing pathetic either in the deed or the intention. The important thing for Aristotle is that there must be a context of relationship. The act of destruction must involve *philoi*, 'dear ones' or 'close blood relatives' (*Aristotle's Poetics*, pp. 412–39). This problem would seem to be insuperable. Obviously, there is no destruction of kin in *Samson*. However, I will try to show later that Samson's destruction of the Philistines is a pathos which a Christian reader can fairly consider Aristotelian.

There are one or two other problems, but this is enough to suggest how out of touch with Aristotle's dramatic theory Milton's practice is said to be. Some of his supposedly un-Aristotelian ideas are blamed on what we are led to believe was a kind of minestrone of Horatian tidbits and neoclassical distortions served up by the Italians and others, which we are told he swallowed with the help of a typically Renaissance habit of syncretism. Thus, Milton's rendering of catharsis is said to be a blending of homeopathic medicine and Puritan theology, mixing *purgatio, lustratio, expiatio*, humours adust, sin, conversion, regeneration, grace, and Christian peace. This vision of a Milton whose adaptation of Aristotle is confused and erratic or willfully idiosyncratic does not accord with the respect approaching veneration with which Milton refers to the philosopher who is "our chief instructer in the Universities" and whose *Poetics* are infused with "sublime art" (YP VII, p. 448; II, p. 404). Many scholars before and since Ruth Mohl would agree with her opinion that Milton's "preoccupation with Aristotle was a fundamental, lifelong pursuit."[8] W. R. Parker considered that Milton followed Aristotle because Aristotle had so effectively "summed up what had previously been thought and done" (p. 69), and W. B. Hunter has shown how Milton entered into the very spirit of the Greek philosopher, adapting his terms subtly to explain such Christian theological concepts as the persons of the Trinity.[9] In precisely this spirit, I believe, Milton adapts Aristotelian poetic theory to set Samson's morality in a Christian context.

Samson's morality is un-Christian and, even in terms of his own limited social economy, is unproductive; that is, he cannot get even temporal deliverance for himself or his people by a massive act of slaughter, let alone achieve what Milton understood by Christian liberty. The young Milton had approached the politics of liberation with a moderately confident commitment to heroic political violence, though even early there were signs that he was troubled by it. Although in *Areopagitica* he was still talking about extirpating influences that were antireligious, first, he insisted "all charitable and compassionat means be us'd to win and regain the weak and the misled" (YP II, p. 565). In his *Commonplace Book* we see an early suspicion of patriotism when it is misused for ethnic hatred and material interest:

This virtue [love of country] should be sought by philosophers cautiously. For a blind and carnal love of country should not carry us off to plundering and bloodshed and hatred of neighboring countries, so that we may enrich our country in power, wealth, or glory; for so did the pagans act. It behooves Christians, however, to cultivate peace. (YP I, p. 422)

The old regicide was necessarily silent on contemporary politics after the return of Charles II. According to DiSalvo, his later views on "our need for the militant resistance" to an ungodly temporal government "may still remain the most uncomprehended dimension of his deeply coded polemical poems" (p. 228). Too many attempts to decode *Samson* are based on earlier statements he made when military success seemed to prove that God was with his militant righteous rebels: "pleas'd to make himselfe the agent, and immediat performer of their desires; dissolving their difficulties when they are thought inexplicable, cutting out wayes for them where no passage could be seene" (YP I, p. 927). After 1660, in what spirit would Milton recall his mocking words in *Eikonoklastes*, written when it seemed that God had delivered into the hands of the New Model Army the enemy and their king? Milton says of the king: "It being now no more in his hand to be reveng'd on his opposers, he seeks to satiat his fansie with the imagination of som revenge upon them from above; and like one who in a drowth observes the Skie, [he] sits and watches when any thing will dropp, that might solace him with the likeness of a punishment from Heavn" (YP III, p. 563).

Early remarks such as these could be applied with cruel accuracy to the later Milton as he is imagined by Christopher Hill, Nicholas Jose, and others.[10] Hill has documented the experience of defeat, the disillusionment, the bitterness, the sense of betrayal or, in some cases, the bewilderment at God's treatment of his people, and *Samson* is a record of all this; but it is also the record of a man who is there the second time. Unlike Lilburne, Simpson, Sedgwick, Fox, and the others, Samson does not have the example of Christ to turn to, away from carnal violence and war, finding Christ in a spiritual realization of peace.[11] This peace in Christ does not preclude hating the enemies of God, that is, hating evil, but it does preclude slaughtering them by the thousands, which achieves nothing for the Danites and nothing for those opposed to the monarchy. Hill's reading here is affected by his determination to believe that Milton "knew" there must be a way forward again (p. 317). For instance, Hill argues that Adam rejoices at Noah's survival and does not lament at the destruction of the wicked. However, if we look at those lines carefully we find Adam only laments "less" at the misery than he rejoices at the emergence of perfection, justice, and God's appeasement. This is an image or analogous instance of the *felix culpa* theme that structures the whole poem. It does not cancel out Adam's misery at the suffering of those who are destroyed: "How didst thou grieve then, Adam . . . Of tears and sorrow a flood thee also drowned."[12]

Lewalski is not persuaded that Christ's nonviolent spiritual mission is to be taken as a model for all creatures. Some are called on to fight, she insists, as Michael and the angels were (p. 247). However, J. A. Winn has shown with beautiful coherence that even the defensive violence of the angels is proved by Milton to be futile. They are willing and submissive fools of God, the foils for Christ. It is the Word that conquers, the creating Word.[13] I will not repeat here the argument I have outlined elsewhere and referred to above that the characters in this play all exemplify the darkened moral consciousness of fallen humanity under the Law, misconceiving heroism, liberty, and redemption, construing these and other concepts in a sense that is literal and limited by their ignorance of Christ and of "the divine excellence of his spiritual kingdom, able without worldly force to subdue all the powers and kingdoms of this world, which are upheld by outward force only" (YP VII, p. 255). That ignorance leads us to Samson's hamartia.

Aristotle's use of the term *hamartia* has resulted in more misunderstanding than any other critical term he uses except *catharsis*. When Hanford said in 1925 that Samson's was "the most dignified of all tragic faults—rebellious pride," he was perhaps unaware of the work that had already been done to discount the old moralistic reading of Aristotle's term. Sixty years later, Milton scholars still seem to cling to the Victorian misunderstanding of the word. J. S. Hill tells us that most of them consider "Samson's *hamartia* was pride, or *hubris*" but he points to "the sin of presumption." Mueller speaks of a "concept of progressive *hamartia*" which is "entirely dependent on the free will" (pp. 163–64), and Mary Ann Radzinowicz says that its meaning in the *Poetics* ranges from "passion or violence affecting other human beings to rashness, negligence, or blundering in relation to supernatural beings" (p. 10). The best corrective to such opinions is Bremer's summary of his full and authoritative analysis of the contextual and philological evidence:

it is justified to define *hamartia* in *Poetics* 1453a10/15 as '*tragic error*', i.e. a wrong action committed in ignorance of its nature, effect etc., which is the starting point of a causally connected train of events ending in disaster. *Hamartia* is not '*tragic flaw*', i.e. a moral weakness, a defect of character which enlarges itself in its successive stages till it issues in crime; nor is *hamartia* equivalent to '*tragic guilt*', i.e. the state brought about by sinning, an inner attitude which stems from the wicked action, and a kind of burden from which one is relieved only by adequate punishment. [14]

In sixteenth-century Italian translations of Aristotle and commentaries, we find support for the reading preferred by modern classical scholars. In Pazzi's 1536 translation, *Poetics* 1453a7–11 is translated, "Is autem erit, qui nec uirtute, nec iustitia antecellat, minimeque per uitium, prauitatemue [sic], in ipsam infelicitatem lapsus fuerit, uerum humano quodam errore, ex magna quidem existimatione, atque felicitate" ("He will be moreover one who is not pre-eminent in either virtue or justice and certainly not one who will have fallen into that misery through a moral flaw or depravity but in fact through some human error, indeed a person of high reputation and good fortune").[15] Else translates the reference to *hamartia* as "because of some mistake" (*Aristotle's Poetics*, p. 376), here "humano quodam errore." A few lines later, Pazzi reads that the shift should be "ex felicitate ad miseriam, errore sanè non leui, minimè verò per dedecus, ex illo quidem virorum, de quo dictum est, genere" (1453a15–17) ("Out of happiness into misery, through an error that is indeed not trifling but certainly not because of evildoing on the part of one of those men of the kind that has been specified"). In the beautiful edition of his 1548 commentary, it is Pazzi's translation, with a few small changes that Robortello uses. In the vernacular in 1588, Denores writes that the tragic "tramutation dalla felicità all'infelicità" should befall a character "illustre tra buona e cattiua, e che trapassi dall'uno stato all 'altro per certi errori humani" ("Illustrious neither good nor bad, who passes over from the one condition to the other because of certain human errors").[16] And to make quite clear that the error is not to be thought of as moral nor sinful in the Christian sense, he goes on to say "questa attion horribile, e miserabile; ò si commetta tutta via per ignoranza; ouero sia per commettersi non sapendola, e poi saputa non si commetta" (f. 47) ("This horrible and pitiable action may either be performed entirely through ignorance or it may be done unknowingly, for knowingly it would not be done"). Denores really does want to make the point clear!

A great deal of learned commentary is available by the seventeenth century to direct a student of Aristotle to read *hamartia* as 'ignorance' rather than as 'sin' or 'tragic flaw'. However, Bremer notices two complications. Some Italians who translate the Greek correctly question Aristotle's judgment, arguing that it is wrong to exclude the guilty error or sin, since many Greek tragedies are constructed around evil or immoral acts which Aristotle appears to ignore. Castelvetro and Beni disagree with Aristotle, but they do not misunderstand him. Milton was free to follow the Stagirite or the preferences of a "puny," modern intellect. Others do seem to misunderstand, as Vettori does, arguing from the *Problems* to criticize Oedipus's rashness, and translating 1453a16 with "propter peccatum magnum." "So for the first time *hamartia* is related to (identified with ?) 'fatal passion'," Bremer points out (pp. 69, 70–71). He sees in this the beginnings of a tendency "to imagine that Aristotle was here saying that in a tragedy there ought to be a proper moral correlation between guilt and consequent disaster" (p. 195). By the time of Dacier, Mesnadière, and Rymer this will harden into a belief in "poetic justice," and later, with the German philosophers, into the theory of "tragische Schuld." However, this is by no means the prevailing opinion in the literature available to Milton.

Even if translations and suggestions that mislead can be found in the sixteenth century, I have not seen it pointed out that many passages in other parts of the *Poetics* reinforce the sense that is once again preferred today, and these serve to clarify the meaning of *hamartia*. In Vettori's own commentary, this is the translation of 1453a8–11: "neque propter vitium et prauitatem mutatur, caditque in res aduersas, sed propter errorem quendam, hominum qui sunt in magna existimatione et abundantia omnium bonorum" ("Neither through a moral flaw nor depravity is he changed, and he falls into evil fortune, but it is on account of some error of men who are of noble reputation and have abundant prosperity"). Piccolomini will provide the last examples of many possible. The tragic action is done "non per malitia, e malvagia volontà, ma più tosto per imprudentia, e per qualche sconsiderato errore" ("Not through malice nor evil intent but rather through ignorance or some unthinking error").[17] The point is even clearer when he explains how the best anagnorisis lies in the recognition of the hamartia: "miglior sarebbe ancora, quando la persona eseguisse la cosa non conoscendo: e poi dopo il fatto riconoscesse il tutto percioche in tal caso il fatto non harebbe dello scellerato" (p. 214) ("It would be still better, when the person performed the business unknowingly: and then after the deed recognised the whole truth since in such a case the deed would not be touched by wickedness").

Now, as Adkins says, if *hamartia* means a mistake of fact, "no theory of tragedy based on a moral flaw in the hero need look to Aristotle for support," which covers the vast majority of interpretations of *Samson* ever published and certainly those put out in the last half-century or so which see Samson as rising from despair to Christian fortitude, or moving through some sort of process of regeneration, or overcoming a series of temptations, or rejecting pride, garrulity, lust, or "effeminacy."[18] In the interpretation I have suggested, however, Samson's hamartia is entirely Aristotelian, but it is profoundly Christian at the same time. Samson is ignorant under the Law of the morality of the New Testament. This process of adapting an Aristotelian term recalls Milton's adaptation of Aristotle's *ousia* to make a Christian theological distinction between *essence* and *substance*.[19] In killing the Philistines, Samson "committed a wrong action in ignorance of its nature." Samson, under the Law, is ignorant of the new covenant, ignorant of the example of Christ, perfect and to be imitated. Then was the "state of rigor" to which force was not unbefitting. As he interprets his duty to God, nothing could be further from his heart than "the sense of charitie":

> The state of religion under the gospel is far differing from what it was under the law: then was the state of rigor, childhood, bondage and works, to all which force was not unbefitting; now is the state of grace, manhood, freedom and faith; to all which belongs willingness and reason, not force: the law was then written on tables of stone, and to be performd according to the letter, willingly or unwillingly; the gospel, our new covnant, upon the heart of every beleever, to be interpreted only by the sense of charitie and inward perswasion. (YP VII, p. 259)

"*Hamartia* is lack of the knowledge which is needed if right decisions are to be taken."[20] Samson, who is so unreservedly committed to "inexpiable hate" (*SA*, 839), cannot know that "who so hateth his brother is a murderer" and he is ignorant of the new covenant's "brother-hood between man and man over all the World" (YP II, p. 470; YP III, p. 214). His ignorance is inevitable because of his place and time in Christian history.

Those who have been determined to present Samson as a Christian hero, redeemed retrospectively by Christ, sanctified in the letter to the Hebrews extrapolating Christian liberty backwards to Adam, have tended

to minimize the importance of Christ's life in human time, with its concrete exemplariness. They have reduced Christ's existence almost to a
technicality, a formality necessary to fulfill certain legal requirements.
This reading reaffirms the centrality of Christ in Milton's theology.

There are two important reservations or qualifications that modern
classical scholars have made with respect to hamartia, but both can comfortably be accommodated by the Christian reading I am suggesting. G. F.
Else argues that the hamartia should involve *philoi:*

The finest mistake for the purposes of tragedy, like its correlate the finest recognition, will have to do with the identity of a 'dear' person, that is, a blood relative,
and will accordingly lead to or threaten to lead to his being slain or wounded. As a
component or cause of the complex plot, such a *hamartia* is inherently fitted to
arouse our pity—and our 'fear', that is, our horror that a man should have killed or
be about to kill a 'dear one'. (*Aristotle's Poetics*, p. 383)

Else's argument has not been universally accepted, though R. D. Dawe
and others who have objected to it do not seem to have noticed an important part of that argument (pp. 391–98).[21] I suggest that the Greek insistence on the importance of blood kinship would in Milton be appropriately replaced by a Christian conception of a universal human bond in
charity, of which Samson would be ignorant under the Law. Even the
Philistines are *philoi* under the new covenant with its new conception of
"brother-hood between man and man over all the World." Recognition
could only come with Christ. Samson could not know this because of
where he is placed in the linear pattern of human history designed by
God, for "then was the state of rigor . . . now is the state of grace."

Interestingly, this is a Christian version of yet another aspect of
hamartia that has been noted by Dawe and Bremer. Trying to explain why
Aristotle has so little to say of the obviously important role of the gods in
fifth-century tragedy, Dawe concludes that the old concept of *ate* has, by
Aristotle's time, been subsumed into the philosopher's conception of
hamartia. So, he explains, "an error of judgement is something which can
be either entirely the responsibility of the man who makes it, or can be
something induced, normally by the gods putting a man in such a position
that he has little choice but to make a decision that will later recoil on him
with disastrous, and above all disproportionate, consequences" (94–95).
Herakles's massacre of his wife and children is a terrible instance of this in
Euripides's tragedy. Bremer states, "*hamartia* and *ate* are correlative: a
man, 'blinded' by divine interference (θεόθεν) does wrong and brings ruin
upon himself and others" (p. 196).

The pagan theology must, of course, undergo a mutation in the Christian Reformation context. Milton did believe that God could send good temptations in the way of the free-willed Christian. He also believed God could harden the heart of the sinner. However, I do not think that either of these is the relevant mutation of *ate;* rather, it is the mystery of the divine ordering of the universe, the unsearchable dispose of omniscience and omnipotence shaping post-Adamic history and containing in its pattern the lives of all human beings, for all their free will. Samson's ethic of violence is repellent and inimical to the ethic proclaimed by Christ in his words and in his life, but Samson is injected into a world and a dispensation shaped by an almighty God. What Samson did in conscience was part of God's plan. Everything is part of God's plan. Yet that terrible act of carnal violence was not only self-destructive—it failed to deliver God's people on earth from the power of the unrighteous. Defeated Puritans in 1671 had no doubt that their cause had been right, and yet their failure was ordained as part of God's larger mysterious plan. Caught up in the fury of righteousness, they had killed and had given up their dead. Did they not fear those deaths might be as futile as Samson's in achieving liberty for God's people? Now, they could only concede that God's plans in which they had played their parts were incomprehensible. Samson's experience mirrored their own. How can he be blamed? He agonized over the encoded signs that he felt were ethical guides and wondered if the motions that roused him were divine. He could not even be certain his "motions" did not originate in his own proud drive for vengeance. He had been wrong before, it seemed.

The terror of Samson's last moments, discounted by so many Milton scholars, is clear in Judges. Would he face a contented God or the horror of a soul dead in one doom with the Philistines? Samson is to be pitied. His terror is to be shared by the audience. "There is only one kind of terror," says Lucas, "that a theatre audience can feel, the terror which they share with those who in the play are aware of their own impending doom." And as Else says, "we feel horror because of the nature of the deed, and pity because it is executed or planned in ignorance." The pathos, then, is not Samson's death.[22] It is the monstrous destructive act perpetrated on the Philistines, in tribal hostility and in ignorance of any higher bond uniting human being with human being in charity. "The ultimate root of the tragic is ignorance," writes Else, "with the proviso that the ignorance must have led or threatened to lead to an act which runs counter to man's deepest moral instincts" (*Aristotle's Poetics*, p. 420). As Barbara Lewalski concludes, though by a quite different route, the tragedy invites "a complex and subtle assessment of the uses of the past" (p. 247). To readers who had just lived through an attempt at political deliverance which had been violent and futile, and who could count and remember the dead, the pity and the terror must have been not only poignant but very personal.

If it is true that Aristotle has "had more bastard opinions fathered upon him than any other writer of influence," then catharsis is among the most seductive of his ideas and Milton scholarship has been the most energetic of sires (Rees, *AT*, p. 1). Catharsis is regularly said by critics of Milton to have occurred on stage rather than as part of the experience of the audience or reader. Samson is frequently assumed to have had a catharsis and so, often, are Manoa and the Chorus. No one has yet suggested that Dalila or Harapha experience catharsis although they must have been purged quite comprehensively at the theater, but without much accompanying delight. Manoa and the Chorus are sometimes spoken of as a kind of audience, and Manoa's purgation has itself been treated by Mueller as "a little drama of its own" in a perfect inversion of what Aristotle is supposed to have suggested. Radzinowicz has said that what has been purged in Samson is remorse or, perhaps it is, as Georgia Christopher has it, his "old and torn identity." Sherman H. Hawkins equates catharsis with regeneration and sometimes with redemption.[23] It has been considered a "theme" (Radzinowicz, "Distinctive Tragedy," p. 277), or a "principle of structure" (Hawkins, p. 223), or "a state of equilibrium achieved at the end of the work" (Mueller, p. 173), and also as "the image of God's providence, his mercy and justice combined" (Radzinowicz, p. 253). Radzinowicz also suggests that "God has behaved toward Samson like an Aristotelian tragic poet . . . life is the tragedy He records from human history; He designs the tragedy to effect the purgation" (*Toward "Samson Agonistes,"* p. 107). This should have silenced Plato's objections to drama more effectively than Aristotle's arguments, but it is different from anything Aristotle does suggest. Critics of *Samson* have felt free to use Aristotle's terminology for a highly inventive and free-floating process of elaboration, weaving the original concepts into other ideas like motifs in designs that have become quite rococo.

It is a useful corrective at this point to turn to the calm common sense of D. W. Lucas, who inquires into the workings of pity and terror in Aristotle's discussion: "Our knowledge that we are seeing a play and not a piece of life affects our feelings" ("Pity, Terror," p. 56). Even if we do not accept Kitto's brilliant suggestion that catharsis was a cleansing of the incidents in the plot, and if we conclude instead that Milton believed that it was an emotional or spiritual or paideutic cleansing, it must come about in the spectators at a dramatic representation of events, not in the participants in the tragic events themselves. Milton insists in his epigraph to the

1671 edition that it is the mimesis, the "imitatio actionis seriae" that has the "power" he describes and that carries with it its tempering delight. Whatever educative effect the sight of real bloodshed or misery may have is beside the point. That is what the fictionalized characters in the play experience. The delight is "stirred up by reading or seeing those passions *well-imitated.*" That is what the observer of a dramatic presentation experiences. Seekers after mere horror are "at fault because their effect is not produced by *imitation* in the proper sense (that is, the representation of human action, character and 'thought')" (Else, *Aristotle's Poetics*, p. 410).

The great Renaissance puzzlement about what exactly Aristotle meant by "mimesis," which is so forcibly expressed by Francesco Patrizi and, to some extent, by most of the great Renaissance commentators, did not prevent those theorists from distinguishing between the effect of an event in life and the effect of its fictional representation.²⁴ That much Aristotle himself had made quite clear:

> τό τε γὰρ μιμεῖσθαι σύμφυτον τοῖς ἀνθρώποις ἐκ παίδων ἐστὶ καὶ τούτῳ διαφέρουσι τῶν ἄλλων ζῴων ὅτι μιμητικώτατόν ἐστι καὶ τὰς μαθήσεις ποιεῖται διὰ μιμήσεως τὰς πρώτας, καὶ τὸ χαίρειν τοῖς μιμήμασι πάντας. σημεῖον δὲ τούτου τὸ συμβαῖνον ἐπὶ τῶν ἔργων· ἃ γὰρ αὐτὰ λυπηρῶς ὁρῶμεν, τούτων τὰς εἰκόνας τὰς μάλιστα ἠκριβωμένας χαίρομεν θεωροῦντες, οἷον θηρίων τε μορφὰς τῶν ἀτιμοτάτων καὶ νεκρῶν. (*Po.*, 1448b5–12)

["Imitation is natural to human beings from the time they are children. They are different from other animals in being more inclined to be imitative, learning their earliest lessons by copying and, as we see, they all get enjoyment from works of imitation. This is proved by what actually happens in our own lives, for we enjoy looking at accurate reproductions of things that are distressful to look at in actuality, repellent animals, for instance, and corpses."]

Horrible and pitiful happenings do not effect catharsis: this comes from witnessing the imitation of such events. Whatever Aristotle meant by *catharsis*, he was not discussing any alteration in the characters who were part of the fictional representation. Yet it is easy to see how this blurring of meaning has come about and has led to the casual interchange of literary-critical and other-than-critical terms such as *catharsis* and *regeneration*. Critics have been inclined to see the effect of tragedy holistically, as being part of an educative, moral, and spiritual process of improvement. For Milton, people who become better are, by definition, better Christians. Thus, all terms relating to spiritual and moral improvements have come to be treated as if interchangeable with all other terms relating to spiritual, moral, and, therefore, emotional improvement. The result, unfortunately, is to make *catharsis* quite useless as a technical, critical term. It has been used as if it is interchangeable with not only purgation, purification, and expiation, but also with calm, peace, relief, grace, conversion, consolation, regeneration, and many other good things.

This confusion of meaning and this devaluation of a critical term are unfortunate. *Catharsis* was more valuable when it more accurately indicated its limited (although undetermined) Aristotelian sense. As Milton read in Guarini's work, "può ben l'huomo per altra, e molto miglior maniera, purgar gli affetti del terrore, e della compassione, che per quella della Tragedia."[25] There are better ways to purge people than tragedy, so it is useful to be able to refer conveniently to the specific kind of purgation tragedy is said to bring about. Besides, *catharsis* could also be useful in indicating a particular intertextual network of links between Milton, Aristotle, and others, whereas now that space is heavily trampled and the tracks are hopelessly blurred. It would be helpful if the Milton Academy could somehow pronounce a moratorium on the use of *catharsis* as designating all the varied forms of Christian self-improvement and limit it to its possible Aristotelian senses of either 'effect on the consciousness of the spectator or reader' or 'aesthetic management of fictional dramatic/poetic material.'

It is conventional to read the last lines of the play as if they are a "correct" Christian assessment of all that has gone before, as if all readers should find peace and consolation in this exemplum of Christian heroism. So, for John F. Andrews, the calm of mind is "our own," that is, the readers'. It is often taken for granted that the *kommos* is Milton's own comment on the completed action. For Radzinowicz, the "lofty" words of Manoa's last speech belong "to the voice which in the last of the three movements of *Lycidas* offered similar assurance and consolation."[26] I am not convinced that the text suggests this. The references in the last seven lines are to characters in the play: to Samson ("the faithful champion"), the Philistines ("Gaza . . . and all that band them"), so that "His servants" are apparently the departing Danites. Their tone is, indeed, psalmic, which is very appropriate for Old Testament speakers pondering the ways of God, but that does not mean that they have read the encoded signs rightly as true Christian experience. It is worth comparing the end of the *Agamemnon*, although the role of the Chorus there is quite different. Clytaemestra speaks the last words. After years of nurturing her hatred, she has sated it in an orgiastic act of vengeance. Her final words are calm, peaceful, and confident. She promises to bring good order to the house of Atreus. The ending of the play is effective, and the sense of closure is false as it is in

*Samson,* for in both plays the audience's knowledge of what lies ahead ironically undercuts the words of the speaker:

Perhaps there is another level of irony undercutting the chorus's optimism: when the angel of Revelation "seals" the one hundred and forty-four thousand who will be saved at the real "close," the tribe of Dan will be omitted. Yet perhaps the most bitter irony is still to be mentioned. It should be considered by those who see the play as a subtle but defiant statement of hope by an undaunted revolutionary, still confident that the Puritan Good Old Cause can prevail, rejecting "quietism," still dreaming of a violent cleansing of England (C. Hill, 439; Jose, 135). For the contrary may be argued: that the play presents the profoundest doubts about the effectiveness of violence and the achievement of the revolutionaries. There is a postscript to the Book of Judges. Its attempt to explain the miserable aftermath to Samson's magistracy would not have given much comfort to the revolutionaries. The reason for all that misery was that "In those days *there was no king in Israel:* every man did what was right in his own eyes" (emphasis added). The Cambridge Commentary makes the point clear: "and so the institution of monarchy emerged. It was an idealistic dream that kingship would prove the solution to Israel's social and religious ills" (225–26). Samson's violent measures led not to deliverance but to the establishment of the monarchy in the hope of relief from anarchy and unrest. The parallel with the events of 1659–60 might be a bitter one for a supporter of the republican cause to contemplate.[27]

For many years critics have been hesitant about the "hopeful claims made by Manoa and the Chorus." Generally, their vision at the end has not been queried by most of those who have doubted their competence earlier in the play, like Andrews, who notes their "limited understanding" (p. 95), and Huntley, who finds them "shallow" and "self-serving," indulging in an "opaque though noble fabric of platitudes." Frye treats many of their early opinions as "doggerel" but believes they "are carried along by the action to genuine profundity and eloquence at the end."[28] The text leaves this in doubt.

It is relevant here to think for a moment about "passion spent." I have not seen an explanation of why this condition is desirable. Radzinowicz's suggestion does not help us: "Milton aims at moderative, not extirpative catharsis, and his tragedy moderates passions" ("Distinctive Tragedy," p. 277). But if "spent" means anything, it means 'extirpated' rather than 'moderated.' If Helen Damico is right that this is a highly encoded poem, we should be especially careful about its conclusions. Milton often insists that the passions are created by God and we need not "empty out" or "expel quite" our predominating passions, but that "each radicall humour and passion wrought upon and corrected as it ought, might be made the proper mould and foundation of every mans peculiar guifts, and vertues"

(YP I, p. 900).[29] His objection to the litany as a way of praying to God was that it was "leane and dry, of affections empty and unmoving, of passion, or any heigth whereto the soule might soar upon the wings of zeale, destitute and barren" (YP I, p. 939). In *Areopagitica* he asks, "Wherefore did he creat passions within us, pleasures round about us, but that these rightly temper'd are the very ingredients of vertu?" and immediately afterwards says that it is the misuse of reason to "wander beyond all limit and satiety" (YP II, pp. 527–28). Satan thinks spent passion, "satiate fury," may explain why their angry victor is not pursuing the fallen angels still (*PL* I, 179). He is wrong; he misconceives the ways of God—not that the Danites are satanic, but they are wrong, they are un-Christian, they misconceive. How different the sated loathing of the Danites is from Christ's "unappalled . . . calm and sinless peace" (*PR* IV, 425). The "calm mood" of Adam, resolved to sin and stoically resigned to punishment, is quite different also from Christ's (*PL* IX, 920); so is the "outward calm" of Satan (*PL* IV, 120). Neither is experience of the same quality as the Chorus's, but these are intertextual warnings to be careful in decoding this complex moment.

The chorus congratulates itself on its "new acquist of true experience" but why is it credited with truly interpreting experience when its perceptions are so flawed and underscored with irony? In unquestioning wish-fulfillment, the Chorus has concluded that Samson was "self-killed / Not willingly" (1664–65) although he had told the Chorus just before leaving that death was the "best" he could desire (1264). The Danites have been accused of blasphemy by some readers for seeing Samson as being "tangled in the fold, / Of dire necessity" (1665–66). Their theology is almost as dubious as that of the devils whose "stubborn patience" is founded in an ideology of "fixed fate" and "chance" and "doom" (*PL* II, 550–69). Also dubious are Manoa's concerns with monuments and laurels, with legends and traditions. "The carnal supportment of tradition" is a guide consistently despised by Milton (YP I, p. 827).

Irony underlines almost every word of the *kommos*. Even as the plans of highest wisdom are said to be "unsearchable," the Chorus presumptuously glosses what each detail of those plans means. Joan Bennett is confident that "a belief in God's inscrutability is in effect a denial of God's justice."[30] We must hesitate to agree, recalling instead how Milton lashed out violently at those who dared to analyze the workings of the mind of God, in these lines from *Eikonoklastes*, lines that suggest Milton justified the ways of God with more humility than he is usually given credit for:

He, who without warrant but his own fantastic surmise, takes upon him perpetually to unfold the secret and unsearchable Mysteries of high Providence, is likely for the most part to mistake and slander them; and approaches to the madness of those reprobate thoughts, that would wrest the Sword of Justice out of Gods [own] hand, and imploy it more justly in thir own conceit. (YP III, p. 564).

In *Christian Doctrine*, Milton describes God as "WONDERFUL and INCOMPREHENSIBLE," and he speaks of God's will as "absolute and inscrutable" (YP VI, pp. 152, 176). If that irony does not help us decode the limitations of Samson's companions, Manoa's incorrect predictions about "honour" and "freedom" for Israel and "eternal fame" for his house should: the tribe of Dan is instead omitted from the book of those who will be saved in Revelation.        25385 /

The Chorus fails to comprehend the nature of the real "close." The Judaic speakers imagine that this is an important and triumphant chapter in Israel's history and cannot see it as the small step it really is on the road of Christian history that will end with the true close, the eschaton. They are not given that knowledge of the true close which is granted to those who have received the promise. In the last lines, the poet has beautifully imitated an Old Testament spirit, a mood of tribal exultation in a bloody slaughter of the enemy, a deep relief at a sign of God's apparent satisfaction with his people. It is difficult to agree with John Arthos that "there is such compassion in it, such awe, and such charity."[31] There is nothing in the text to confirm that the voice of Milton has preempted the voices of the fictional characters except the splendid resonance and contentment in the closing lines, and those are qualities that are freely available to speakers whose understanding of heroism is pre-Christian.

It remains now to enquire whether this reading admits of peripeteia and anagnorisis in an Aristotelian sense. Ulreich considers the peripeteia is the "reversal of fortune" which he locates in Samson's revival, although Aristotle distinguished a "change of fortune" as a *metabasis* (*Po.*, 55b28). Radzinowicz also seems to consider it as Samson's "restoration to health." They are undeterred by Rees, who states flatly that it is "an unpardonable misuse of a key Aristotelian term" to use it of character, when Reversal could only be an element of plot.[32] The problems associated with peripeteia are well outlined by D. W. Lucas (1962): the complexity of its meaning, whether it refers to the audience's expectations or the characters', its relation to the main dramatic climax, and above all its special connection with the protagonist's hamartia. The last is especially important in an Aristotelian "complex" plot "because actions based on misapprehension lead to complication" (p. 60). The peripeteia is a special form of change (*metabole*): it is "an *unexpected* yet *logical* shift in the events of the play from happiness to unhappiness or the reverse."[33] The peripeteia is not, as is often suggested, Samson's decision to go with the officer. In the most powerfully dramatic fashion, it is situated in the pathos. It is unexpected by the "unsuspicious" guide (1635), by all the revelers who were struck with "amaze" (1645), thinking "their dreadful enemy their thrall" (1622). The unhappiness of the Philistines and their "years of mourning" (1712) are not in doubt; but Manoa, to lessen "the sorrow" (1564) and quench the tears, must take comfort in a heroic code that is un-Christian. The peripeteia is logical because it follows from Samson's un-Christian ethic that is unflinchingly revealed in the preceding action.

It may appear, then, that there is no anagnorisis in *Samson Agonistes*. The discussions we have had in recent years of self-recognition, moral progress, and intimations of prophetic insight follow from a determination to see the protagonist as a model for Christian self-improvement. But the play is not about the regenerative process, that is, if what Milton says of that process in *Christian Doctrine* and *Paradise Lost* is to be our guide.[34] Samson's penitence began some time after he waked to "guilty shame" (*PL* IX, 1058), and regeneration was well on its way before this play began. Rees's translation of *Poetics* 1452a29–31 is "a change from ignorance to knowledge, affecting one's relationships with one's kin or one's enemies" (*AT*, p. 15), and elsewhere he has glossed it as "the discovery of the true identity of other persons in relation to oneself, though sometimes it might be described more correctly as the realization of the circumstances in which one is placed and of which one has hitherto been ignorant" ("Pathos," p. 1). There can be no doubt that Milton considered true Christ's teaching about Christian relationships in a universal human family, moved by a love that is to be extended to one's enemies. "Death the gate of life" will bring recognition even to Samson, "for those who have died, all intervening time will be as nothing, so that to them it will seem that they die and are with Christ at the same moment" (YP VI, p. 410). For Samson, recognition will seem to come instantaneously at the moment of death. In that moment, this hero of faith will be with Christ, will recognize the futility of his violence, of his hope for the liberation of Israel, of the status of Israel itself. He will recognize his brotherhood with his *philoi*, the Philistines. This is a uniquely Christian anagnorisis in a uniquely Christian tragedy. There is, indeed, "a scene of great concentration marking the passage from ignorance to knowledge."[35] Because of the nature of Christian time, the pre-Christian survivors must remain in ignorance of it.

Margaret Arnold suggests that Milton "compressed the action of a trilogy into *Samson Agonistes,*" transcending the scope of any one Attic drama.[36] If I may disagree slightly and adapt this suggestion, it seems that Milton simulates precisely the effect of one play within a trilogy. The *Agamemnon* must serve again as an example, since our knowledge of trilogies other than the *Oresteia* is incomplete. That drama has its own unity and it appears to have closure. It is unnecessarily schematic to suggest that Milton arranged his last three poems with the idea of an Attic trilogy in mind. It is true, nonetheless, as it might be in the first or second play in a Greek trilogy, that the dramatic action in Milton's play appears to be complete, but the predicate lies in the future with the unfolding of Christian history. There is a tropic formal appropriateness about the lack of closure since no human event can be more than an episode in the linear historic progress toward the eschaton. It seems to me (to echo Margaret Arnold's conclusion) that Milton has done in his own language, with even more precision, understanding, and inventiveness than he has been given credit for, "what the greatest and choycest wits of Athens [etc. did in theirs . . . ] with this over and above of being a Christian" (YPI, p. 812).

St. Francis Xavier University

NOTES

Work done in Florence to prepare this essay was made possible by grants from St. Francis Xavier University and the Social Sciences and Humanities Research Council of Canada, for which this writer is very grateful.

1. Barbara Kiefer Lewalski, "Milton's *Samson* and the 'New Acquist of True [Political] Experience,'" *Milton Studies,* XXIV, ed. James D. Simmonds (Pittsburgh, 1988), p. 233.

2. Derek N.C. Wood, " 'Exil'd from Light': The Darkened Moral Consciousness of Milton's Hero of Faith," *UTQ* LVIII (1989), 244–62. See p. 246 for discussion of the reference to Salmasius in *Complete Prose Works of John Milton,* ed. Don M. Wolfe et al. (New Haven, 1953–82), vol. VI, p. 583, hereafter cited as YP.

3. Jacqueline DiSalvo, "Make War Not Love: On *Samson Agonistes* and the *Caucasian Chalk Circle,*" *Milton Studies,* XXIV, ed. James D. Simmonds (Pittsburgh, 1988), pp. 213, 214.

4. Aristotle, *Aristotelis de arte poetica liber,* ed. R. Kassel (Oxford, 1965), 49b27, hereafter cited as *Po.* in the text; Mary Ann Radzinowicz, *Toward "Samson Agonistes": The Growth of Milton's Mind* (Princeton, 1978), p. 346.

5. M. E. Grenander, "*Samson*'s Middle: Aristotle and Dr. Johnson," *UTQ* XXXIV (1955), 388; William R. Parker, *Milton's Debt to Greek Tragedy in "Samson Agonistes,"*

(1937; rpt. Hamden, 1963), p. 70; Martin E. Mueller, "*Pathos* and *Katharsis* in *Samson Agonistes*," *ELH* XXXI (1964), 170–74.

6. See Daniel C. Boughner, "Milton's Harapha and Renaissance Comedy," *ELH* XI (1944), 297–306; Helen Damico, "Duality in Dramatic Vision: A Structural Analysis of *Samson Agonistes*," *Milton Studies* XXII, ed. James D. Simmonds (Pittsburgh, 1978), pp. 91–116; Anthony Low, *The Blaze of Noon: A Reading of "Samson Agonistes,"* (New York, 1974), pp. 158–62, 306.

7. B. R. Rees, "*Pathos* in the *Poetics* of Aristotle," *Classical Quarterly* XXII (1972), 11, referred to as "*Pathos*" in the notes and in the text; Gerald F. Else, *The Origin and Early Form of Greek Tragedy* (Cambridge, Mass., 1965), p. 88; *Aristotle's Poetics: The Argument*, trans. Gerald F. Else (Cambridge, Mass., 1957), p. 356.

8. B. R. Rees, *Aristotle's Theory and Milton's Practice: "Samson Agonistes"* (Birmingham, 1972), p. 15, referred to as *AT* in the notes and in the text.

9. Ruth Mohl, *John Milton and His Commonplace Book* (New York, 1969), p. 39; W. B. Hunter, "Milton's Theological Vocabulary," in *Bright Essence: Studies in Milton's Theology*, ed. W. B. Hunter, C. A. Patrides, and J. H. Adamson (Salt Lake City, 1972), pp. 15–25.

10. Christopher Hill, *Milton and the English Revolution* (London, 1977); *The Experience of Defeat: Milton and Some Contemporaries* (New York, 1984); Nicholas Jose, "*Samson Agonistes:* The Play Turned Upside Down," *Essays in Criticism* XXX (1980), pp. 124–50.

11. Hill, *Experience of Defeat*, pp. 32, 102, 115, 161, and throughout text.

12. *Paradise Lost* XI, 754–57. All references to Milton's poetry are to *The Poems of John Milton*, ed. John Carey and Alastair Fowler (London, 1968).

13. James A. Winn, "Milton on Heroic Warfare," *The Yale Review* LXVI (1976), 70–86.

14. James Holly Hanford, "*Samson Agonistes* and Milton in Old Age," *Studies in Shakespeare, Milton and Donne* (New York, 1925), p. 183; J. S. Hill, "Vocation and Spiritual Renovation in *Samson Agonistes*," *Milton Studies* II, ed. James D. Simmonds (Pittsburgh, 1970), p. 154; Jan Maarten Bremer, *Hamartia* (Amsterdam, 1969), p. 63.

15. Alessandro Pazzi, *Aristotelis Poetica* (Venice, 1536), f. 14.

16. Francesco Robortello, *In librum Aristotelis de arte poetica explicationes* (Florence, 1548); Iason Denores, *Poetica* (Padua, 1588), f. 44–44ᵛ.

17. Pietro Vettori, *Petri Victorii commentarii, in primum librum Aristotelis de arte poetarum* (Florence, 1560), p. 123; Alessandro Piccolomini, *Annotationi . . . nel libro della poetica d'Aristotele* (Venice, 1575), p. 195.

18. A.W.H. Adkins, "Aristotle and the Best Kind of Tragedy," *Classical Quarterly* XVI (1966), 101.

19. See Hunter, "Milton's Theological Vocabulary," p. 25.

20. D. W. Lucas, *Aristotle Poetics: Introduction, Commentary and Appendixes* (Oxford, 1968), p. 302.

21. R. D. Dawe, "Some Reflections on Ate and Hamartia," *Harvard Studies in Classical Philology* LXXII (1968), 91.

22. D. W. Lucas, "Pity, Terror, and *Peripeteia*," *Classical Quarterly* XII (1962), 56; Else, *Aristotle's Poetics*, p. 383n; see also Mueller, "*Pathos* and *Katharsis*," p. 170.

23. Mueller, "*Pathos* and *Katharsis*," p. 169; Mary Ann Radzinowicz, "The Distinctive Tragedy of *Samson Agonistes*," in *Milton Studies* XVII, ed. Richard S. Ide and Joseph Wittreich (Pittsburgh, 1983), p. 254; Georgia Christopher, "Homeopathic Physic and Natural Renovation in *Samson Agonistes*," *ELH* XXXVII (1970), 373; Sherman H. Hawkins, "Samson's Catharsis," in *Milton Studies* II (Pittsburgh, 1970), p. 219.

24. See, for instance, chapters 2 and 3 in Baxter Hathaway, *The Age of Criticism: The*

*Late Renaissance in Italy* (Ithaca, 1962). See especially, *passim*, Francesco Patrizi da Cherso, *Della Poetica*, 3 vols, ed. Danilo Aguzzi Barbagli, Istituto Nazionale di Studi sul Rinascimento, (Florence, 1969–71).

25. Battista Guarini, *Il Verato Secondo* (Ferrara, 1593), p. 63.

26. John F. Andrews, " 'Dearly Bought Revenge': *Samson Agonistes, Hamlet*, and Elizabethan Revenge Tragedy," in *Milton Studies* XIII, ed. James D. Simmonds (Pittsburgh, 1979), p. 96; Radzinowicz, "Distinctive Tragedy," p. 260.

27. Wood, " 'Exil'd from Light,' " pp. 251–52.

28. Daniel T. Lochman, " 'If There Be Aught of Presage': Milton's Samson As Riddler and Prophet," in *Milton Studies* XXII, ed. James D. Simmonds (Pittsburgh, 1986), p. 213. See also the following discussions: G. Finney, "Chorus in *Samson Agonistes*," *PMLA* LVIII (1943), 649–63; Virginia R. Mollenkott, "Relativism in *Samson Agonistes*," *SP* LXVII (1970), 89–102; Joan S. Bennett, "Liberty Under the Law: The Chorus and the Meaning of *Samson Agonistes*," in *Milton Studies* XII, ed. James D. Simmonds (Pittsburgh, 1978), pp. 141–63; John Huntley, "A Revaluation of the Chorus' Role in Milton's *Samson Agonistes*," *MP* LXIV (1966–67), 137; Northrop Frye, "Agon and Logos: Revolution and Revelation," in *The Prison and the Pinnacle*, ed. Balachandra Rajan (London, 1973), p. 159.

29. See J. Arthos, "Milton and the Passions: A Study of *Samson Agonistes*," *MP* LXIX (1971–2), 209–21.

30. Joan Bennett, "A Reading of *Samson Agonistes*," in *The Cambridge Companion to Milton*, ed. Dennis Danielson (Cambridge, 1989), p. 232.

31. John Arthos, "Milton and the Passions: A Study of *Samson Agonistes*," *MP* LXIX (1971–72), 221.

32. John C. Ulreich, Jr., " 'Beyond the Fifth Act': *Samson Agonistes* as Prophecy," in *Milton Studies* XVII, ed. Richard S. Ide and Joseph Wittreich (Pittsburgh, 1983), p. 285; Radzinowicz; *Toward "Samson Agonistes*," p. 61; Rees, *AT*, p. 6;

33. Else, *Aristotle's Poetics*, p. 344.

34. See, for instance, G. A. Wilkes, "The Interpretation of *Samson Agonistes*," *Huntington Library Quarterly* XXVI (1962–63), 363–79; Mason Tung, "Samson Impatiens: a Reinterpretation of Milton's *Samson Agonistes*," *TSLL* IX (1967–68), 475–92. Hill, *Milton and the English Revolution*, p. 433, does not believe regeneration is the main structural principle in the play. See also *Christian Doctrine*, especially YP VI, pp. 461–70, but also 189–97 on reprobation. See also John Carey, *Milton* (London, 1969); Irene Samuel, "*Samson Agonistes* as Tragedy," in *Calm of Mind*, ed. Joseph A. Wittreich, Jr. (Cleveland, 1971), pp. 235–57; Joseph Wittreich, *Interpreting "Samson Agonistes"* (Princeton, 1986).

35. Lucas, *Aristotle Poetics*, p. 294. See also I. M. Glanville, "Note on Peripeteia," *Classical Quarterly* XLI (1947), 73–78; Glanville, "Hamartia and Tragic Error," *Classical Quarterly* XLIII (1949), 47–56; S. H. Butcher, *Aristotle's Theory of Poetry and Fine Art*, 4th ed. (New York, 1951); M. Ostwald, "Aristotle on *Hamartia* and Sophocles' *OT*," in *Festschrift Kapp* (Hamburg, 1958), pp. 93–108; *Aristotle's "Poetics" and English Literature: A Collection of Critical Essays*, ed. Elder Olson (Chicago, 1965); H.D.F. Kitto, "Catharsis," in *The Classical Tradition: Literary and Historical Studies in Honor of Harry Caplan* (Ithaca, 1966), pp. 133–47; G.M.A. Grube, *The Greek and Roman Critics* (Toronto, 1968); T.C.W. Stinton, "*Hamartia* in Aristotle and Greek Tragedy," *Classical Quarterly* XXV (1975), 221–54; John Moles, "Notes on Aristotle, *Poetics* 13 and 14," *Classical Quarterly* XXIX (1979), 77–94; D. Armstrong and C. W. Peterson, "Rhetorical Balance in Aristotle's Definition of the Tragic Agent: *Poetics* 13," *Classical Quarterly* XXX (1980), 62–71; Charles B. Schmitt, *Aristotle and the Renaissance* (Cambridge, Mass., 1983).

36. Margaret Arnold, "*Graeci Christiani*: Milton's Samson and the Renaissance Edi-

tors of Greek Tragedy," in *Milton Studies* XVIII, ed. James D. Simmonds (Pittsburgh, 1983), pp. 247–49. Other works not cited above that should be consulted in relation to this discussion are Paul R. Sellin, "Sources of Milton's Catharsis: a Reconsideration," *JEGP* LX (1961), 712–30; Martin Mueller, "Sixteenth-Century Italian Criticism and Milton's Theory of Catharsis," *SEL* VI (1966), 139–50; Paul R. Sellin, *Daniel Heinsius and Stuart England* (London, 1968); Annette C. Flower, "The Critical Context of the Preface to *Samson Agonistes*," *SEL* X (1970), 409–23; J. M. Steadman, "Passions Well Imitated: Rhetoric and Poetics in the Preface to *Samson Agonistes*," in *Calm of Mind*, ed. J. A. Wittreich, Jr. (Cleveland, 1971), pp. 175–207; R. B. Waddington, "Melancholy Against Melancholy: *Samson Agonistes* as Renaissance Tragedy," in *Calm of Mind*, ed. J. A. Wittreich, Jr., (Cleveland, 1971), pp. 259–87.

# IMAGINING DEATH: THE WAYS OF MILTON

## Arnold Stein

M ANY GOOD writers have contributed to the remarkable body of
eloquence inspired by death, and much of that eloquence is immediately responded to and understood. Milton's eloquence for the most part
works differently. Many of his expressions need the ampler space of prepared context and field of reference in order to speak at full power. In
contrast, for example, we understand Sir Walter Raleigh at once when he
declares that "great lords of the world" "neglect the advice of God . . . but
they follow the counsell of Death, upon his first approach."[1] We may not
feel competent to judge the spirituality of Raleigh's performance on the
scaffold but he seems to have a special dispensation to ignore the standard
"counsell of Death." In some of his poems Raleigh deliberately displays
brief but correct piety and an emphatically untroubled conscience. To be
one of Raleigh's enemies and to read these poems was to feel clumsy and
be furious, and perhaps be driven to thoughts that gambled recklessly
with one's own salvation. At dying, fictive or actual, Raleigh was a virtuoso
player. The passage of time and the resistance of his own genius make it
difficult to judge Raleigh's postures or to detect and measure the presence
of morbidity.

The personal strangeness of another virtuoso player, John Donne,
does not give itself away easily, but he commands our immediate response
to the arresting image:

> Thinke then, my soule, that death is but a Groome.
> Which brings a Taper to the outward roome,
> Whence thou spiest first a little glimmering light,
> And after brings it nearer to thy sight.[2]

Donne had a hundred ways of saying it. George Herbert, a master of
eliciting the immediate response, marvelously diverts and transforms materials of morbidity, as when he addresses pre-Christian death as an "un-
couth, hideous thing," aptly imaged by bones and skull: "Thy mouth was
open but thou couldst not sing."[3]

But my subject is Milton, whose mature thoughts on death are most
clearly available in *Paradise Lost*, an epic that creates a rich world of

internal and external reference. The hero of *Paradise Regained* does not fear death at all, and the hero of *Samson Agonistes* is, or thinks he is, looking for death. Only *Paradise Lost* needs to tell the fuller story. I think I overstate matters very little to say that Milton's God "Knew it not good" for fallen man to live without sound instruction concerning death. The content and emphasis of that instruction I shall try to follow through toward the end of my essay. But other matters will come first.

According to my personal scale for estimating these matters, Milton shows considerable moderation toward the subject of death. As theologian he seems to have settled his thoughts and to have reserved his best attention and energy for other matters. As poet he did not encourage his imagination to rove freely or linger hopefully in unknown territory. This is not to be taken as my last word on the subject. I am now emphasizing the kind of poetic imagination that has accepted certain tasks, for instance in *Paradise Lost* that of teaching Adam how to live, conscious of death, in the world outside the original garden. That task will require an imagination responsive to choices preferred by reason and characterized by certain restraints. I hasten to add: imaginative excitement will not be simply sacrificed. In the meantime, I offer an isolated example, that of the dramatic use of an untrustworthy character to philosophize upon instinctual feeling. In Pandemonium, Belial (not yet slipped into his later career of lurking and waylaying, but poet, orator, and spokesman for the life of thought and feeling) asks:

> for who would lose,
> Though full of pain, this intellectual being,
> Those thoughts that wander through eternity,
> To perish rather, swallowed up and lost
> In the wide womb of uncreated Night,
> Devoid of sense and motion?          (II, 146–51)[4]

At the end of his speech time is both life and hope, set to the music of a siren song: "Besides what hope the never-ending flight / Of future days may bring, what chance, what change / Worth waiting" (II, 221–23). I am illustrating Milton's resourcefulness in expressing, for particular situations, strong but deliberately limited views of death.

I turn now to the beginning of *Paradise Lost* to illustrate something of the kind of power Milton can generate by making and using a field of reference:

> Of man's first disobedience, and the fruit
> Of that forbidden tree, whose mortal taste
> Brought death into the world, and all our woe.          (I, 1–3)

What is death here? As physical state it is the cessation or absence of life—what we mean in an ordinary sense. But as something brought into the world, not created with the world, death requires a conceptual effort. It comes with a cause and a history, from an act of disobedience, the first one, an act both simple and comprehensive. The tree is forbidden and all the related meanings of its *fruit* are transferred to the "mortal taste" and "Brought . . . into the world" as death. "All our woe" is a large addition— not death itself, but freely related in obvious ways and also in subtle or remote ways to be found out by thought and experience. Milton's imagination is here making its choices in known territory. The items evoked draw their figurative life from the story to which they belong.

According to the story, this death is *the* death, the primary one. It is expressed by no single authoritative image but is a fertile source of images. When Milton's Eve eats the apple, we are told that she "knew not eating death"(IX, 792). The syntactical compression and exoticism require an attentive reader to expand the brevity and follow up the meanings. Frank Kermode has provided an instructive demonstration of some of the possibilities:

"She knew not that she was eating death"; "she knew not Death even as she ate it"; "although she was so bold as to eat Death for the sake of knowledge, she still did not know—indeed she did not even know what she had known before, namely that this was a sin." Above all she eats Death, makes it a part of her formerly incorruptible body, and so explains the human sense of the possibility of incorruption, so tragically belied by fact.5

To receive the benefit of this communication we must be willing to forgo our pleasure in striking visual images; we must also be willing to treat seriously language that strains our sense of propriety. Ignorance, eager ignorance, and death are part of the character of the first disobedience as Milton writes the story. The trivial and the tragic find themselves together as Eve unconsciously imitates the monster Death for whom Milton has written a special part in the poem. A dozen lines before the intensity of "eating death" we are given the facts: "she plucked, she eat," and notices nothing outside herself but only inner experience: the taste, the rapture of immediate delight, and the surging expectations that rise in her consciousness just before the act of eating comes around again and is characterized. We return to the eating and concentrate on it as if it were really beginning now, or rather seen only now in a well-prepared moment: "Greedily she engorged without restraint, / And knew not eating death" (IX, 791–92).

The greedy eating echoes and anticipates the monster Death and his

almost unbounded hunger. In hell Death grins a "ghastly smile" when
Satan promises that on earth "all things shall be your prey" (II, 846, 844).
When he arrives in Paradise, Death acknowledges the appearance of
plenty but doubts that he will be able to satisfy his famine, "To stuff this
maw" (X, 601). Milton combines the familiar attribute of Death as a raven-
ous devourer with the remarkable service of Death (and Sin) as the original sanitation department. Furthermore, they themselves become the
material means of fulfilling the prophecy to be made in good time by St.
Paul: "The last enemy that shall be destroyed is death" (1 Cor. XV, 26). Or
as Milton's God explains,

> till crammed and gorged, nigh burst
> With sucked and glutted offal, at one sling
> Of thy victorious arm, well-pleasing Son,
> Both Sin and Death, and yawning grave at last
> Through Chaos hurled, obstruct the mouth of hell
> For ever, and seal up his ravenous jaws.          (X, 632–37)

The Son's vision in Book III contained the essential point: "While by thee
raised I ruin all my foes, / Death last, and with his carcass glut the grave"
(258–59).

So Eve reflects a special affinity with Death that seems to come from
no discernible previous cause influencing her will. Death serves the story
as a kind of nightmare mythic source, a general field of reference, and a
preview of things to come. There may be a bitter universal message in
that connection between the beauty of the first woman and the repulsive
horror of Death—though however we figure such a malediction we must
not forget that Satan is the matchmaker. In any case, after Eve's first
excitement over the fruit, her thoughts and speech exhibit a rich flow and
counterflow of symptoms recognizable as having been released by sin and
as placing her in the way of punishment. Later, in Book XI, a renewal of
Eve's connection with Death emerges, and she will be assigned specific
culpability for one kind of distress leading to death among her descendants. The occasion is Adam's being presented with a full display of human maladies—"A lazar-house it seemed" (XI, 479)—and Adam protests
against such "inhuman pains" and "deformities." Michael rigorously rejects Adam's argument and explains that these miseries are the punishment of serving "ungoverned appetite / . . . a brutish vice, / Inductive
mainly to the sin of Eve" (XI, 517–19). It is her "inabstinence" that will
bring on these calamities. One would like to feel that Adam's unhesitating
answer—"I yield it just . . . and submit" (526)—owes nothing, or next to
nothing, to the announcement of Eve's blame. If we regard this particular

judgment against Eve as unduly harsh and cleaving closely to the letter, we may also think that she is not being humiliated, bullied, lectured, and painfully rebuilt, as Adam is. We shall return to the strenuous education Adam receives on the subject of death.

I have been offering examples and illustrations by way of introducing some of "the ways of Milton." I continue by drawing materials from the early Milton, especially from *Lycidas*.

In some early poems Milton imagines his own death directly; in the later poems the author does not stage himself so. In *Lycidas* the reference to his own death is employed casually in passing, as a reason for joining the continuity of poets elegizing poets:

> So may some gentle Muse
> With lucky words favor my destined urn,
> And as he passes turn,
> And bid fair peace be to my sable shroud.　　　　　(19–22)

The statement echoes convention, and certainly offers no unmediated intimacy, but it does not feel casual. A year later, writing to Manso, Milton ends with a formal scene picturing a peaceful, satisfied death, all the literary life's work completed, the faithful friend standing by, sympathetic and helpful:

Then, too, if faith has meaning, if rewards are assured for the good, I myself, carried away to the home of the heavenly gods to which labor and a pure mind and ardent virtue lead, shall see these things, as far as the fates allow, from some part of that secret world, and, with my mind wholly serene and my smiling face suffused with rosy light, I shall in joy know myself blessed in ethereal Olympus.[6]

The passage is a sculptured moment of tenderness and delicacy of feeling, formal, "literary," and diplomatic in sending song across religious borders. All irritants of modern religious controversy are freely translated into the pleasing language of Greek mythology. A variation occurs a year or two later in the elegy for his close friend, Charles Diodati. There a piece of mimetic naivety expresses a compulsive part, as grief and loneliness interrupt the magnum opus of the shepherd-author. His great project of an Arthurian epic (perhaps already troubled by intimations of its own decease) he nevertheless manages to sketch out in order to bring the departed friend up to date. The sense of strain is ragged and, like other things in the elegy, for a moment out of control or almost out of control.

I return to *Lycidas*, for the poem is highly wrought and does wonderful things by using an externally established field of reference, the pastoral elegy. Milton also presents effects that are immediate and physical, emergıng from under a veil of conventional manners. I want to emphasize that capacity for directness in a context, for I shall illustrate a similar capacity on a larger scale when we come to fallen Adam's intensive instruction on the subject of death. In *Lycidas* Milton composes his fullest response to the death of another and to the sense of loss that compels the questioning of life as if it were directly answerable to the ways of death. The richness of the poem makes it difficult to limit one's attention to particular subordinate matters, but I do not intend to dilate upon the great beauties and active intricacies of the poem. I want to concentrate on Milton's handling of death, and especially on the ways he imagines it.

Some of the poet's deep involvement in his subject takes the turn of imagining death in hateful forms, abruptly and nakedly, or almost so. For instance, "Who would not sing for Lycidas?" (10) would seem to be an introduction that invites a ceremonial response, perhaps elaborate. Instead, the practical answer is that Lycidas was a poet and should be mourned in poetry. Furthermore, that answer provides the transition and initiative to visualize the dead friend as he is: "He must not float upon his wat'ry bier / Unwept, and welter to the parching wind" (12–13). "Wat'ry bier" is a kind of embellishment, perhaps trivial in its play of wit, yet nevertheless for a moment or more lessening the shock of the invoked dead body plainly floating before the mind's eye. The rhythm of "upon his wat'ry bier" may add a painfully realistic rocking motion to that imagined floating body, but the formal protest against the grotesquely improper "bier" can also deflect at least some of our attention from the unqualified deadness of "float." Still, the deadness is emphasized and held in protracted view by two supplementary actions: "welter" and "parching." That next line is utterly unsparing: "and welter to the parching wind." It is then followed by a line that is lavishly embellished: "Without the meed of some melodious tear" (14).

Other examples repeat, vary, and extend these imaginative actions: "Where were ye, Nymphs, when the remorseless deep / Closed o'er the head of your loved Lycidas?" (50–51). To readers who recognize the live metaphor in the etymology of "remorseless," the single effect of the epithet is opened up and made more active. The imagining of a head going under is stimulated to see the closing action as that of a mouth, just then, as the moment is evoked, biting once and for all. The sea is remorseless because it bites, as it were, and swallows, from an above-water perspective, but the sea is not itself bitten by any feeling. A brief, self-conscious elaboration ("remorseless . . . Closed . . . loved") provides some indirectness as a brutal directness produces the mental image of a head disappearing. Another image of death then follows, that of Orpheus. He is not drowned and not presented in a mental image requiring some time to evolve, but Milton accords six lines to the case of Orpheus. The embellishing indirectness comes first, and like a brief obituary introduces the lineage, the fact that he was "enchanting" and that he was lamented by "universal nature." Then we get the direct view, but after the raging mob have killed and dismembered him:

> When by the rout that made the hideous roar
> His gory visage down the stream was sent,
> Down the swift Hebrus to the Lesbian shore. (61–63)

The example of Orpheus, besides illustrating the vulnerability of poets, also provides a complimentary analogue to the still-promising young poet, but the ancient figure also varies and then cuts across the general atmosphere of ceremony. Though the event itself is recalled from the dimly remote past, the head of Orpheus comes into the poem with the credentials of an immediate horror.

I have two more related examples to offer. First, the lines inquiring into the present whereabouts of the drowned Lycidas:

> Ay me! whilst thee the shores and sounding seas
> Wash far away, where'er thy bones are hurled,
> Whether beyond the stormy Hebrides,
> Where thou perhaps under the whelming tide
> Visit'st the bottom of the monstrous world;
> Or whether thou, to our moist vows denied,
> Sleep'st by the fable of Bellerus old,
> Where the great Vision of the guarded mount
> Looks toward Namancos and Bayona's hold:
> Look homeward, Angel, now, and melt with ruth;
> And, O ye dolphins, waft the hapless youth. (154–64)

"Visit'st" is extraordinary: "Visit'st the bottom of the monstrous world." Since it is a word strongly attached to activities of the living—as in making purposive social calls or enjoying the recreational privileges of pleasing sights—we must be shocked when the "visiting" takes place entirely outside the possibility of living purpose or response. The underwater body drifts according to the movement of water and in ways painful to imagine as we recognize how to our minds the dead seems, though clumsily, to imitate the alive, perhaps bumping and retreating from objects, or sidling, or being deflected by them, seldom staying long in one place, as if animated by a restless curiosity, perhaps responding to sights at "the bottom of the monstrous world." Milton has been very hard on us and probably on himself, but he is about to make amends by the immediate

alternative to "Visit'st": "Or whether thou . . . Sleep'st by the fable of
Bellerus old." That venerable image of death as sleep signals a retreat
from harsh surprises and embellishments and after-effects toward a stage
of melting with pity and invoking dolphins to "waft the hapless youth."
Wafting interposes more than "a little ease."

Finally I point to that early episode when hope for success in our
writing leads us to expect "to burst out into sudden blaze," that is, fame.
But just then "Comes the blind Fury with th' abhorrèd shears, / And slits
the thin-spun life" (75–76). The directness of the violence here most
resembles that surrounding the "gory visage" of Orpheus, but the directness also resembles effects produced by "float," "welter," "parching," "remorseless," "visit'st"—those unmitigated views of death. By embellishment and other contrasting effects Milton both opposes and accentuates
hateful views of death. The occurrences are easier to identify and describe
than to comprehend. They seem to be not so much part of a technique of
writing as a way of sensing an imaginative experience in the making.

After the flower passage and before the healing vision of Lycidas in
heaven, the poet presents himself in a moment of confessed personal weakness: "For so to interpose a little ease, / Let our frail thoughts dally with false
surmise" (152–53). The acts of embellishment may spring from the same
desire. The vision in heaven serves to authorize the end of mourning. It
does not, however, rescue, unite, or complete all previous affirmations of
"frail thoughts"; it does not confirm expressions of hopefulness that are
subject to faltering and fading. But as the sun goes down and the song for
Lycidas comes to its formal close, we return to normal time, the ordinary
world, and the rediscovery of good in the expectations of life. The great
words of release are common ones: "To-morrow . . . fresh . . . new." The
ways Milton engages conflicts in the poem look forward to *Paradise Lost*.
Indeed, the end of *Paradise Lost* may seem to be a partly reimagined end of
*Lycidas*.

What I have been saying of *Lycidas* moves away from one of my
introductory descriptions of Milton's ways of imagining death—that he
did not encourage his imagination to rove freely, and that he preferred
strong but deliberately limited images of death chosen for particular purposes and answerable to reason. But in *Lycidas* the conditions are different: a process of formal questioning is both interrupted and advanced by
open moments of searching that seem unrestricted and are intense but are
also unsustained. To speak in general: Images that startle may turn from
quick stimulants of attention to vehicles of transition; among other potentialities they may haunt us. If such images remain relatively isolated and yet
haunt us, they are rare and resist discussion. What I am getting ready to
say is that the first impression of an image as original and as opening

unknown territory will also create further expectations, and how these are met will determine what we come to think of that image. Whether immediately striking or not, an image that seeks and makes connections is telling a story; its ways and its pace must be learned while reading. We cannot assume that the story will be tame, predictable, and lacking force. For example, and by way of returning to *Paradise Lost:* the image of Eve who "knew not eating death" owes more to its power to expand while revealing significant connections than to the startling novelty of the earliest stages of the image. The moment that brings together greed, ignorance, and death becomes a story; its obviousness may be considered self-evident and perhaps universal. The unfolding narrative will show how and why it happened, and with more suspense and subtlety and surprise and pleasure than we dared to expect. My last point is that the story is also mysterious; traces of the unexplained persist and may attract.

In *Paradise Lost* death has many shapes and is elicited in many ways: by images, or references, or suggestions at one or more removes; and by anticipations, memories, glimpses. The loss of happiness necessitates the withdrawal of immortality. That is the official word of the poem and the world it recreates and engages itself to justify. Moreover, in Milton that link of happiness lost and death found stimulates a prolific imagination. Things related to the black, cold "dregs / Adverse to life" (VII, 238–39) may exhibit various degrees of relationship to death. After the fall there is war, a direct relationship, but also peace and its perverse luxury, riot, and decay. Exile, solitude, derision may raise thoughts of death. The mind acting as if wholly in possession of itself and of everything thinkable can mythologize law and the nature of things; so Adam declares to Eve: "if death / Consort with thee, death is to me as life" (IX, 953–54). Thoughts of death, besides being a rich source of feelings apt for expressive purposes, have worked themselves thoroughly into the common language. So Eve, deciding whether to share the forbidden fruit with Adam, remembers that sentence of death:

> Then I shall be no more,
> And Adam wedded to another Eve
> Shall live with her enjoying, I extinct;
> A death to think. (IX, 827–30)

Or simpler still, Eve, overhearing the sentence of their banishment from the Garden, begins her touching lament: "O unexpected stroke, worse than of Death! / Must I thus leave thee, Paradise?" (XI, 268–69). The angel interrupts her and gently redirects her thoughts. Somewhat later Adam will hear of Paradise banished from itself, as it were, and exhibiting a degree of change that may seem to approach death. During the Flood

Paradise will have its "verdure spoiled and trees adrift," and will become "an island salt and bare, / The haunt of seals and orcs, and sea-mews' clang" (XI, 832, 834–35).

Familiar images may possess a latent power to travel unanticipated paths. In *Samson Agonistes* the hero can call his blindness "a living death" (100), "exiled from light (98) . . . yet in light" (99). Not until line 575, however, toward the end of his father's visit, do we hear him declare that he desires and has been desiring death, which has been "oft invoked"— though not directly and not in our hearing. But after Manoa leaves, Samson's long lament ends:

> This one prayer yet remains, might I be heard,
> No long petition—speedy death.
> The close of all my miseries, and the balm.          (649–51)

Samson's death is felt as an impending issue of the poem, a center of problems and their resolution, an issue that is expressed by many masked or indirect references to death. The most familiar image, sleep, participates in a strange story. In Samson's great lament after the departure of Manoa, he speaks these lines:

> Sleep hath forsook and giv'n me o'er
> To death's benumbing opium as my only cure,
> Thence faintings, swoonings of despair,
> And sense of Heav'n's desertion.          (629–32)

There was an earlier time when his relations with sleep were interrupted and were the source of a personal problem, serious enough but common, potentially a subject for crude jokes, but far removed from "swoonings of despair." Dalila's "feminine assaults"

> surceased not day or night
> To storm me over-watched, and wearied out,
> At times when men seek most repose and rest,
> I yielded, and unlocked her all my heart.          (404–07)

At last Samson has one more opportunity to play the scene, now revised. During the "intermission" of his labors to give pleasure to the Philistines, Samson requested permission,

> As over-tired to let him lean a while
> With both his arms on those two massy pillars
> That to the arched roof gave main support.          (1632–34)

When he stands "with head a while inclined," we may wonder, briefly, about the humble display of public weariness, but we are not likely to imagine his rest as a kind of dozing, and whatever the exact content of his prayer (if he is indeed praying), we are not invited to think that he still is mentally where he has been before, whether in bed with Dalila or repeating his petition for "death's benumbing opium as my only cure" (630).

I come now to the course of instruction Milton prepared for the fallen Adam. As the angel Michael begins the educational retraining that will prepare Adam to live in the world outside, the main purposes named to Adam are these: "to learn / True patience" (XI, 360–61), "to temper" extremes and bear contrary states:

> Prosperous or adverse: so shalt thou lead
> Safest thy life, and best prepared endure
> Thy mortal passage when it comes.     (XI, 364–66)

Training for the new life is directed toward the new end of life, enduring "Thy mortal passage when it comes." Nothing in the course description leads one to expect easy pleasure, or to fill relaxed moments by contemplating the prospect of graduation. Some unhurried preliminaries have already taken place, and Michael has been "mild" and "benign" in answering Eve and Adam. Now Adam learns in an aside that a special kind of sleep has been arranged for Eve; he then is furnished with a brief vision of the future Kingdoms of the world, after which his eyesight is purged and he is directed to behold "Th'effects which thy original crime hath wrought" (XI, 424). This is the death of Abel, which begins as pastoral and ends as something else. When we witness the first human death in the world, and through the eyes of the father-to-be, whose responses to the sight are still governed by his having lived almost all his life in the state of innocence, we see an Adam deeply troubled but only half understanding the violence and apparent injustice. He cries out:

> O Teacher, some great mischief hath befall'n
> To that meek man, who well had sacrificed;
> Is piety thus and pure devotion paid?     (XI, 450–52)

Though "also moved," like Adam and like us, the angel explains the incident in a calm manner and assures Adam that justice will be done.

In spite of the dismaying prospect of unborn sons murdering and dying, the central shock to Adam is the personal discovery:

> But have I now seen Death? Is this the way
> I must return to native dust? O sight
> Of terror, foul and ugly to behold,
> Horrid to think, how horrible to feel!     (XI, 462–65)

Though Michael has explained that there will be revenge and reward, it is the death itself that grips Adam's attention, that and the instant imaginative transference to seeing, thinking, and feeling his own death. In this Adam anticipates Raleigh's insight and responds at once to the "counsell of Death." To move Adam from this demonstrated human base of terror and revulsion, Michael, though clearly working against a set time, needs to order and apply his lessons gradually. He chooses, first, to acknowledge but limit the terror and, second, to discipline the revulsion by repeating the basic experience through significantly progressing variations of the "foul and ugly." He begins by reminding Adam that he has thus far observed only death's "first shape on man." There are many shapes:

> and many are the ways that lead
> To his grim cave, all dismal; yet to sense
> More terrible at th'entrance than within.          (XI, 468–70)

Michael has the intuitive equipment of a master diplomat. He admits the undeniable truth at once: the cave is "grim" and all the ways to it are "dismal." But it is worse at the entrance than within. That piece of half-information may be worth something later. Besides, judgment is now limited to the report of sense and the difference between "More terrible at th'entrance" and less terrible "within." This leaves room for reports from the higher faculties contributing to judgment, and anticipates a more propitious time when the more fully informed listener may be ready to respond to a whole situation.

Fire, flood, and famine are added to the list, with no elaboration. Then one further cause of death is introduced, "Diseases dire," and only one cause is mentioned, intemperance "In meats and drinks." A private showing is promised of the "misery" attributed to Eve's "inabstinence." (We may add this far-reaching effect to "Greedily she engorged.") The comparison is hurried and pinched, but Michael seems to be saying that more will die of intemperance than by violence supplemented by fire, flood, famine. The "sad, noisome, dark" place comes to Adam "immediately" (XI, 478, 477). "A lazar-house it seemed" (XI, 479). Many diseases are named and sparely but effectively characterized. They add up, and Milton remembered a few more for the second edition. Amidst the suffering sick there is an emblematic figure of Death, triumphant and shaking his dart, "but delayed to strike, though oft invoked" (XI, 492). Adam's revulsion receives strong medicine (of a homeopathic sort); his response is to return to a vein of thought first discovered after his inner decision to join Eve in eating the forbidden fruit, and further developed in the long meditative soliloquy of Book X, where he tried to argue with God and speculated on the meaning and nature of death. Now in Book XI he says in part:

> Why is life giv'n
> To be thus wrested from us? Rather why
> Obtruded on us thus?
> . . . . . . . .
> Can thus
> Th'image of God in man, created once
> So goodly and erect, though faulty since,
> To such unsightly sufferings be debased
> Under inhuman pains? Why should not man,
> Retaining still divine similitude
> In part, from such deformities be free,
> And for his Maker's image sake exempt? (XI, 502–14)

Michael's instruction is bearing fruit, and Adam has turned up a wrong question that is timely and useful. Some of Michael's next replies are punitive rebukes apparently aimed to move Adam out of empty, belated arguments that slip from compassion to self-pity to self-serving—arguments based on original human worth but veering away from problems of justice and responsibility. The style of Adam here is one Milton perfected for Satan, and the speech is punctuated with comic self-revelations, such as: "though faulty since," "inhuman pains," "Retaining still divine similitude / In part." The angel administers his punishment not as a warrior or philosopher but as one kind of good teacher, one who seems to understand how Adam feels and thinks. Michael does not need to be as restrained and careful as the angel Raphael, lest something be said inappropriate to the freedom of the innocent human being. So Michael reads out an unsparing interpretation of human vice and ends at the place he wants Adam to start from next. Michael concludes: while men abuse "Nature's healthful rules," they deserve their sicknesses, "since they / God's image did not reverence in themselves" (XI, 523, 524–25).

Is there no other way to death, Adam then asks, "besides / These painful passages?" (XI, 527–28). The angel is ready, and Adam hears a lecture on good diet and the rule of *"Not too much,"* and the rewards of a temperate life in yielding access to the easy and "mature" death, dropping "like ripe fruit," "not harshly plucked" (XI, 535, 537). That is the affirmative part, followed almost without transition by an account of old age, an inventory of symptoms chiefly not attractive but not made "foul and ugly" like the inventory of diseases:

This is old age, but then thou must outlive
Thy youth, thy strength, thy beauty, which will change
To withered weak and gray; thy senses then
Obtuse, all taste of pleasure must forgo
To what thou hast, and for the air of youth
Hopeful and cheerful, in thy blood will reign
A melancholy damp of cold and dry
To weigh thy spirits down, and last consume
The balm of life.                                    (XI, 538–46)

Nothing in old age is presented as in itself good, nothing to be hoped for, no meliorative touch. As the concentrated first stage of his instruction approaches its end, Adam shows how he feels at the news of the best destiny offered him, the luck of arriving at old age:

Henceforth I fly not death, nor would prolong
Life much, bent rather how I may be quit
Fairest and easiest of this cumbrous charge,
Which I must keep till my appointed day
Of rend'ring up, and patiently attend
My dissolution.                                    (XI, 547–52)

In view of what still must be done in the last thousand lines, there is much to be said in favor of Adam's tempered pessimism. We have traveled barely a hundred lines since the death of Abel, and Michael has guided Adam through the crucial early lessons on how to think and feel about his own death to come. Michael now concludes with an aphorism anticipating a piece of Stoic wisdom and makes it clear that this part of the discourse is over:

Nor love thy life, nor hate; but what thou liv'st
Live well, how long or short permit to Heav'n:
And now prepare thee for another sight.           (XI, 553–55)

A synoptic history then follows, in which Adam can train himself against the "foul and ugly" in life—represented not only by such death-bringers as war, tyranny, and persecution, but also by the exposed aspects of peace and wealth leading to corruption and perversity. These experiences constitute a path of practical education in a rational sequence, unfolding like a history. A second educational path is not continuous; its theological vision works through types, a system of recognition and symbolic reasoning which discovered various fulfillments of Old Testament examples in the New Testament. Some events do not need to follow each

other in a rational, temporal order, but one event may prefigure a latent truth to be further revealed in another event. That second path was opened up early in *Paradise Lost* by the great first scene in heaven, where prophecy and dramatic action expressed events foreknown by God but held back, as it were, from full realization.

I shall return now only as far as Michael's early conversation with Adam. Before the first harsh lessons regarding death, Michael had encouraged Adam by announcing that his prayers had been heard and his death postponed. There would be time for him to repent and time for good deeds to cover the one bad act. Then just before he announced their banishment from Eden, Michael mentioned a new possibility: "well may then thy Lord appeased / Redeem thee quite from Death's rapacious claim" (XI, 257–58). This is a latent truth which will be brought forward again, somewhat further forward, advanced by being more definite, like a picture of improved clarity. The truth will finally be understood by Adam himself, who will participate in the revelation as his personal path of education converges with the working of typology. But not yet. The lament that immediately follows the news of banishment leaves the news of possible rescue from death unremarked, as if it were not heard or were less important than the threat of eviction. As a result, the possibility of rescue has no discernible effect on Michael's teaching and Adam's learning the rigid facts of death. The timing of Michael's optimistic suggestion belongs to the marvelous rationality of narrative and dramatic art cooperating with a kind of theological vision that exceeds the rational. The signal of hope that is passed by now will emerge in a later fulfillment.

After his death Jesus will rise: "Thy ransom paid, which man from Death redeems" (XII, 424). Adam's own life and the judgment of death upon him are not for certain directly and fully involved here but are, to some degree, related to the prophesied redemption. A few lines later, however, the mention of "temporal death" adds a degree of clarification that would include Adam, or—not to be hasty in greeting the emergence of typological significances—Adam could infer his potential eligibility to join those whom Christ redeems from "a death like sleep, / A gentle wafting to immortal life" (XII, 434–35).

The educational path that we may recognize as being largely secular, continuous, and rational has been carefully followed and honored. The basic method is an open one, that of dialogue. Its capacity for promoting personal growth is represented by Adam's increased participation in the dialogue. His questions and responses improve greatly. On his own initiative he acknowledges his Redeemer and declares himself "Taught . . . by his example" that death is "to the faithful . . . the gate of life" (XII, 572,

571). The emotions that rise in Adam and correspond to both parts of his educational experience are those of joy and love.

At the heart of Milton's process is a standard Renaissance agreement concerning Christian death. The inherent fear of death could best be answered and removed by an opposing deep emotion, the love of God. There were well-known ways of assisting and easing that process, but for Adam, the pioneer, all the problems of his progress were unique. As we have seen, Michael first prepared his student in a hundred lines; and then, some eight hundred lines later, with no direct mention made, the fear is gone. One imagines that many of Milton's early readers would have recognized and enjoyed the play of similarity and difference between their own modern practices and the tutoring Adam received when he still had some nine hundred years to live but was nevertheless obliged to follow an immensely accelerated and packed schedule of learning.

At the very end of the poem Adam walks away from his past and the irretrievable part of his loss, "with wand'ring steps and slow," but with some restoration of optimism and with Providence as his guide and the world "all before them, where to choose"; yet this is a world that in his preview scrambled after joy and was pursued by sorrow. Nevertheless, when Adam walks away he is walking hand in hand with the woman who will share his life and who, like himself, is almost as good as new yet also worse and better.

University of Illinois, Urbana

NOTES

1. Sir Walter Raleigh, *The History of the World* (London, 1614), p. 776.
2. John Donne, *The Second Anniversarie*, 85–88, in *The Poems of John Donne*, ed. H.J.C. Grierson (Oxford, 1933).
3. George Herbert, "Death," 1–4, in *The Works of George Herbert*, ed. F. E. Hutchinson (Oxford, 1945).
4. My quotations from Milton are taken from *The Complete Poetical Works of John Milton*, ed. Douglas Bush (Boston, 1965).
5. Frank Kermode, *The Living Milton* (London, 1960), p. 117.
6. Bush, *Poetical Works*, pp. 154–55.

# MILTON AND TRADITION

## E. R. Gregory

THE PRECISE percentages of change and continuity in tradition can never be agreed on. Edward Shils, who has written lovingly and acutely of *Tradition*, is unimpressed by such studies as *The Socialist Tradition, The Tradition of the New, The Tradition of Modernity,* or *The Symbolist Tradition:*

> Those who argue for tradition nowadays turn out . . . to be very progressivistic in the traditions they support; it is the "tradition of change" which they praise and they do not think about what is involved in this paradox. More substantive traditions, traditions which maintain the received, receive less support. The "tradition of traditionality" has few supporters.

Other scholars, however, have found that very paradox to be the essence of tradition. The distinguished medieval historian Karl F. Morrison, for example, has pointed to "the duality of conservatism and change" as constituting "the fundamental character of tradition"; while our century's most distinguished apologist for tradition, T. S. Eliot, implied as much when he wrote that "the difference between the present and the past is that the conscious present is an awareness of the past in a way and to an extent which the past's awareness of itself cannot show." Thus, living artists can find patterns of meaning in dead writers that those writers themselves were not aware of, and their incorporation of the dead into their own work, if well done, must perforce result in art that is like and yet unlike its predecessors, art unrecognizable perhaps to its predecessors as their progeny.[1]

Of this possibility, John Milton was well aware. Arguing in *Tetrachordon* that spiritual and mental companionship were as important as the physical dimension in marriage, he concluded that his position for all its seeming boldness and novelty was well grounded in an ancient tradition of interpretation:

> we conclude no more then what the common Expositers themselves give us, both in that which I have recited and much more hereafter. But the truth is, they give us in such a manner, as they who leav their own mature positions like the eggs of an Ostrich in the dust; I do but lay them in the sun; their own pregnancies hatch the truth; and I am taxt of novelties and strange producements, while they, like that inconsiderat bird, know not that these are their own naturall breed.[2]

In the attitude revealed by this passage lies the power that enabled Milton so radically to transform the past in his poetry. Learned and careful readers have long recognized that, like tradition itself, Milton's great poems embody continuity and change. Thus William Hazlitt's oft-quoted comment that Milton "is a writer of centos, and yet in originality scarcely inferior to Homer."[3] Whence this paradox? Precisely in a cast of mind that recognized no less surely than Eliot's that "the difference between the present and the past is that the conscious present is an awareness of the past in a way and to an extent which the past's awareness of itself cannot show" (p. 6).

Unlike Eliot, Milton never made a definitive pronouncement on tradition. His seventy-eight references to tradition and traditional matters were made over a number of years and in quite different contexts. An overwhelming majority of them, however, appear in a context of religious controversy, forty-three of them in the antiprelatical pamphlets alone. The few that have nothing to do with religion indicate that he was at home with such modern definitions as "the passing down of elements of a culture from generation to generation" or "cultural custom or usage" and that outside religious controversy, his usage was often neutral or even favorable.[4] He is neutral, for example, in the *History of Britain* when he observes that "from the first peopling of the Iland to the coming of *Julius Cæsar,* nothing certain, either by Tradition, History, or Ancient Fame hath hitherto bin left us" (YP V, p. 2). Here tradition is merely one way whereby information about the past can be transmitted to the present, not the best means surely, but not to be despised when other material is lacking. Or again in *Areopagitica* he objects to Plato's reduction of all learning to "practicall traditions" (YP II, p. 522), but it is the reduction he objects to and not the traditions. Indeed, he hints in *Of Education* that a certain amount of tradition is necessary in order to create a truly rich culture, for he defends Latin and Greek as the cornerstones of education on the ground that "every nation affords not experience and tradition anough for all kinde of learning, [and] therefore we are chiefly taught the languages of those people who have at any time been most industrious after wisdom" (YP II, p. 369).

In religion, however, his attitude was hostile. For him, religious tradition was the oral transmission of doctrine and practice closely allied with a belief that such doctrine and practice were valid beyond their confirmation in the written Scriptures. The immediate source of his hostility was, of course, the argument over episcopacy that held center stage in English politics during the early 1640s, but the issues that engaged him and his Anglican opponents were neither new nor simple. A part, though not all, of the vehemence with which Milton attacked tradition rooted itself in his heritage as a Protestant; for during the sixteenth century as the Roman Catholic Church found the concept more and more under attack, it defended it with greater and greater stridency. Thus, when in 1545 the theological faculty at Louvain formulated an orthodox set of articles for the Catholic faith, the twenty-fifth was a specific vindication of tradition's authority:

Not only those things must be held in certain faith which are expressly revealed in the Scriptures, but also those which we must accept as things to be believed according to the tradition of the Catholic Church and which have been defined with respect to acts of faith and morals by the See of Peter or legitimately convened general councils.[5]

This position the Council of Trent fully concurred with a year later:

It [the Council of Trent] also clearly perceives that these truths and rules [of the Christian faith] are contained in the written books and in the unwritten traditions, which, received by the Apostles from the mouth of Christ Himself, or from the Apostles themselves, the Holy Ghost dictating, have come down to us, transmitted as it were from hand to hand. Following, then, the examples of the orthodox Fathers, it receives and venerates with a feeling of piety and reverence all the books both of the Old and New Testaments, since one God is the author of both; also the traditions, whether they relate to faith or to morals, as having been dictated either orally by Christ or by the Holy Ghost, and preserved in the Catholic Church in unbroken succession.[6]

At the very fountainhead of Protestantism, Milton observed a hostility to tradition so reverenced, noting in *A Treatise of Civil Power* that the term itself had first been used to designate those German reformers who objected to "imposing church-traditions without scripture" (YP VII, p. 243). The writings of Calvin and Luther both were chock-full of hostility toward tradition as exalted by the Roman Catholic Church. In the *Institutes*, Calvin wrote that God's eternal truth is "a truth that cannot be dictated to by length of time, by long-standing custom, or by the conspiracy of men." He summed up "Evil custom," that is, custom or tradition unsupported by Scripture, as "nothing but a kind of public pestilence in which men do not perish the less though they fall with the multitude."[7]

Because their scholastic training had ingrained the citation of sources in them, Calvin and Luther continued to quote the church fathers as frequently and as knowingly as their Catholic opponents, but as ancillary support to arguments whose truth was validated in the Bible. That some of the fathers similarly stressed the primacy of Scripture thus led to the fathers' use to undercut the fathers' authority. Augustine in particular proved a powerful spokesman for the primacy of Scripture. In a letter to Jerome, Augustine had written:

it is from those books alone of the Scriptures, which are now called canonical, that I have learned to pay them such honor and respect as to believe most firmly that not one of their authors has erred in writing anything at all. If I do find anything in those books which seems contrary to truth, I decide that either the text is corrupt, or the translator did not follow what was really said, or that I failed to understand it. But, when I read other authors, however eminent they may be in sanctity and learning, I do not necessarily believe a thing is true because they think so, but because they have been able to convince me, either on the authority of the canonical writers or by a probable reason which is not inconsistent with truth.[8]

In writing to Fortunatianus, Augustine had further declared that

we are not obliged to regard the arguments of any writers, however Catholic and estimable they may be, as we do the canonical Scriptures, so that we may not— with all due respect to the deference owed them as men—refute or reject anything we happen to find in their writings wherein their opinions differ from the established truth, or from what has been thought out by others or by us, with divine help. I wish other thinkers to hold the same attitude toward my writings as I hold toward theirs. (III, pp. 235–36)

Passages such as these had shaped Luther's response to the articles of Louvain. With regard to the twenty-fifth article, cited above, he wrote: "Neither did St. Augustine want his books or those of others to be made equal to sacred Scriptures or his sayings to be held for articles of faith" (*Luther's Works* XXXIV, p. 356).

Milton then felt himself to be on solid ground in concluding that "it is the general consent of all sound protestant writers, that neither traditions, councels nor canons of any visible church, much less edicts of any magistrate or civil session, but the scripture only can be the final judge or rule in matters of religion, and that only in the conscience of every Christian to himself" (YP VII, p. 243). Milton's championing of the individual's right to judge all matters for himself thus rooted itself in a Protestant "tradition" of denigrating tradition. The particular fervor with which he himself attacked it, however, is explicable in terms of the specific controversial situation in which he found himself; for his Anglican opponents by no means endorsed the Roman Catholic exaltation of tradition. The very moderation of their appeal to tradition made it in a sense harder to counter and thus led to more sweeping denunciations on Milton's part than he might otherwise have engaged in.

With regard to tradition, as elsewhere, the Anglican Communion had sought the *via media*, maintaining the Bible as the ultimate authority and yet not discarding customs, ceremonies, or institutions that lacked specific biblical authority. The fourth of the Thirty-Nine Articles stated: "Holy Scripture, conteineth all thynges necessary to saluation: so that whatsoever is not read therin, nor may be proued therby, is not to be required of any man, that it should be beleued as an article of the fayth, or be thought requisite necessary to saluation." The thirty-fourth article, on the other hand, while granting that tradition varied according to time and place, affirmed that the challenging of tradition was not to be taken lightly:

It is not necessarie, that traditions and ceremonies, be in all places one, or utterly lyke, for at all tymes they haue ben dyvers, and maye be chaunged, according to the diuersitie of countries, tymes, and mens maners: so that nothyng be ordayned agaynst Gods worde. Whosoeuer through his priuate iudgement, willyngly and purposely doth openlie breake the traditions and ceremonies of the Church, which be not repugnant to the worde of God, and be ordayned and approued by common aucthoritie, ought to be rebuked openly (that other may feare to do the lyke) as one that offendeth agaynst the common order of the Churche, and hurteth the aucthoritie of the magistrate, and woundeth the consciences of the weake brethren.⁹

Milton's most noted adversary, Bishop Joseph Hall, exemplified in his writings on episcopacy precisely the combination of reverence for tradition coupled with its subordination to Scripture that the Articles embody. In his treatise *The Old Religion*, Hall devoted an entire chapter to "The Newness of the Doctrine of Traditions," attempting to show how dangerous and misguided a too great emphasis on tradition can be in religious matters. In *Episcopacy by Divine Right*, Hall indicated an awareness of how deeply compromised any argument from tradition was by the excessive authority, as he saw it, that the Roman Catholic Church had endowed the concept with. Having quoted Tertullian's view that continuing practice in the church proved apostolic endorsement and Augustine's that universal practice similarly proved such endorsement, he continued:

Let not any adversary think to elude this testimony with the upbraiding to it the patronage of the popish opinions concerning traditions. We have learned to hate their vanities, and yet to maintain our own truths without all fear of the patrocination of popery. We deny not some traditions (however the word, for want of distinguishing, is from their abuse grown into an ill name,) must have their place and use.¹⁰

The more concessions he made, however, the more trenchantly Milton argued that tradition was of no value at all in religious controversy; for to Milton, Hall's concessions were not signs of intellectual honesty, the inevitable results of a learned and subtle, albeit conservative, mind at work on difficult problems, but rather dishonest and dangerous controversial ploys:

> who can be a greater enemy to Mankind, who a more dangerous deceiver then he who defending a traditionall corruption uses no common Arts, but with a wily Stratagem of yeelding to the time a greater part of his cause, seeming to forgo all that mans invention hath done therein, and driven from much of his hold in Scripture, yet leaving it hanging by a twin'd threed, not from divine command but from Apostolicall prudence or assent, as if he had the surety of some rouling trench, creeps up by this meanes to his relinquish't fortresse of divine authority againe. (*Animadversions*, YP I, p. 663)

Thus freed as he saw it from any need to meet a genuine temperance with like temperance, Milton often made it sound as if getting rid of tradition were merely a matter of sweeping a few moth-eaten rags out of the Temple of Truth.

In truth, however, the issues surrounding tradition in the 1640s were as complex as they were ancient, the latest responses in an ongoing debate involving a whole nexus of related questions that can never be answered to everyone's satisfaction: What significance, if any, does the past hold for the present? Who is to determine that significance? Is there any sense in which present thought can represent a genuine advance in understanding over past thought? In Christianity, the relevance of the past to the present was unclear even in New Testament days as the quarrel between the parties of circumcision and uncircumcision recounted in Acts, chapter xv, makes clear. Nor did the problems involved in institutionalizing a revelation abate as the apostles died and were replaced by men who had no first-hand knowledge of Jesus' life, death, and resurrection. Indeed, they intensified as the gospel spread over an ever-enlarging area and enlisted an ever-growing number of converts. The New Testament canon itself was an attempt to stabilize doctrine and practice, but inevitably it was highly selective in what it included. As the author of John wrote, "there are also many other things which Jesus did, the which, if they should be written every one, I suppose that even the world itself could not contain all the books that should be written" (John xxi, 25). Nor did what was written automatically interpret itself. As the central events of the Christian faith faded into the long ago and far away, it became ever more urgent to establish how and by whom their truth had been validated and transmitted and who in the present age would be entrusted to preserve, interpret, and pass on "the faith which was once delivered unto the saints" (Jude 3).

Although the church fathers continued to assert the primacy of Scripture, it was tradition that became for the Roman Catholic Church the guarantor of the processes whereby religious truth was established, preserved, and transmitted, a view of tradition argued, for example, by Irenaeus and Vincent of Lerins. Vincent, who was quoted and much utilized by Bishop Hall, gave a particularly compelling argument for how and why tradition ought to be used in establishing church practice. He started, as virtually all the fathers did, from the same point that Milton did, that "the canon of Scripture is complete, and sufficient of itself for everything, and more than sufficient."[11] Granting this, however, Vincent then asks, "what need is there to join with it the authority of the Church's interpretation?" His answer: "because, owing to the depth of Holy Scripture, all do not accept it in one and the same sense, but one understands its words in one way, another in another; so that it seems to be capable of as many interpretations as there are interpreters" (p. 132). For Vincent, as for Bishop Hall over a thousand years later, this clearly was undesirable. The remedy as he saw it to many interpretations lay in the institution of the church, where

all possible care must be taken, that we hold that faith which has been believed everywhere, always, by all. For that is truly and in the strictest sense "Catholic," which, as the name itself and the reason of the thing declare, comprehends all universally. This rule we shall observe if we follow universality, antiquity, consent. We shall follow universality if we confess that one faith to be true, which the whole Church throughout the world confesses; antiquity, if we in no wise depart from those interpretations which it is manifest were notoriously held by our holy ancestors and fathers; consent, in like manner, if in antiquity itself we adhere to the consentient definitions and determinations of all, or at the least of almost all priests and doctors. (P. 132)

Milton, on the other hand, while not denying that the Scriptures contained complexity, yet felt that in its essentials, that is, in what men and women needed to know to secure their salvation, it was clear enough: " 'tis true there be some Books, and especially some places in those Books that remain clouded; yet ever that which is most necessary to be known is most easie; and that which is most difficult, so farre expounds it selfe ever, as to tell us how little it imports our *saving knowledge*" (YP I, p. 566). Sufficiently a child of his age to sympathize with Calvin's observation that "the affairs of men have scarcely ever been so well regulated that the better things pleased the majority" (*Institutes* I, p. 23), he was certainly to find in the course of his life abundant evidence that men and women can know the truth and yet ignore it. Yet so strong was his conviction that they can know the truth that the disappointments of a lifetime were insufficient to dissuade him from believing that they should be given the chance to determine for themselves what the truth is, a conviction strongly reaffirmed in his prefatory epistle to *Christian Doctrine*.

The result was a tremendous acceleration in the amount of both variety and change in interpretation that he was prepared to countenance. As his image of the ostrich egg demonstrates, the changes that he envisaged in some cases appeared to others to involve a total break with the truth as previously conceived, though such was Milton's confidence in the essential unity of truth that he could see continuity where others did not. His opponents, while not denying the possibility of change and development, were far less perceptive in identifying organic development where surface appearance was different. Thus, the imagery that Vincent of Lerins used to portray the development of doctrine that he regarded as properly organic furnishes an interesting contrast to Milton's; for instead of truth emerging ostrichlike from her egg, he shows it growing, maturing, and changing in the manner of the human body as it goes from infancy to full maturity:

The growth of religion in the soul must be analogous to the growth of the body, which, though in process of years it is developed and attains its full size, yet remains the same. There is a wide difference between the flower of youth and the maturity of age; yet they who were once young are still the same now that they have become old, insomuch that though the stature and outward form of the individual are changed, yet his nature is one and the same, his person is one and the same. Men when full grown have the same number of joints that they had when children; and if there be any to which maturer age has given birth, these were already present in embryo, so that nothing new is produced in them which was not already latent in them when children. (XI, p. 148)

No less than Milton's, Vincent's image portrays organic unity beneath surface difference, but the change in emphasis from underlying continuity to surface disjunction is significant. Vincent conveys the satisfaction that a father feels in seeing his son develop from a baby boy to a fully adult male, the parent perceiving and taking pleasure in each successive stage of development beautifully fulfilling the promise inherent in the preceding one. It also contains the idea that only one organic development is contained in the embryonic organism and that any departure from that development, any addition or subtraction of limbs, will result in the body's becoming "either a wreck or a monster, or, at the least . . . impaired and enfeebled." Milton's, on the other hand, focuses on the parent's failure to recognize himself in his offspring, surely as common a feature of human experience as the satisfaction in fulfillment Vincent adumbrates, and therefore suggests that the process of maturation in ideas can sometimes seem stranger and more shocking to its observers and even participants than Vincent's would imply. And although the egg/bird metaphier implies that only one course of development is possible for its metaphrand, the emergence of truth, Milton's emphasis is on the intellectual acuity and openness of mind necessary to perceive the continuity in radical change. Knowing first-hand that men and women did not always recognize the truth the moment they saw it, he was more prepared to tolerate a diversity of opinion than Vincent or his seventeenth-century followers.

In *Episcopacy by Divine Right*, Hall demonstrated his innate conservatism by quoting with approval Vincent's formula: "*Quod semper et ubique*, 'always and everywhere,' was the old and sure rule of Vincentius Lirinensis; and who thinks this can fail him is well worthy to err" (IX, p. 242). Within the context of his time, his was an enlightened and flexible conservatism. Certainly his appeal to tradition was moderate in comparison to the Roman Catholic one, and yet his defense of episcopacy was grounded in a sense that any great change in church doctrine or organization was undesirable and unlikely to accord with the truth as perceived in the past. Milton's realization that the truths of the past and present could be the same though not easily perceived as such did not recommend itself to Hall. For him, Tertullian's axiom, "*quod primum verum*, that 'the first is true,' " precluded the new from being so and militated against his identifying the old in the seemingly new. If the first was true, it followed for Hall "then [that] the latest is seldom so where it agrees not with the first. After the teeming of so many ages it is rarely seen that a new and posthumous verity is any other than spurious" (IX, p. 184). Unfortunately for Hall, arguments based on Vincent's criteria are hard to sustain in controversy. No matter how impressive they may be in totality of presentation, they are always vulnerable to attack in their details. "Semper et ubique," what the church at all times and in all places has taught, is by its nature an appeal to consensus and a denial that airtight evidence is desirable or indeed available as a basis for argument; for it is one thing to prove that a practice was widespread and approved by many a church father and quite a different matter to prove that it has been practiced at all times and in all places with the approval of all or even "almost all priests and doctors."

In ranging over the evidence, then, Milton had no difficulty in finding gaps and inconsistencies in the historical records, untrustworthy witnesses, and signs of corrupting self-interest, all of which weakened tradition as a defense for prelaty. The records tracing prelaty back to New Testament practice were sketchy. Both parties agreed that the words *episcopus* and *presbyteros* had been used interchangeably in New Testament times but disagreed as to the point when they began to be applied to different orders. For those arguing in favor of prelaty, the charges given by Paul to Timothy and Titus in his epistles seemed evidence that the offices were early differentiated. Milton challenged this, claiming that Timothy and Titus "had rather the vicegerency of an Apostleship committed to them, then the ordinary charge of a Bishoprick, as being men of an extraordinary calling" (*Of Prelatical Episcopacy*, YP I, p. 626). Yet even granting that Timothy was a bishop in the sense that the seventeenth century understood the term, where, Milton wanted to know, was the evidence that the office had continued thereafter in unbroken succession?

The records of apostolic succession were far too fragmentary to constitute a cast-iron case that the office of bishop as currently understood had been a feature of church organization at all times and in all places. Controversy thus came to focus on what constituted fair and reasonable evidence that bishoping had existed in unbroken line from apostolic days on. Archbishop Ussher had made much out of the fact that at the Council of Chalcedon in 451, an otherwise obscure bishop, Leontius of Magnesia, had claimed in debate that an unbroken line of twenty-seven bishops originating with Timothy had served in Ephesus, the implication being that a lack of challenge to the statement in its debating context confirmed its truth.[12] If this reasoning was accepted, then one piece of evidence suggested that episcopacy originated in New Testament times and continued in Ephesus at least for four hundred years or so thereafter. This one piece was, of course, only a tiny part of a body of evidence impressive, if so, by cumulative weight; but Milton's response is instructive in that it implies what he felt could be done with all the evidence if it were subjected to the same critical scrutiny.

What, after all, do we know about Leontius, he asked; he is only a name: "neither the praise of his wisedome, or his vertue hath left him memorable to posterity, but onely this doubtfull relation, which wee must take at his word; and how shall this testimony receive credit from his word, whose very name had scarse been thought on, but for this bare Testimony?" (YP I, p. 628). His presence at the council tells us nothing about him. Neither does the lack of response from his peers, for we know nothing of them either. Very likely, some of them were "bad and slippery men," just as some of the participants in contemporary convocations were; but assuming they were all good and wise, their testimony has no value in determining what went on four hundred years earlier.

Turning back to a much earlier writer on church history, Eusebius, Milton notes that he confesses "that it was no easie matter to tell who were those that were left Bishops of the Churches by the Apostles, more then by what a man might gather from the *Acts* of the Apostles, and the Epistles of St. *Paul,* in which number he reckons *Timothy* for Bishop of *Ephesus*" (YP I, p. 631). If Eusebius, then, who was well known, can tell us no more than this, why, Milton asks, should we place any credence in a so much more obscure figure like Leontius; and why, furthermore, should we place much credence in either of them when they interpret as the creation of a bishop what in reality "was only an intreating him to tarry at *Ephesus,* to do something left him in charge"? The point that he strongly emphasizes, then, is that, "while we leave the Bible to gadde after these traditions of the ancients, we heare the ancients themselvs confessing, that what knowledge they had in this point was such as they had gather'd from the Bible" (YP I, p. 631).

Leontius's testimony thus cannot bear the weight Ussher imposed on it. Unfortunately, because Milton did not build his case with scholarly detachment, he sometimes overlooked the chinks in his own armor. The editors of the Yale *Prose,* for example, point out correctly that Eusebius himself named as bishops persons who were not so identified in the New Testament.[13] Sometimes, too, he takes as a given what needs to be proven as above where his assumption about Paul's charge to Timothy is no more provable than the opposition's assumption that Paul made Timothy a bishop.

Rising above the lapses in his own arguments, however, Milton's exaltation of critical independence and rigor in judging the past is still worth pondering. The valuable point that he makes concerning Leontius, Eusebius, and the Bible has little to do with whether there were twenty-seven bishops in Ephesus from Timothy to Leontius, or twenty-six, or none. It has rather to do with a cast of mind that he identifies as dangerous when it applies the lessons of the past to the present. Of the bishops and their supporters, he writes:

they cannot think any doubt resolv'd, and any doctrine confirm'd, unlesse they run to that indigested heap, and frie of Authors, which they call Antiquity. Whatso-ever time, or the heedlesse hand of blind chance, hath drawne down from of old to this present, in her huge dragnet, whether Fish, or Sea-weed, Shells, or Shrubbs, unpickt, unchosen, those are the Fathers. (YP I, p. 626)

The key word is *indigested.* It is not antiquity that he objects to and certainly not the church fathers. In order to convey their particular wisdom, however, their works have to be read carefully, placed in the context of their time, and weighed in comparison with other writers. What he sees in his opponents is a kind of rifling through a random "heap, and frie of Authors" in order to find data that may or may not be accurate and may

or may not apply to the argument they are conducting. The randomness
suggested by "heap, and frie" is then amplified in the next sentence where
the reader is reminded that not all the surviving works of the church
fathers are of equal value, that blind chance in her dragnet has pulled
along considerable rubbish as well as pearls of great price and that until
the mass is sorted through and the good disentangled from the fish and
seaweed, the pearls cannot be properly appreciated.

Inevitably, the sorting through involved critical judgments as to the
abilities and motives of tradition's witnesses. If nothing was known about
Leontius, what was known in other cases was far from reassuring. In the
"very ancient writer" Papias, Milton found, he thought, an excellent example of how reliance on sources other than the Bible could corrupt Christian doctrine. A contemporary of the apostles, Papias had placed greater
emphasis on what he heard than on what he read:

If, then, any one who had attended on the elders came, I asked minutely after
their sayings,—what Andrew or Peter said, or what was said by Philip, or by
Thomas, or by James, or by John, or by Matthew, or by any other of the Lord's
disciples: which things Aristion and the presbyter John, the disciples of the Lord,
say. For I imagined that what was to be got from books was not so profitable to me
as what came from the living and abiding voice. [14]

A response to "the living and abiding voice" was not in itself repugnant to
Milton. In his view, as we shall see, such a response was built into the
freedom that the Gospel as opposed to the Law bestowed on its believers.
He did, however, recognize its danger when the believer possessed insufficient intellectual weight properly to rank what he heard and what he read:

Papias a very ancient writer, one that had heard St. *Iohn*, and was known to many
that had seen, and bin acquainted with others of the Apostles, but being of a
shallow wit, and not understanding those traditions which he receiv'd, fill'd his
writings with many new doctrines, and fabulous conceits . . . that divers Ecclesias-
ticall men, and *Irenaeus* among the rest, while they lookt at his antiquity, became
infected with his errors. (YP I, p. 641)

It was after all the doctrine that the apostles taught that made anything else about them worth remembering; and by concentrating instead
on their lives and personalities, Papias and those he influenced spread
"idle traditions" that neglected the Gospel in favor of anecdotal and supernatural materials that focused men's minds on the inessential, the undocu-
mentable, and finally the unbelievable and discreditable:

with lesse fervency was studied what Saint *Paul*, or Saint *Iohn* had written then
was listen'd to one that could say here hee taught, here he stood, this was his

stature, and thus he went habited, and O happy this house that harbour'd him, and that cold stone whereon he rested, this Village wherein he wrought such a miracle, and that pavement bedew'd with the warme effusion of his last blood, that sprouted up into eternall Roses to crowne his Martyrdome. (YP I, pp. 641–42)

Interspersed with such material might be some elements that deserved preservation; but for Milton, the "eternall Roses" were mostly so much fish and seaweed to be discarded if the past were properly to be understood.

Finally, in addition to incomplete evidence and inadequate witnesses, Milton found tradition suspect because all too often he observed that it had been used as a convenient cover for self-interest. This he found to be true in New Testament days, in the days of the church fathers, and in his own day. Thus Christ had taught that the Pharisees' traditions concerning divorce were useless either as a gloss on the Law's original intent or as a guide in applying it to their own lives:

Moses because of the hardness of your hearts suffered you to put away your wives: but from the beginning it was not so.

And I say unto you, Whosoever shall put away his wife, except it be for fornication, and shall marry another, committeth adultery: and whoso marrieth her which is put away doth commit adultery. (Matt. xix, 8–9)

Christ's maintenance of tone in speaking to his disciples about divorce Milton interpreted not as a universalizing of the above ban but rather as a further demonstration that traditions based on self-interest can have a pernicious effect extending far beyond the original group and including persons we would expect to be more perceptive and selfless:

But if it be thought that the Disciples offended at the rigor of Christs answer, could yet obtain no mitigation of the former sentence pronounc't to the Pharises, it may be fully answer'd, that our Saviour continues the same reply to his Disciples, as men leaven'd with the same customary licence, which the Pharises maintain'd; and displeas'd at the removing of a traditional abuse wherto they had so long not unwillingly bin us'd. (*Doctrine and Discipline of Divorce*, YP II, p. 311)

As for "Prelaticall tradition," he found it early and late no less tainted with self-interest than the Pharisaical. Of the "tradition of the Church" toward the close of the second century A.D., he wrote that if it

were now grown so ridiculous, & disconsenting from the Doctrine of the *Apostles*, even in those points which were of lest moment to mens particular ends, how well may we be assur'd it was much more degenerated in point of *Episcopacy*, and precedency, things which could affor'd such plausible pretenses, such commodious traverses for ambition, and Avarice to lurke behind. (*Of Prelatical Episcopacy,* YP I, p. 646)

Throughout church history, he found some bishops more interested in lining their own pockets and advancing their own importance than in preaching the Gospel or serving the people. As in the second century, so in his own time he found bishops only too willing to use tradition as a justification for the abuses that allowed them to satisfy their "canary-sucking, and swan-eating palats" and for the church-building and ceremonies that amplified their own position (*Of Reformation,* YP I, p. 549). To convey the danger always latent in tradition used as a defense for prelaty, he resorted once again to the image of the egg and what emerges from it:

The soure levin of humane Traditions mixt in one putrifi'd Masse with the poisonous dregs of hypocrisie in the hearts of *Prelates* that lye basking in the Sunny warmth of Wealth, and Promotion, is the Serpents Egge that will hatch an *Antichrist* wheresoever, and ingender the same Monster as big, or little as the Lump is which breeds him. (*Of Reformation,* YP I, p. 590)

Human traditions, be it noted, are not the worst part of the nauseous mess described, being merely "soure levin" in comparison to the "poisonous dregs" in the prelates' hearts. They are, however, the agents that activate and enlarge the potential for evil inherent in the institution of prelaty and therefore in the present context, whatever their potential elsewhere, must be regarded as pernicious.

  In religious disputation, then, Milton concluded that "Tradition hath had very seldome or never the gift of perswasion" (YP I, p. 648). So deeply ingrained in his controversial position was this negative view of tradition that he described it as "deceivable" (YP I, p. 520); "abusive" (YP II, p. 317); "obscure" (YP II, p. 639); and "idle" (YP I, p. 641). He linked it with "fleshly ceremony" (YP I, pp. 829–30); "degenerate corruption" (YP I, pp. 601–02); "abuse" (YP II, p. 311); and "Heresie" (YP VIII, p. 421). His imagery even more conveys how strongly his feelings are engaged. Fortified, as he thought, by the example of Christ himself, who, "speaking of unsavory traditions, scruples not to name the Dunghill and the Jakes" (YP I, p. 895), Milton described tradition not only as "soure levin" but also as a "broken reed" (YP I, p. 624); the "old starting hole" of "errour and fond Opinion" (YP I, p. 648), "the perpetuall canker-worme to eat out Gods Commandements" (YP I, p. 779); "old vomit" (YP I, p. 912); "a muddy pool" (YP II, p. 543); and "corrupt, and poysonous waters" (YP I, p. 649).

  In all of this, however, it is the authority of tradition as opposed to that of the Scriptures that Milton so adamantly opposes. Tradition is a "broken reed" when used to prop up the "*Divine* constitution" of episcopacy; for "to satisfie us fully in that, the Scripture onely is able." It is a "starting hole" for "errour, and fond Opinion, when they find themselves outlaw'd by the Bible, and forsaken of sound reason." It is "perpetuall canker-worme to eat out Gods Commandements." It is "old vomit" to those who have backed away from "the purity of Scripture which is the only rule of reformation." It is "the mixt confluence of so many corrupt, and poysonous waters" when compared "with the sincere milke of the Gospell."

The context of religious controversy, then, is of crucial importance in evaluating the hostile language Milton used to describe tradition. In a larger sense, however, he considered it, like all learning and all history, as valuable to those men and women whose character and scale of values enable them independently and honestly to judge what they read. Acutely aware of the dangers of pedantry and antiquarianism, he nevertheless believed firmly that the past can teach lessons to the present. Believing, as noted above, that Latin and Greek afforded "experience and tradition anough for all kind of learning," he made it clear that "language is but the instrument convaying to us things usefull to be known" (YP II, p. 369) and that the criterion for determining such usefulness lay in whether scholars could apply the lessons learned from the past to the situations in which they found themselves: "I call therefore a compleate and generous Education that which fits a man to perform justly, skilfully and magnanimously all the offices both private and publike of peace and war" (*Of Education,* YP II, pp. 377–79).

The Bible, no less than the classics, he felt was not the record of something that had happened long ago and far away but rather, as Foxe's *Book of Martyrs* had taught Englishmen for over eighty years, the record of themselves and of their time. As William Haller has written, "Every individual case [in Foxe] was charged with the whole meaning of history as he conceived it. The blood of English martyrs of yesterday was shown to be one with the blood of all the martyrs back to Nero."[15] This sense of contemporaneity with the past, Haller shows, was particularly strong in the Puritans of the 1640s so that it was entirely in keeping with his education and sympathies that Milton again and again related the past to the situations in which he and his countrymen found themselves. Thus in condemning the prelates of his day for their perfidy and worldliness, he found it entirely natural to quote Spenser's *Shepheardes Calender,* noting as he quotes that Spenser inveighs "not without some presage of these reforming times":

The time was once, and may again returne
(For oft may happen that hath been beforn)
When Shepheards had none inheritance
Ne of land, nor fee in sufferance,
But what might arise of the bare sheep,
(Were it more or lesse) which they did keep. [16]

Applying the lessons of the past to the present, however, is always problematic; and Milton realized that while no shortcuts to infallibility exist, a concentration on minutiae and externals guarantees a worse fallibility than total ignorance of the past would entail. Thus, immediately after enjoining the study of languages, he cautioned that, "though a linguist should pride himselfe to have all the tongues that *Babel* cleft the world into, yet, if he have not studied the solid things in them as well as the words and lexicons, he were nothing so much to be esteem'd a learned man, as any yeoman or tradesman competently wise in his mother dialect only" (YP II, pp. 369–70). Throughout his career, he had much to say about the misuse of lexicons, phrasebooks, sources, his comments there paralleling those that he makes about the misuse of tradition; for always what he objects to is their use as a substitute for genuine learning and understanding. While still in his teens, he wrote a letter to his former teacher, Alexander Gill, highly critical of his fellow students for "learning barely enough for sticking together a short harangue by any method whatever and patching it with worn-out pieces from various sources" (YP I, p. 314). Years later, his criticism of Salmasius was essentially the same:

A scholar, I suppose, who till old age has spent his time thumbing anthologies and dictionaries and glossaries, instead of reading through good authors with judgment and profit; and so all your talk is of manuscripts and variant readings, of displaced or corrupt passages: you reveal that you have never tasted a drop of honest scholarship. (*First Defence*, YP IV, p. 338)

Honest scholarship, in Milton's view, was not incompatible with anthologies and dictionaries. We know that he used them himself and indeed worked off and on for many years on his own thesaurus "according to the manner of Stephanus."[17] Still, without a sure sense that such works are means rather than ends and that manuscripts, variant readings, and corrupt passages do a scholar no good unless he has a larger sense of the work's significance, all such endeavors become for Milton so much pedantic bric-a-brac, so many exercises in futility.

As with dictionaries and anthologies, so with tradition. The person invoking it must employ tact and intelligence in determining its limitations and uses; or to use Milton's own images, it must be well and thoroughly digested before it can be properly utilized. Else, it remains an "indigested heap, and frie of Authors," or worse yet, "old vomit." If we look, however, at another of Milton's images, the simile taken over from Scripture in *Areopagitica* wherein truth is compared to a streaming fountain, we find a more favorable possibility for tradition. True enough, "if her waters flow not in a perpetuall progression, they sick'n into a muddy pool of conformity and tradition" (YP II, p. 543). But what if the stream remains unblocked and perpetually flowing? Tradition itself then can become the metaphrand in an image that radically alters its significance. No longer viewed as a bulwark for the status quo, it becomes rather the embodiment of our necessarily changing apprehensions of the past and of truth itself.

Such an image Milton had encountered in Ignatius and quoted with approval in *Of Reformation*. "The head, and beginning of divine tradition" was, of course, the Bible; and when the channel carrying divine tradition clogged, the remedy was to return to its source (YP I, p. 563). Ignatius's image did not suggest, however, that the waters of divine tradition must be permanently frozen in order to ensure conformity with the Scriptures. The river image carries with it perforce the idea of constant change. The change can be for the worse, for the vein may "be stopt, or turn'd aside in the midcourse" (p. 563). But it also implies the possibility of change for the better, that men and women through their reason can unclog the stream's course and make its waters flow again if they understand its true source; and for so long as the stream's waters flow in consonance with their source, "divine tradition" can carry the eternal truths of the Scriptures in a medium of constant change.

We noted above that Milton was more sanguine than his conservative opponents in his estimate of men and women's abilities to read the Bible for themselves. In extension, this becomes a major tenet in his philosophy— that truth can only become truth for each of us as we individually possess it through the agency of our reason and faith. Immediately prior to quoting Ignatius, he quotes Lactantius on the importance of independence in reading and how it militates against excessive reverence for the ancients:

not because they went before us in time, therefore in wisedome, which being given alike to all Ages, cannot be prepossest by the Ancients; wherefore seeing that to seeke the Truth is inbred to all, they bereave themselves of wisedome the gift of God who without judgement follow the Ancients, and are led by others like bruit beasts. (YP I, pp. 561–62)

The ancient writers and the stream of tradition from New Testament times on are thus to be challenged and challenged vigorously, but this is a measure of their value rather than their lack of value. Within the Bible itself, Milton found, he thought, the pattern for the proper valuing of tradition itself. Comparison of the Law and the Gospel emphasized to him the granitic and unchanging character of the Law as compared to the fluid and dynamic Gospel. The former demanded reverence, but demanded it in a formal, unchanging, legalistic way; the latter challenged its readers to respond to it in love, thus guaranteeing that their response would change, develop, enlarge. Noting that "the christian arbitrement of charity is supreme . . . resolver of all Scripture" and that Eusebius had compared "the state of Christians to that of *Noah* and the Patriarkes before the Law," he continued:

this indeede was the reason, why *Apostolick* tradition in the antient Church was counted nigh equall to the writt'n word, though it carried them at length awry, for want of considering that tradition was not left to bee impos'd as law, but to be a patterne of that Christian prudence, and liberty which holy men by right assum'd of old. (*Tetrachordon*, YP II, pp. 637–38)

Such liberty brings with it the possibility of error. Looking back at the passage on Papias quoted above, we note that nothing wrong inhered in "those traditions which he receiv'd." Indeed, we may sense that Papias's preference for the personal as opposed to the doctrinal, for the spoken as opposed to the written, was for Milton to some extent a legitimate expression of his Christian freedom, vitiated only by a lack of prudence commensurate with the liberty he rightfully possessed. If Papias's "shallow wit," however, deformed and obscured the traditions he transmitted to others, the same liberty that permitted him to go awry likewise enabled others not only to transmit tradition faithfully but to enrich it; for Milton always allows the possibility that those of a penetrating intellect can reveal a truth in Scripture or tradition not formerly apparent.

His own interpretation of Christ's teachings on divorce Milton believed to be just such an enrichment: "Thus med'cining our eyes wee neede not doubt to see more into the meaning of these our Saviours words, then many who have gone before us" (YP II, p. 639). And yet, however radical his interpretation might seem to his contemporaries, Milton insisted that it was congruent with the writings of "many who have gone before us." Granted, he could find few men who had advanced his argument as he did; but still he maintained that his argument was just that—an advancement, a clarification, an enrichment of what was implicit in the "common Expositers" though they themselves were unaware of it.

The key to using tradition intelligently, then, lay for Milton in that same independence and reason that he exalted in reading classical literature and even the Bible itself. In his hierarchy of sources, tradition obviously lay at the bottom, more open by its nature to corruption and degradation than the others. Still, save only the Bible, all writing, however illustrious its reputation, might in his view be a source of error. The only way to perceive such error, he thought, lay in independence of mind. With approval, he quoted St. Augustine's recommendation to count "it lawfull in the bookes of whomsoever to reject that which hee finds otherwise then true, and so hee would have others deale by him" (YP I, p. 562).

In the light of such approval, Christ's rejection of pagan learning in *Paradise Regain'd*, so long a stumbling block in Miltonic criticism, seems far more of a piece with Milton's thought, differing in degree more than in kind from thoughts expressed elsewhere. Containing within himself all human wisdom, Christ properly affirms that he does not need to look elsewhere for what he already fully possesses:

> who reads
> Incessantly, and to his reading brings not
> A spirit and judgment equal or superior
> (And what he brings, what needs he elsewhere seek)
> Uncertain and unsettl'd still remains,
> Deep verst in books and shallow in himself.[18]

For those of us who are merely mortal, a less austere response is appropriate; for not possessing within ourselves all reason, we may well look without, finding some books at least an enhancement to our understanding of ourselves and of life. Our search is futile, however, unless we approach our task as mature men and women capable of exercising independent and reasonable judgment.

Our exercise of these qualities enables us finally to possess the truth for ourselves. For Milton, this is far more than the merely negative virtue of avoiding error. Parting company with the skeptics in his commitment to a truth that exists independently of our perception of it, he nonetheless affirms that truth does not become truth to us until we make it our own through personal discovery and commitment. No other person, author, or tradition will suffice: "A man may be a heretick in the truth; and if he beleeve things only because his Pastor sayes so, or the Assembly so determins, without knowing other reason, though his belief be true, yet the very truth he holds, becomes his heresie" (*Areopagitica*, YP II, p. 543).

For those of us who still believe that the past has lessons to teach the present, Milton thus stands as a challenging, yet encouraging, taskmaster. Tradition, he believed, cannot be "impos'd as law," nor are there any infallible touchstones or painless shortcuts in determining what to keep and what to discard. For Milton, tradition at its best was the record of men and women responding freely and lovingly to a living message. Without freedom, without love, he found tradition as comfortless and forbidding a monument as the Law itself to a Christian believer. With these qualities, he saw all the elements that hinder humanity in its quest for a living past—inadequate knowledge, inadequate intellect, inadequate character even—as surmountable. The task, he knew, was not easy, involving the many and painful mistakes that he saw as the inevitable price of freedom. It was, he thought, possible. Discursively and exemplarily, his work yet argues powerfully that he was right.

The University of Toledo

## NOTES

1. Edward Shils, *Tradition* (Chicago, 1981), p. 4; Karl F. Morrison, *Tradition and Authority in the Western Church, 300–1140* (Princeton, 1969), p. xi; T. S. Eliot, "Tradition and the Individual Talent," in *Selected Essays* (New York, 1960), p. 6.

2. *Complete Prose Works of John Milton*, 8 vols., ed. Don M. Wolfe et al. (New Haven, 1953–82), vol. II, p. 598. All references to the prose cite this edition as YP.

3. William Hazlitt, "On Shakespeare and Milton," in *The Complete Works of William Hazlitt*, 21 vols., ed. P. P. Howe (London, 1930–34), vol. V. p. 58.

4. The definitions are from William Morris's *American Heritage Dictionary* (New York, 1969).

5. Quoted in *Luther's Works*, 55 vols., ed. Lewis W. Spitz and Helmut T. Lehmann (Philadelphia, 1955–86), vol. XXXIV, p. 351.

6. *Canons and Decrees of the Council of Trent: Original Text with English Translation*, trans. H. J. Schroeder, O.P. (St. Louis, 1941), p. 17.

7. John Calvin, *Institutes of the Christian Religion*, 2 vols., trans. Ford Lewis Battles, ed. John T. McNeill (Philadelphia, 1960), vol. I, p. 23.

8. St. Augustine, *Letters*, 5 vols., trans. Sr. Wilfrid Parsons, S.N.D. (New York, 1951–56), vol. I, p. 392.

9. Quoted from *Articles, wherevpon it was agreed by the Archbysshops, and Bishops . . .* [The Thirty-Nine Articles of the Church of England] (London, 1564), n.p.

10. Joseph Hall, *The Works of the Right Reverend Joseph Hall*, 10 vols., ed. Philip Wynter (1863; rpt. New York, 1969), vol. IX, p. 168.

11. For Irenaeus's view, see *Against Heresies*, bk. III, chap. 2, in *The Ante-Nicene Fathers*, 10 vols., ed. Alexander Roberts and James Donaldson (1899–1900; rpt. Grand Rapids, Mich., 1979), vol. I, p. 414; Vincent of Lerins, *The Commonitory*, in *A Select Library of Nicene and Post-Nicene Fathers*, 2d ser., 14 vols., ed. Philip Schaff and Henry Wace (1894; rpt. Grand Rapids, Mich., 1973), vol. XI, p. 132.

12. James Ussher, *Judgement of Doctor Rainoldes Touching the Originall of Episcopacy* (London, 1641), pp. 4–5.

13. The passage in Eusebius, *Ecclesiastical History*, bk. III, chap. 4, may be con-

sulted in the Loeb edition, 2 vols., ed. Kirsopp Lake (London, 1926), vol. I, pp. 195–97. The Yale editors' observations are contained in footnote 19 to *Of Prelatical Episcopacy*, (YP I, p. 630–31).

14. Papias, *The Ante-Nicene Fathers* I, p. 153. Only fragments of Papias's work survive, embedded in other writers. The above is quoted from Eusebius's *Ecclesiastical History*, bk III, chap. 39. Another version of the passage appears in the Loeb edition, vol. I, pp. 291–93.

15. William Haller, "John Fox and the Puritan Revolution," in *The Seventeenth Century by Richard Foster Jones and Others Writing in His Honor* (Stanford, Calif., 1951), p. 217.

16. Edmund Spenser, "May Eclogue," 103–08, quoted in *Animadversions*, YP I, p. 723.

17. Edward Phillips, "The Life of Mr. John Milton" (1694), in *The Early Lives of Milton*, ed. Helen Darbishire (London, 1932), p. 72.

18. *PR* IV, 321–27, in *Complete Poetry and Major Prose*, ed. Merritt Y. Hughes (New York, 1957), p. 523.

# MILTON CATCHES THE CONSCIENCE OF THE KING: *EIKONOKLASTES* AND THE ENGAGEMENT CONTROVERSY

## *Sharon Achinstein*

---

CRITICS HAVE looked at Milton's arguments for liberty of conscience in the context of the struggle in the seventeenth century over
religious toleration, and indeed, Milton's insistence that the individual
conscience ought to be free from outward constraint or coercion is a
touchstone of his political theory.[1] Milton held that individual conscience
was an ultimate moral authority, a God-given guide to ethical behavior.
God speaks of his gift of conscience in *Paradise Lost:*

> And I will place within them as a guide
> My Umpire *Conscience,* whom if they will hear,
> Light after light well us'd they shall attain,
> And to the end persisting, safe arrive. (III, 194–97)[2]

Throughout his work, Milton seems to uphold a firm commitment to
freedom of conscience and to the idea that the voice of conscience is the
voice of God in humans.

Yet in one of his works, Milton turns back on his sense of conscience
as an autonomous and supreme judge, the "umpire" of human affairs, and
denies it a role in national politics. In *Eikonoklastes,* Milton writes, "This
we may take for certain, that [the king] was never sworn to his own
particular conscience and reason, but to our condition as a free people"
(YP III, p. 519). While Milton means here that the king's loyalty is to the
public and not to his own private morality, as is conventional in sixteenth-
century constitutionalist thought, the phrasing does disturb the notion of
conscience as an inviolate principle of human action. The difficulty is:
What does Milton think ought to be the place of conscience in political
affairs?

Part of the answer is that the term *conscience* is itself unclear. What,
after all, is it that must be left free? In Milton studies, conscience has
generally been regarded either as a religious concept or as a rational one,
and the idea of conscience in Milton has been subsumed into a discourse

either about reason or about free will, not about its place in politics. The
Miltonic conscience, the "rational" argument goes, is the expression of
"right reason," a Platonic concept denoting the ability to distinguish right
and wrong. An example of this understanding of the term is William B.
Hunter's *Milton Encyclopedia,* in which the reader who looks up the word
*conscience* in volume two is directed to the entry called *reason* in volume
nine. Arthur E. Barker and A.S.P. Woodhouse also equate conscience
with reason in their discussions of the movement for toleration for the
sects during the civil war period, and they align Milton with a tradition of
Renaissance humanism. The civil war Milton, in this reading, becomes a
protoliberal, like John Lilburne and Roger Williams, who fought for freedom of speech and for religious toleration when speaking of freedom of
conscience. *Areopagitica* asserts this equation between conscience and
reason: "Give me liberty to know, to utter, and to argue freely according to
conscience, above all liberties," Milton cries (YP II, p. 560). Conscience is
a principle of free choice over any reading material, political and religious.
Even Andrew Milner, writing from a Marxist perspective, sees Milton's
idea of conscience as part of a nascent "rationalist epistemology," the
avatar of the *cogito* of the "new bourgeois man." As the equivalent of right
reason, conscience is the philosophic premise of moral individualism,
expressing a "fixity" in Milton, "which comes to characterize the humanist
definition of subjectivity," according to the materialist critic Catherine
Belsey.[3]

On the other hand, there are critics and historians who have elided
the Miltonic notion of conscience with the religious concept of free will or
the Holy Spirit. Discussions of Milton's "Christian Liberty" have focused
on liberty of conscience as a marker of free will. For Maurice Kelley,
conscience in Milton is a "divine impulse," centered on the heart, a sign of
God's gift of inward liberty to humans. John R. Knott gives conscience a
more "mysterious" formulation, aligning it with the Holy Spirit which
informs a right reading of Scripture. Conscience verifies the inner law
only in accordance with the dictates of the Spirit. Though that Spirit is not
identical to reason, it is also not contrary to it. The religious notion of
conscience is found in Milton's *Treatise of Civil Power* (1659), where
conscience is defined as an equivalent to "religion, that full perswasion
whereby we are assur'd that our beleef and practise, as far as we are able
to apprehend and probably make appeer, is according to the will of God &
his Holy Spirit within us, which we ought to follow much rather then any
law of man" (YP VII, p. 242). This late interpretation of conscience follows
the quietistic ending of *Paradise Lost,* where spiritual freedom is found in
the "paradise within."[4]

Though these readings outline the intellectual suppositions of Milton's writings on conscience, they fail to account for the biographical element that shapes Milton's arguments. In this essay, I give more attention than previously has been paid to Milton's biography, and particularly to Milton's politics, since I see his arguments about conscience as a response to contemporary debates in the English Revolution.[5] Milton's political uses of conscience are clear in his Commonwealth writings, where he champions conscience as a principle of national self-determination, asking in *The Tenure of Kings and Magistrates* (1649): "By what conscience, or divinity, or Law, or reason, a State is bound to leave all these sacred concernments under a perpetual hazard and extremity of danger, rather then cutt off a wicked Prince, who sitts plotting day and night to subvert them" (YP III, p. 254). But Milton's defense of freedoms of conscience (both political and religious) runs aground when the king's book is published because the king himself is defended on the grounds of conscience in *Eikon Basilike.* Milton faced a real difficulty as he rejected the king's appeal to conscience: How could a protector of free conscience like Milton refuse to allow the king those freedoms? In *Eikonoklastes,* Milton seems to negate his earlier claims for conscience, revealing a real ambivalence about the place of conscience in justifying political positions. For all its claims to a truth which transcends politics, the idea of conscience owes a great deal to Milton's contemporary political arena.

The persistent tension throughout Milton's work between the understanding of conscience in its personal sense and its proper place in public affairs is no better exemplified than in *Eikonoklastes. Eikonoklastes* addresses the consequences of the admission of conscience into the political sphere, but it does so not as a work of theory but rather as a nasty polemic designed to kill the image of the king after the king himself had been killed. As a practical instance where Milton's theory of conscience may be tested, *Eikonoklastes* shows it comes up short, or at least requires decent revision. The king's invocation of conscience as the bedrock of political action in *Eikon Basilike* exposes a conceptual difficulty for Milton who agrees that conscience is a fundamental guide of human conduct, but who refuses to exempt the king from his responsibilities to his people on the grounds of such a guide. Milton is forced to adapt his understanding of the role of conscience so that he can exclude the king's conscience from political argument.

This essay examines the idea of conscience in *Eikonoklastes* and in the contemporary Engagement controversy, showing that the terms Milton used in *Eikonoklastes* to exclude the king's conscience from the political arena are those formally presented in the Engagement controversy.

Both *Eikonoklastes* and the Engagement controversy raise the question of the role of conscience in political affairs. Yet the use of conscience was equivocal; when the Parliament of the new Commonwealth required citizens to swear the loyalty oath, both those who subscribed and those who resisted made use of the idea of conscience to justify their actions. The rhetoric of conscience in the Engagement controversy supplied contradictory justifications, and could justify almost any position.

*Conscience* became a radical self-authorizing term, at once meaningful and meaningless. Milton did not give an unequivocal answer to the practical question of the place of conscience in political affairs, but he did put himself at the center of a party that exacted public and political expressions of conscience in the Engagement oath. Milton's role in the Engagement controversy is an example of just how vexing a concept conscience came to be, and it makes the task of understanding the Miltonic notion of conscience all the more difficult. The reading of *Eikonoklastes* that follows should supplement those that have focused on the iconic and antitheatrical elements of the treatise by addressing the issue of hypocrisy in the religious and political terms of the day.[6]

### EIKON BASILIKE AND PURITAN CONSCIENCE

*Eikon Basilike* relied heavily on the king's prayers in his drama of self-justification. Compiled and probably written by the cleric John Gauden, *Eikon Basilike* was issued the day of the king's execution, and it was an immediate publicity success, appearing in forty English editions in its first year alone. The book presented a defense of the king, a narration of the events from the meeting of the Long Parliament in 1641 up until the king's imprisonment, and it was supplemented by the king's personal reminiscences and feelings. With the brilliance of a master propagandist, Gauden had presented the king's prayers at the end of each chapter, and these prayers called upon God to bear witness to the rightness of his actions. In fact, the prayers became the most popular portions of the book itself, surviving in printed Royalist collections well into the eighteenth century in translations, versifications, and musical settings. *Eikon Basilike* was received by its contemporary readers less as a work of polemical persuasion than it was as a remembrance for a martyr.[7]

Aside from their appeal as popular songs, the prayers offered an airtight piece of propaganda for the king: How could anyone quarrel with his prayers, the utterances of the king's own conscience? The testimony of the king's conscience was a powerful tool because conscience was thought to be an irrefutable locus of authority, unassailable since it derived power from a source outside politics, from God. The king insisted again and again on the primacy of his conscience in justifying his actions: "I know no resolutions more worthy a Christian King than to prefer his own conscience before his Kingdom's."[8] For Milton, the image of the king was not only dangerous as an instance of theatricality, but because that image was a specific representation—the king at prayer. Prayer held special meaning for a Protestant; it was the direct and, above all, the sincere communication between humans and God, and it represented the voice of conscience. In *Eikonoklastes*, Milton exchanged the religious meanings of conscience for political ones as he sought to catch the conscience of the king, hoping to expose the "facil conscience [which] could dissemble satisfaction when it pleas'd" (YP III, pp. 371–72).

The king insisted on the propriety of his actions on the unimpeachable grounds of conscience: "I may, without vanity, turn the reproach of my sufferings, as to the world's censure, into the honour of a kind of martyrdom, as to the testimony of my own conscience" (p. 163). By fashioning himself as a martyr, the king presents a self-authorizing exemption from the ordinary strictures of civil behavior.[9] A martyr answers to a higher law, and the king goes so far as to justify his opposition to Parliament's requests on the grounds that they would "wound that inward quiet of my conscience, which ought to be, is, and ever shall be, by God's grace, dearer to me than my Kingdoms" (p. 53). Like the conventional martyr, the king owes his allegiance to God, not to the humans who have judged him: "Thou, O Lord, art my witness in heaven and in my heart if I have purposed any violence or oppression against the innocent or if there were any such wickedness in my thoughts" (p. 13). Repeatedly stressing his inward piety over his outward circumstances, the king concludes, "I am confident the justice of my cause and clearness of my conscience before God and toward my people will carry me as much above [my enemies] in God's decision as their successes have lifted them above me in the vulgar opinion" (p. 178).

Given that the language of conscience was so often used during the English Revolution as justification for opposition to the king, it is surprising that the king himself employs this defense. Milton and many others had preached resistance to an "unjust" king like Charles on ground of conscience.[10] In justifying rebellion against unjust kingship in the *Tenure of Kings and Magistrates*, Milton argued that "God put it into mans heart to find out that way at first for common peace and preservation, approving the exercise therof" (YP III, p. 209), and he applied the theory that citizens could judge rulers by the workings of an inner natural law, the law of conscience. Milton himself had subscribed to such a view of conscience in his poetry and prose and would present figures who exemplified conscientious resistance (Abdiel and Enoch are two) in *Paradise Lost*. Because conscience made humans answerable to God alone, it could not be refuted on ordinary civil grounds, as Milton was well aware, and it could provide a defense of unprecedented actions like a tyrannicide, as in *Tenure of Kings and Magistrates* (YP III, p. 237).

As it was for Milton, conscience was considered by many Protestants to be a bedrock of human action, an irrefutable justification for dissent. Seventeenth-century writers developed their conceptions of conscience from John Calvin and Martin Luther as an "extra-political factor" that operated as a direct link between humans and God.[11] In Calvinism, conscience was a human faculty of discernment which partook in elements of the divine:

When [men] have a sense of divine judgment, as a witness joined to them, which does not allow them to hide their sins from being accused before the Judge's tribunal, this sense is called "conscience." For it is a certain mean between God and man, because it does not allow man to suppress within himself what he knows.[12]

The image here is the judge's tribunal, like Milton's "umpire" in *Paradise Lost* which hears cases. Milton consistently draws upon the judicial metaphor in his own writings on conscience, mentioning "the barre of conscience" and "the jurisdiction of conscience" in the divorce tracts (YP II, pp. 337, 657). In Calvin, however, the conscience is closer to the truth, called the "guardian," the "keeper" (*Institutes* I, p. 848); conscience is also "a thousand witnesses" (p. 1182) and associated with the idea of natural, or inward law, "written, even engraved, upon the hearts of all" (p. 367). For Calvin, conscience is not just a faculty, it is a joint action between God and humans, "when men have an awareness of divine judgment adjoined to them as a witness which does not let them hide their sins but arraigns them as guilty before the judgment seat" (p. 1181).

Most important, conscience is an inward guide, as Calvin puts it, "Dictat lex illa interior" (*Institutes* I, p. 367), an inward law. "A good conscience," writes Calvin, "is nothing but inward integrity of the heart" (p. 849). Milton's description of conscience, in *Reason of Church Government*, as God's "Secretary" depends on this sense (YP I, p. 822). A "secretary" is one who is entrusted with private or secret matters in addition to being the name for one whose office it is to write for another. Conscience is a secretary in that it is entrusted with the commands of God, also in the sense that it takes down God's dictation on the heart of the individual. Conscience as a secretary is "written," and the metaphor Milton uses in an echo of Calvin is "engrave," a form of writing that is lasting, as on stone. In opposing those prelates who would force conscience, Michael in *Paradise Lost* describes to Adam that forcing conscience violates that inner writing:

> from that pretense,
> Spiritual Laws by carnal power shall force
> On every conscience; Laws which none shall find
> Left to them inroll'd, or what the Spirit within
> Shall on the heart engrave.                    (XII, 520–24)

Like the words on the tablets of stone of the Ten Commandments, the words of conscience are written by God.

Puritans commonly translated their sense of conscience into an image of a physical guide, as Milton does in his sonnet, *To Mr. Cyriack Skinner upon his Blindness*, where his image of the conscience follows Calvin's usage. Even though the poet is now blind,

> Yet I argue not
> Against heav'n's hand or will, nor bate a jot
> Of heart or hope; but still bear up and steer
> Right onward. What supports me, dost thou ask?
> The conscience, Friend.                    (6–10)

Conscience is that inner faculty which liberates the poet from the need for external sight. He is "content though blind" (14), and "yet" he harbors hopes about the future. The short, sharp words (bate, jot, heart, hope, bear, steer) are pricks and prods which portray that journey as an uneven, even a stumbling one, as if the way is strewn with sharp stones. Conscience provides a steady help through these, a kind of internal navigational device, both in land as it is in the "blindness" sonnet, and at sea, as it is in the most memorable of Milton's lines on conscience, where the "umpire Conscience" leads humans to "safe arrive" (*PL* III, 195–97).

According to Luther, conscience is relegated to the spiritual, as opposed to the civil, sphere, in line with his famous distinction between the two kingdoms.[13] In Milton's early poem, *On the New Forcers of Conscience Under the Long Parliament*, the poet sought to protect the spiritual freedom of conscience from encroachments by the civil realm. Milton railed against "the new forcers of conscience" in 1646, against those who seemed to tread upon the freedoms of individual conscience to decide how to practice religion. Milton asked the civil authorities, "Dare ye for this adjure the Civil Sword / To force our Consciences that Christ set free" (5–6). The poem makes a clear distinction between the "Civil Sword" and that which "Christ set free," two spheres of action which Milton's two separate lines of poetry tried to keep apart.

But this distinction between civil and spiritual was not always so sharp in Calvinism. According to Calvin, conscience was a component of Christian liberty, the freedom to decide matters deemed inessential to proper Christian teaching, and this could mean civil matters. The problem, as Calvin had accurately forecast, was when civil laws seemed to threaten a Christian conscience. To resolve this difficulty, Calvin went back to the key text, Paul's command in Romans, chapter xiii, that "every soul be subject unto the higher powers" on grounds of "conscience" to provide justification for obedience to the civil magistrate. Calvin, like Luther, read in Paul a firm distinction between human and divine laws: Paul "does not teach that the laws framed by [magistrates] apply to the inward governing of the soul," since "human laws . . . do not of themselves bind the conscience" (p. 1184). Yet even though Calvin makes a separation between the two kingdoms, nevertheless he admits that difficulties arise in the application of the principle because many "do not sharply enough distinguish the outer forum, as it is called, and the forum of conscience" (p. 848).[14]

During the civil war, the distinction between inner and outer spheres of action was further weakened as fighters used conscience as grounds for their political activism. The English Puritans built on Calvin's sense of conscience as the locus of Christian liberty, giving it a practical component, first to decide "cases of conscience" in the form of traditional casuistry, and then to register political claims against their king within a constitutional framework. William Ames formulated the idea of conscience in an active way in 1643: "It appeareth that conscience is not a *contemplative judgment*, whereby truth is discerned from falsehood: but a *practical* judgment," and that meant conscience could lead to a form of knowledge that "may be a rule to him to direct his will." In their drive to construct a "holy commonwealth," civil war reformers sought to create a political system based on rules acceptable to free consciences. According to many of the radicals of the English Revolution, conscience was a sovereign faculty, incapable of subordination to higher secular authority, and must be left free. The Levellers' "Agreement of the People" from 1647 preserved freedoms for conscience for humans, resolving "that matters of religion and the ways of God's worship are not at all entrusted to us by any human power, because therein we cannot remit or exceed a tittle of what our consciences dictate to the mind of God." This idea was used to justify opposition to human powers.[15]

When applied politically, conscience could be a radical concept because of its unimpeachable authority. As an innate faculty of humans, it could without external constraint judge right and wrong. The Puritan notion of conscience, as the theologian William Ames pleaded, was based on the idea that only divine agency could give the gifts of faith or salvation: "The conscience is immediately subject to God, and his will, and therefore it cannot submit it self unto any creature without Idolatry."[16] Liberty of conscience from civil authorities was therefore necessary. If the abolition of episcopacy in 1646 served only to establish what Milton saw as a prelatical—national—church system, then this was a burden upon the conscience. The discussion about conscience during the civil war period took on increasingly more political and less theological tones.

The difficulties of this position are obvious. Conscience becomes its own authorizing principle. The doctrine of conscience is as potentially politically subversive as it is irrational: there is no way to ensure standards of political action, nor to distinguish an erring conscience from a true one. For the king to use this defense is an interesting alliance with the more radical reformers of his day. In writing his answer to *Eikon Basilike* in 1649, Milton is put in the awkward position of having to explain why conscience may not always authorize political actions. The king's invocations of conscience were deeply troubling to Milton who was fighting for freedom of conscience but who saw in the king's words a terrible hypocrisy.

### CATCHING THE KING'S CONSCIENCE

In *Eikonoklastes* Milton sought to demystify the king's rhetoric by countering the king's "idolatrous" tactics with rational argument. To accomplish this, Milton consistently showed that while *Eikon Basilike* patently defended the king's actions before God, it was really a crafty defense before the citizens of England. Milton registered that his enemy's motive was to achieve "that what he could not compass by Warr . . . by his Meditations" (YP III, p. 342), arguing that those still loyal to the king,

Intend it not so much the defence of his former actions, as the promoting of thir own future designes, making thereby the Book thir own rather then the Kings, as the benefit now must be thir own more then his, now . . . to corrupt and disorder the mindes of weaker men, by new suggestions and narrations. (YP III, p. 338)

Milton was worried that the king's book would corrupt "weaker men" because it disarmed readers by rhetorical tricks and would thus strengthen the royalist cause.

Milton's main strategy was to to cloud the testimony of the king's conscience by proving that the king was an utter hypocrite. The king's plagiarism was a flagrant example of this hypocrisy, and Milton used the famous example of the stolen prayers, both from Sidney's *Arcadia* and from David's psalms, to discredit the account of the king's conscience. The biblical heist is more opprobrious than the literary one in Milton's mind because of the connection between prayer and conscience in Puritan theology in general and in civil war minds in particular. Milton, like the reforming godly of the English Civil War period, saw the language of prayer as an especially inflammatory issue, not only as a religious issue, but also as a political one. The first actions of those who opposed the king were to reject his imposition of the prayer book by prerogative in Scotland in 1637, and the dissidents, including Milton, called Charles's desire for a uniform church to be dictated by set forms of worship, the forcing of conscience. Set prayers, along with all the other signs of ritual, seemed to reformers to smack of idolatry. [17] These Puritans, echoing Jesus' attack on Pharisaic hypocrisy in the New Testament, viewed institutionalized forms of worship as evil, as interrupting the conversation between an individual's conscience and God.

Not only did Milton see the stolen prayer as another sign of the king's general usurpation of his people's right, of his false dramatic role as a penitent martyr, and of his odious prayer book reforms, but most important, it was a sign of the dangerous gap between the king's words and his intentions: "Had he borrow'd *Davids* heart, it had bin much the holier theft" (YP III, p. 547). Especially in prayer, there ought to be a correlation between the inner condition of the soul and the outward use of forms, but Milton claimed the truth was that one's inner condition was unreadable. The king had no right to the words spoken by others because of this gap between inner thoughts and outward manifestations of those thoughts. Only God can know to whom the property, literary and otherwise, properly belongs: "It is not hard for any man, who hath a Bible in his hands, to borrow good words and holy sayings in abundance; but to make them his own, is a work of grace onely from above" (YP III, p. 553). [18] Inner spirit must accord with external presentation: "But transported with the vain ostentation of imitating *Davids* language, not his life, observe how he brings a curse upon himself and his Fathers house (God so disposing it) by his usurp'd and ill imitated prayer" (YP III, p. 555).

The theft of Jesus' words was an ultimate act of hypocrisy because the king was not at all like Jesus: "Eev'n his prayer is so ambitious of Prerogative, that it dares ask away the Prerogative of Christ himself" (YP III, p. 502). Milton used the familiar language of Parliament to attack the king's abuse of prerogative, here, surprisingly, in a religious sense. The king's literary borrowing was the same type of usurpation as both his religious and his political acts of usurpation, tyrannical because it depended upon the king's will alone. The stolen words were proof that the king's piety was an artful construction. As Milton saw it, the king was proving nothing in using Jesus' last words on the cross, since "it is an easie matter to say over what our Saviour said"; instead, Milton demanded that the king be judged by his actions, "how he lov'd the People, other Arguments then affected sayings must demonstrat" (YP III, p. 447). Though the king has spoken the same words as Jesus, his inner worth was in no way the same.[19]

Further, in politics, prayers alone do not count: "But Kings, above all other men, have in their hands not to pray onely but to doe. To make that prayer effectual, he should have govern'd as well as pray'd. To pray and not to govern is For a Monk and not a King" (YP III, p. 531). Milton works himself into the position of denying the king any rule by conscience at all, drawing the reader's attention to the disparity between the king's words and his actions and claiming that by those actions alone can the king be judged: "As for the truth and sinceritie which he praies may be alwaies found in those his Declarations to the people, the contrariety of his own actions will bear eternal witness how little carefull or sollicitous he was, what he promis'd, or what he utterd there" (YP III, p. 469). Words should not substitute for facts. Milton here replaces the Calvinist "witness" of conscience with the "eternal witness" of actions. Since actions occur in the public realm, they alone can be subject to public evaluation. The danger of judging the king by his words alone is that they cannot be trusted: "Meer words we are too well acquainted with," Milton remarks with a sneer (YP III, p. 497).

Milton discounts the king's claim that conscience may act in the public realm at all: "To wipe off jealousies and scandals, the best way, had bin by clear Actions, or till Actions be clear'd, by evident reasons" (YP III, p. 497). The king especially is not entitled to follow the callings of his private conscience because he is not a private man. In *Treatise of Civil Power*, and also in the two poems on conscience, Milton separated the realms of civil and ecclesiastical jurisdiction, allowing each human to preserve a private inner space for conscience, as Luther had done before him. But Milton presses this distinction: Kings do not enjoy the same privacy of conscience as private citizens do. A king in *Eikonoklastes* is a wholly public figure; his conscience is not admitted to resolve political situations. Milton proposes a model for political justification that is based upon "evident reasons," not upon inner faith, where English citizens, rather than God, must act as judges of the king's actions.

Rather than accept the private calling of the king's conscience, Milton sought to place *Eikon Basilike* firmly in the public realm so that it could be refuted, explaining that since the king was "making new appeal to Truth and the World," he would offer a counterappeal to the king in an "op'n and monumental Court of his own erecting" (YP III, pp. 340–41). That court would be the court of public opinion rather than the private court of the king's conscience. Because he believed that the real audience for *Eikon Basilike* is the English citizenry, Milton rejects the king's claims that God is his authority and judge of his actions. Milton substitutes the English nation as judge, insisting that the king's actions must be evaluated in the public realm. Milton denies that conscience may stand as an authority for a public man like the king in his account of the political responsibilities of the magistrate: "This we may take for certain, that he was never sworn to his own particular conscience and reason, but to our condition as a free people" (YP III, p. 519). The king's loyalty is to public, not to his private morality. As Milton writes in *Tenure of Kings and Magistrates*, "to say Kings are accountable to none but God, is the overturning of all Law and government" (YP III, p. 204). The king's conscience then is not free.[20]

Yet if Milton seeks to catch the conscience of the king, he must be careful not to bind his own. Milton's way out of this difficulty follows still another tack: he makes a distinction between true and false conscience. Milton does not mean here (as he will in his later writings) to exclude conscience entirely from the political arena. Rather, true consciences do not force others, and the king has violated this principle: "He calls the conscience *Gods sovrantie*, why then doth he contest with God about that supreme title? Why did he *lay restraints*, and force enlargements upon our consciences in things for which we were to answer God onely and the Church?" (YP III, p. 501). The king has used his conscience contrary to its purpose, as an implement of manipulation over others. With scorn, Milton remarks, "But the *incommunicable Jewell of his conscience* he will not give, *but reserve to himself.* It seemes that his conscience was none of the Crown Jewels; for these we know were, in *Holland*" (YP III, p. 459). Bitterly accusing the king of valuing his own conscience above his subjects' freedoms, Milton charges that the king "would have his conscience not an incommunicable, but a universal conscience, the whole Kingdoms conscience" (p. 459). Milton reviles the king for hastening to protect that which he would not hesitate to steal from others: "Thus what he seemes to feare least we should ravish from him, is our chief complaint that he obtruded upon us; we never forc'd him to part with his conscience, but it was he that would have forc'd us to part with ours" (p. 459). Milton turns the king's language against him: what kind of "jewel" is a soul's conscience, he asks, if the king is willing to force the conscience of others?

Milton attacks the king's program for a unified church, which would force, "ravish," other soul's consciences, and he takes the language of sexual conquest: the conscience is as dear to one as a woman's sexual "honor." "The more our evil happ, that three Kingdoms should be thus pesterd with one Conscience" (YP III, p. 459), Milton continues; a "universal" conscience is an imperial, intolerant conscience. Milton points out that the king's logic here does not make sense: If conscience is an "incommunicable jewel," then the king would have no right to "ravish" others. Yet Charles has done just that: "It was he that would have forced us to part with ours." The metaphor of a rape here is essential; it displaces the king's own rhetoric of martyrdom, a passive, feminine world of images, with an overtly aggressive, masculine one. This is part of Milton's general strategy to demystify the king's image in order to remystify it in new terms.[21] The image highlights Milton's emphasis on the irretrievable value of conscience, and his opposition to the coercive nature of the king's efforts is presented with graphic clarity.

Another sign of the king's erroneous conscience is his profession to know the consciences of others. To Milton the appeal to other humans' consciences smacks of popery, true heresy:

In the mean while they to whom God gave Victory, never brought to the King at *Oxford* the state of thir *consciences*, that he should presume without confession, more than a Pope presumes, to tell abroad what *conflicts and accusations*, men whom he never spoke with, have *in thir own thoughts*. (YP III, pp. 530–31)

Milton rejects the possibility that the king can know other men's consciences, and he sharpens his attack with the example of the pope, who, by exacting confession, forced his way in to the matter of individual souls: "But they who will not stick to slander mens inward consciences, which they can neither see nor know, much less will care to slander outward actions, which they pretend to see, though with senses never so vitiated" (YP III, p. 531).

Milton's exclusion of the king's conscience then takes several forms. The king is a hypocrite, and therefore the testimony of his conscience is false. The king's conscience is also in error since it has shown two prime faults: attempting to force the consciences of others and claiming to know the consciences of others. The latter prong of attack on the king reveals a rather different side to Milton than the "proto-liberal" fighter for free conscience. Yet Milton's notion of conscience here represents an alert response to the rhetoric of his day; would he be so flexible as to elude its definition altogether?

### THE ENGAGEMENT: THE POLITICAL MEANING OF CONSCIENCE

The questions of liberty of individual conscience and of the civil enforcement of uniformity in religious matters came to a crisis in the days following the king's execution. The rest of this essay offers yet another interpretation of the Miltonic role of conscience in political affairs in light of one of Parliament's first acts which made conscience a serious political issue, the Engagement oath. Soon after the king's execution and the establishment of the Commonwealth, Parliament passed an order requiring oaths of allegiance to its new regime in January 1650, after considering such action since the previous March. After months of discussion, Parliament ruled that all men over the age of eighteen years of age were to subscribe to "be true and faithful to the Commonwealth of England as it is now established." Many royalists and Puritans rejected this oath, and it is the unlikely fact that both groups did so on the grounds of conscience. Both groups held that it compelled a public expression that could not accord with inner beliefs. Because it was a public oath, engagement was deemed to involve not just passive acquiescence, but active loyalty.[22]

The controversy surrounding Engagement that ensued in the press shows that the theories of conscience were headed on a collision course. Those who opposed the Engagement oath questioned the legitimacy of "forcing" obedience to the new regime, and they doubted whether the state should exert coercive powers over the individual to secure such an oath. On the other hand, the leaders of the commonwealth held they had the right to demand allegiance from their subjects, and this included loyalty in matters that were religious as well as political. Opponents to the oath of allegiance charged that such a demand encroached upon the subjects' freedom to think and believe as they wished. Both sides, moreover, explained their opposing positions on the grounds of conscience. John Dury, for example, defended the taking of the Engagement based on rules "agreeable to sense, to reason, and to conscience." Dury defined conscience so that it could enter the public realm of politics: conscience was "God's vicegerent over the society of those to whom his administration doth extend itself." Likewise, the anonymous author of *A Disengaged Survey of the Engagement* urged subscription based upon "immediate necessity" which would "satisfy the conscience."[23]

But opponents of the Engagement also used arguments from conscience to support their positions. They saw conscience as the bedrock of justification of all human actions, especially for swearing oaths. Robert Sanderson opposed the Engagement, arguing that neither the principle of self-interest nor the necessity of loyalty to the state were sufficient grounds to take the oath. These are "two desperate Principles" he wrote, which lead ultimately to atheism, where "every man, by making his own Preservation the Measure of all his Duties and Actions, maketh himself thereby an Idol." Sanderson saw that justifications on the ground of conscience led to a kind of dangerous individualism. John Aucher refused to take the oath which he saw as "the justification, an abetting, or owning (at least in part) of all those irregular and horrid acts, which have been committed for the bringing about of this change," and his refusal was on the grounds of conscience, explaining that one does not swear to oaths lightly: "Yet religious and godly men will make Conscience of what they engage in, declare for, promise, subscribe (much more) swear unto, and dare not take Gods name in vain, abuse his Ordinance, delude God or man by seeming to engage in, or swear that in which they do not really engage." Aucher admitted that the oath would not "tie the Conscience of the Taker," but that "it will trouble it, though it do not bind it, it will burden it." His understanding of the oath agrees with Calvin's reading of the Pauline injunction that "human laws . . . do not of themselves bind the conscience" (*Institutes* I, p. 1184), but Aucher maintains that such a civil order could conflict with conscience in some way.[24]

Milton was at first an ardent supporter of the Commonwealth, one of the first to defend the regicide to Europe. But his position in the Engagement controversy is a curious one, especially in light of his earlier writings on the inviolability of conscience. Milton subscribed to the oath himself in 1650 and went so far as to write a public defense of it. Milton explained in a letter to the senate of Hamburg that the oath was entirely legitimate in terms of political necessity; designed "to the end that we may test and know the loyalty of those whom we are appointed to govern, as is proper and necessary," the chief aim of the framers of the oath was to "stabilize peace and the Commonwealth" (YP V, p. 497). This public justification of the oath was part of his job as secretary for foreign tongues, yet scholars have assigned its composition to Milton since the draft is in his hand.[25] Milton defended the oath because he believed the cause was a true cause. It was in part irenism, a common political expedience, but most of all it was his absolute faith in the rightness of his cause that motivated Milton's rethinking of the supremacy of conscience:

Nothing was more just or would better serve to stabilize peace and the Commonwealth than that those who either have obtained their liberty through us (with God as our leader always) or have recovered life and property through our gift and favor after their heinous actions in the civil war, should in return, if need be, solemnly swear to us their governors their allegiance and duty, and should keep their faith. (YP V, p. 497)

Milton is clear about the conscientious nature of the demonstration of civil obedience: it is an oath which must be "solemnly" sworn in an act of good "faith." The need for this oath is pressing, as Milton notes: "We feel this especially at a time when so many men, being restless and disaffected, though sheltered under our protection more than once, continue to act as traitors" (YP V, p. 497).

Milton bases his theory of obligations on the security that God is acting "as their leader always." With this certainty, Milton iterates the notion of a true conscience. Milton, like other Commonwealth leaders, believed in the doctrine of "particular providences," the external signs of success that the Puritans took to be God's approval. In contrast to the true cause of the Commonwealth, the king's cause was evil, and the king's conscience was evil in enforcing that cause. Milton firmly believed that the king's conscience was in error: "For if the conscience be ill edifi'd, the resolution may more befitt a foolish [rather] then a Christian King, to preferr a self-will'd conscience before a Kingdoms good" (YP III, p. 418).

With the distinction between true and erroneous conscience, Milton is caught in his own trap: God has become the authorizing principle for conscience's role in human affairs, but just as for the king in *Eikon Basilike*, there is no way of knowing God's true meanings. There is no public, stable authority that humans can know to ground conscience, and the question threatens to turn otherworldly, something the political fighters of the English Revolution are too willing to allow while they are striving to enlist support for their causes. To ignore the epistemological difficulty of the meaning of conscience at this time is an act of necessary forgetfulness. But the difficulty of grounding conscience does give Miltonic conscience greater flexibility than the "umpire" of *Paradise Lost* would lead us to believe. It is one thing to hear the voice of the "umpire," and it is another thing to act on it.

Seeing Milton's actions in the Engagement controversy gives a more complex understanding of Miltonic conscience. Where he was convinced of the rightness of the Commonwealth cause, Milton seems willing to exclude certain false consciences from their rights to participate in politics. Though a notion of true conscience does not seem to sit right with the idea of liberty of conscience, still Milton held these contradictory views. The juxtaposition of Milton's writings on liberty of conscience with the critique of conscience in *Eikonoklastes* reveals a difficulty in Milton's understanding of this concept, and this forces us to rethink Milton's use of the concept in his great poems. Conscience in Milton is constructed not in the abstract ruminations of the theologian, nor in the flights of his poetry, but in the heat of the civil war fires, and will prove to be a more flexible force than has previously been thought.

On a final note, it is instructive to compare Milton's approach to the Engagement to that of Thomas Hobbes, writing *Leviathan* about the same time as Milton was writing *Eikonoklastes*. Hobbes also urged subscription to the oath, but unlike Milton, he severed the connection between the internal state of conscience and any public expression. In a commonwealth, Hobbes writes, "the Law is the publique Conscience . . . Otherwise in such diversity, as there is of private Consciences, which are but private opinions, the Commonwealth must needs be distracted, and no man dare to obey the Sovereign Power, farther than it shall seem good in his own eyes."[26] Hobbes seems alone at this time in understanding the real political implications of such an antinomian concept as conscience, and he sees it is necessary to exclude conscience from all political discussion. Milton's letter to the senate of Hamburg gives a theory of the state in miniature, and if it were not for a single parenthetical clause, the invocation of God, this theory would resemble that in Hobbes's *Leviathan*. The theory is one of the simple exchange upon which a civil society is built, which Hobbes set out to explain in *Leviathan:* "the mutual Relation between Protection and Obedience" (p. 728).[27] Milton too figures the relation between individual and the state as one of exchanging protection (of "life and property") for obedience, "duty" to the governors, and he contends that those whose liberty and safety were achieved through the efforts of the present governors now owe their allegiance to them. Though Milton explains the equation between protection and obedience in much the same way as Hobbes does, Milton bases his theory of obligations on the security that God is acting "as their leader always," something Hobbes refuses to do. Rather, Hobbes gives a sustained critique of all politics that require God as an authority. Hobbes resolves the conflict between the individual and the state by excluding conscience from the public realm more completely than Milton's awkward and malleable conception of conscience could ever do. An understanding of Milton's ambivalent sense of conscience in his Commonwealth writing should direct us to see Milton in a line with Thomas Hobbes and, finally, John Locke, who came to reject conscience from the realm of politics completely.

Northwestern University

### NOTES

1. For the toleration arguments and their relation to Milton, see Ernest Sirluck, "Introduction," in *Complete Prose Works of John Milton*, 8 vols., ed. Don M. Wolfe et al.

(New Haven, 1953–82), vol. II, pp. 53–130, hereafter cited as YP. William Haller, *Liberty and Reformation in the Puritan Revolution* (New York, 1955); Don M. Wolfe, *Milton in the Puritan Revolution* (New York, 1941). I wish to express gratitude to Constance Jordan, Gordon Schochet, and Martin Mueller for their helpful comments on earlier drafts of this essay, and to acknowledge a longstanding debt to Earl Miner, whose conversations about conscience have given me much enlightenment.

2. References to Milton's poetry are from *John Milton: Complete Poems and Major Prose*, ed. Merritt Y. Hughes (Indianapolis, 1984). C. A. Patrides traces the image of conscience as the ship coming into harbor back to Augustine in *Milton and the Christian Tradition* (Oxford, 1966), p. 111.

3. William B. Hunter, *A Milton Encyclopedia* (Lewisburg, Pa., 1979), vol. II, p. ix; Arthur E. Barker, *Milton and the Puritan Dilemma* (Toronto, 1942), pp. 143–44; A.S.P. Woodhouse, *Puritanism and Liberty* (London, 1966), pp. 187–91; Andrew Milner, *John Milton and the English Revolution: A Study in the Sociology of Literature* (Totowa, N.J., 1981), p. 101; Catherine Belsey, *John Milton: Language, Gender, Power* (Oxford, 1988), p. 86. These notions of conscience owe a tacit debt to Max Weber, whose *Protestant Ethic and the Spirit of Capitalism*, trans. Talcott Parsons (London, 1989), traced the idea of "one's duty to a calling" to Protestant religious principles, including "wordly asceticism" which "placed the individual entirely on his own responsibility," and which promoted "the sense of methodically rationalized ethical conduct" (pp. 54, 109, 125).

4. Maurice Kelley, *This Great Argument: A Study of Milton's "De Doctrina Christiana" as a Gloss upon "Paradise Lost"* (Princeton, 1941), p. 167; John R. Knott, Jr., "Milton and the Spirit of Truth," in *The Sword of the Spirit: Puritan Responses to the Bible* (Chicago, 1980), p. 121. On "Christian Liberty," see also Barbara K. Lewalski, "Milton: Political Beliefs and Polemical Methods, 1659–60," *PMLA* LXXIV (1959), 191–202, for a discussion of Milton's unswerving dedication to Christian liberty, despite his political shifts; Laurence Sterne and Harold H. Kollmeier, eds., *A Concordance to the English Prose of John Milton* (Binghamton, 1985) is invaluable for tracking usage; on the "paradise within" as a poetical frame, see Louis Martz, *The Paradise Within: Studies in Vaughan, Traherne and Milton* (New Haven, 1964); as a theological position, see Robert L. Entzminger, "Michael's Options and Milton's Poetry," *ELR* VIII (1978), 197–211; and as a political retreat, see Christopher Hill, *Milton and the English Revolution* (New York, 1978), p. 421, and N. H. Keble, *The Literary Culture of Nonconformity in Later Seventeenth-Century England* (Athens, Ga., 1987), p. 24: "quietude is not quiescence: Michael points to continuing moral and spiritual effort as Adam's only way to regain paradise."

5. Hill, *Milton*, does restore Milton to his context, more to the social than to the political. Milton is presented there as the radical revolutionary whose attachment to liberty places him alongside the Levellers, though Andrew Milner is right to point out in his *John Milton*, chap. 6, that Hill overlooks the Independents in his search for the radical Milton. These recent attempts to place Milton in his ideological and political context suffer from serious neglect of the intersection of religion and politics during the English Revolution, the approach here in my search for an understanding of the idea of conscience.

6. Attention to the notion of conscience in *Eikonoklastes* has been scant. Rather, its modern readers have emphasized Milton's attacks on the prayers stolen from Sidney and on the king's theatricality in general. See, for example, Richard Helgerson, "Milton Reads the King's Book: Print, Performance, and the Making of a Bourgeois Idol," *Criticism* XXIX, no. 1 (1987), 1–25; Florence Sandler, "Icon and Iconoclast," in *Achievements of the Left Hand: Essays on the Prose of John Milton*, ed. Michael Lieb and John T. Shawcross (Amherst, 1974), pp. 160–84; and Lana Cable, "Milton's Iconoclastic Truth," in *Politics, Poetics, and*

*Hermeneutics in Milton's Prose,* ed. David Loewenstein and James Grantham Turner (Cambridge, 1990), pp. 135–51.

7. On the occasion and background for *Eikonoklastes,* see Merritt Hughes, "Introduction," chap. 8, in YP III. See also Ernest Sirluck, "*Eikon Basilike, Eikon Alethine* and *Eikonoklastes,*" *MLN* LXIX (1954), 497–502; on the popularity of the prayers, see *The Divine Penitential Meditations and Vowes of his Late Sacred Majestie at Holmby House, Faithfully Turned Into Verse, by E.R., Gentleman* (21, June 1649); later set to music as *Psalterium Carolinum,* by John Wilson (1657); on contemporary reaction, see Francis F. Madan, *A New Bibliography of the "Eikon Basilike"* (London, 1950); Christopher Wordsworth, *Documentary Supplement to "Who Wrote Eikon Basilike?"* (London, 1825), p. 16; a review is provided in Hugh Trevor-Roper, "*Eikon Basilike:* The Problem of the King's Book," *History Today* I (1951), 7–12.

8. *Eikon Basilike: The Pourtraiture of His Sacred Majesty in His Solitudes and Sufferings,* ed. Philip Knachel (Ithaca, 1966), p. 28. All further references are to this edition.

9. For the king's self-fashioning as a martyr, see John R. Knott, Jr., " 'Suffering for Truths sake': Milton and Martyrdom," in *Politics, Poetics,* pp. 53–170, though Knott fails to note the importance of conscience as a self-authorizing, "idolatrous" aspect of martyrdom.

10. For the development of the justification for resistance based on conscience from Luther and Calvin, see Quentin Skinner, *The Foundations of Modern Political Thought* (Cambridge, 1978), vol. II, pp. 206–38; Michael Walzer's discussion of the Calvinist "sacred duty to resist" in *The Revolution of the Saints: A Study in the Origins of Radical Politics* (Cambridge, Mass., 1965), and his "Puritanism as a Revolutionary Ideology," *History and Theory* III (1963), 59–90. The older conceptions of conscience as personal practical wisdom are treated in Timothy C. Potts, *Conscience in Medieval Philosophy* (Cambridge, 1980).

11. Sheldon Wolin, *Politics and Vision: Continuity and Innovation in Western Political Thought* (Boston, 1960), p. 187, discusses the notion of conscience in political theory, yet it is important to distinguish between the ideas of Calvin and the ideas of the English Calvinists, whose sense of Calvin was imbued with Lutheran notions of free will. Perry Miller reminds us of this in *The New England Mind* (Cambridge, Mass., 1982), p. 186. Two fascinating treatments that have creatively misread the Calvinist conscience are Friedrich Nietzsche, " 'Guilt,' 'Bad Conscience,' and the Like" in *On the Genealogy of Morals,* trans. Walter Kaufmann and R. J. Hollingdale (New York, 1989), pp. 57–96; and Max Weber, *The Protestant Ethic and the Spirit of Capitalism,* trans. Talcott Parsons (London, 1930), pp. 108–125, who stresses the connections between Calvinism and radical individualism.

12. John Calvin, *Institutes of Christian Religion,* 2 vols., trans. Ford Lewis Battles, ed. John T. McNeill (Philadelphia, 1960), vol. I, p. 848.

13. W. Cargill Thompson, *The Political Thought of Martin Luther* (Totowa, N.J., 1984); Bernhard Lohsee, "Conscience and Authority in Luther," in *Luther and the Dawn of the Modern Era,* ed. Heiko A. Oberman (Leiden, 1974), pp. 158–83.

14. Arthur Barker, "Christian Liberty in Milton's Divorce Pamphlets," *MLR* XXXV (1940), 153–61, relates Milton's writings on liberty of conscience to Calvin and argues that Milton defends divorce on the grounds of the Calvinist liberty of conscience over things indifferent. Though Luther's position did change on the right to resist unjust authority, especially after 1530, personal conscience was not the authority for resistance, but rather a conception of public versus private duties of the magistrate. See W. Cargill Thompson, "Luther and the Right of Resistance to the Emperor," *Studies in Church History* XII (1975), 159–202; and his *The Political Thought of Martin Luther,* pp. 99–111; also Wolin, *Politics and Vision,* pp. 161–164.

15. On conscience as grounds for political activism, see Walzer, *Revolution of the*

*Saints,* pp. 58–59, 64; Skinner, *Foundations,* vol. II, p. 233; on the casuistical tradition, see Albert R. Jonsen and Stephen Toulmin, *The Abuse of Casuistry: A History of Moral Reasoning* (Berkeley, 1988), esp. pp. 122–75; and Camille Wells Slights, *The Casuistical Tradition in Shakespeare, Donne, Herbert, and Milton* (Princeton, 1981), which addresses the issue of conscience, but considered as a kind of practical divinity, an exercise in intellection or moral arithmetic, not of political action; William Ames, *Conscience with the Power and Cases Thereof* (London, 1643), p. 2; Christopher Hill, *The World Turned Upside Down* (Harmondsworth, Middlesex, 1972), discusses the radicals of the revolution. James Tully, "Governing Conduct," in *Conscience and Casuistry in Early Modern Europe,* ed. Edmund Leites (Cambridge, 1988), pp. 12–71, traces the movement in political thinking away from the radical claims of conscience to the rational theories of assent of Locke that replaced them in the eighteenth century; on the Levellers' "Agreement of the People," see J. P. Kenyon, *The Stuart Constitution, 1603–1688* (Cambridge, 1966), p. 309.

16. Ames, *Conscience with the Power,* p. 5. See also William K. Jordan, *The Development of Religious Toleration in England,* 4 vols. (Cambridge, Mass., 1932–40), vol. II, p. 212.

17. The Scottish Covenanters opposed the prayer book violently, suspecting the king of popery. The prayer book itself became the focus and symbol of the rebellious, and the attack on Laud was due in large part to the work of nonconformists in opposing it. The book was banned formally in January 1645 as part of Parliament's program to purify churches of popish superstition, which included many other measures: removal of altar rails, destruction of candles, tapers, and basins from communion tables, crucifixes, crosses, images, and objects relating to the Virgin Mary, the Trinity, and saints; as well as vestments and organs. See Derek Hirst, *Authority and Conflict: England 1603–1658* (Cambridge, Mass., 1986), pp. 183–85; K. Sharpe, "The Personal Rule of Charles I," in *Before the English Civil War,* ed. H. Tomlinson (London, 1978), pp. 53–78, on Charles's "innovative" model for reforming church and state; in contrast, H. R. Trevor-Roper, "Archbishop Laud," *History* XXX (1945), 181–90), argues that the Laudian mission for the Church was "retrograde."

18. On the notion of an author's work as literary property, see Martha Woodmansee, "The Genius and Copyright: Economic and Legal Conditions of the Emergence of the Author," *Eighteenth Century Studies* XVII, no. 4 (1984), 425–48, esp. 443.

19. For the identification of Charles with Christ, see John R. Knott, Jr., " 'Suffering,' " in *Politics, Poetics;* pp. 159–63); Milton's attack on the king's plagiarism is analogical to the parliamentary interpretation that the king had stolen authority which was originally in the people. Just as the king had stolen from his people "in whom the power yet remains fundamentally, and cannot be taken from them, without a violation of their natural birthright" (YP III, p. 202), he had stolen their literary works, having none of his own to provide for his own sufferings.

20. Hardin Craig, "An Ethical Distinction by Milton," in *The Written Word and Other Essays* (Chapel Hill, 1953), pp. 78–88, proposes an Aristotelian distinction in Milton's system in *De Doctrina* between "duties one owes to oneself and the duties one owes to one's neighbors" (pp. 78–79), but this distinction is unsupported by evidence. In my forthcoming book, *Milton and the Fit Reader in the English Revolution,* I explore this idea of the public as a judge in the context of mid-century political rhetoric.

21. David Loewenstein, *Milton and the Drama of History: Historical Vision, Iconoclasm and the Literary Imagination* (Cambridge, 1990), p. 68, explains how Milton's *Eikonoklastes* substitutes a myth of the tyrant for Charles's myth of the martyr.

22. Blair Worden, "Toleration and the Cromwellian Protectorate," in *Persecution and Toleration: Studies in Church History,* ed. W. J. Sheils (London, 1984), vol. 21, pp. 199–233; and John M. Wallace, *Destiny His Choice: The Loyalism of Andrew Marvell* (Cam-

bridge, 1968), chap. 1; the oath was designed to create a bond between the Rump and the Presbyterians by isolating the royalists who, it was thought, surely would not agree to it. The outcome of the controversy was contrary to expectations, however. The royalists who refused could not support the enemy regime, and the Presbyterians refused to do so on the ground that their prior oath of allegiance (the Solemn League and Covenant) still bound them to the king. Many royalists, however, willingly swore the oath (disingenuously). See Hirst, *Authority and Conflict*, p. 298; D. Wootton, *Divine Right and Democracy* (Harmondsworth, Middlesex, 1986), p. 68; and Blair Worden, *The Rump Parliament, 1648–1653* (Cambridge, 1974), pp. 228–31.

23. John Dury, *Considerations Concerning the Present Engagement* (7 February 1650), p. 15; *A Disengaged Survey of the Engagement. In Relation to Public Obligations* (4 December 1649), pp. 9, A2. An essential tool in research in the pamphlet literature is John M. Wallace, "The Engagement Controversy, 1649–1652: An Annotated List of Pamphlets," *Bulletin of the New York Public Library LXVIII*, no. 6 (1964), 384–405; Quentin Skinner, "The Ideological Context of Hobbes's Political Thought," *The Historical Journal IX*, no. 3 (1966), 286–317, provides another useful survey.

24. Robert Sanderson, *A Resolution of Conscience* (1 December 1649), pp. 5–6. It is a temptation for historians to doubt the sincerity of the appeal to liberty of conscience made by those who were to be persecuted for their religious views, as does Jordan, in *The Development*, p. 212, yet the appeal to conscience was based on a general philosophical reasoning that did not give way after the royalists came back to power with the Restoration. See also John Tulloch, *Rational Theology and Christian Philosophy in England in the Seventeenth Century*, 2 vols. (London, 1874), vol. I, pp. 155–66. My thanks to Richard Kroll for providing references; John Aucher, *Arguments and Reasons to Prove the Inconvenience and Unlawfulness of Taking the New Engagement* (14 February 1650), pp. 3, 8.

25. *The Life Records of John Milton*, 5 vols., ed. J. Milton French (New Brunswick, N.J., 1949–58), vol. II, p. 300.

26. Thomas Hobbes, *Leviathan*, ed. C. B. Macpherson (Harmondsworth, Middlesex, 1983), p. 366.

27. See also Skinnner, "The Ideological Context"; Quentin Skinner, "Conquest and Consent: Thomas Hobbes and the Engagement Controversy," in *The Interregnum: The Quest for Settlement, 1646–1660*, ed. G. E. Aylmer (London, 1972), pp. 79–98; and Gordon Schochet, "Intending (Political) Obligation: Hobbes and the Voluntary Basis of Society," in *Thomas Hobbes and Political Theory*, ed. Mary G. Dietz (Kansas City, 1990), pp. 55–73.

# FALLEN WOMBS: THE ORIGINS OF DEATH IN MILTONIC SEXUALITY

## Mary Adams

T HE IMAGE of the womb, as Milton uses it in *Paradise Lost*, seems at first reading to be a little terrifying. The huge void of Night and the noisy infestations of Sin could lead some to rank Milton among ascetics and women-haters. It is important to realize, however, that he also used the womb as a positive image. Like all created things, the womb has its good and bad uses. The fallen womb becomes a metaphor and an emblem of fallen sexuality and through it the origin of mortality and of the fallen state itself. I believe Milton used this emblem intentionally in order to justify created sexuality in the context of an ongoing theological debate.

Milton was part of a long tradition that addressed the question of the intrinsic value of sexuality. I will briefly present the substance of this tradition in order to suggest an environment in which Milton's specific use of sexual imagery would be especially cogent and will trace its origins in his earlier poetry. My purpose here is to suggest that, from his first use of the imagery that would come to be associated with the "fallen" womb, Milton dealt consistently with a "type" of sexual appetite or libido. While it was created as good, this sexuality became evil as it was perverted from its original use. The womb, then, becomes the metaphor both of this appetite—the state of sin—and its punishment—the state of death.

I will then turn to a discussion of Milton's "cosmic" wombs in order to illustrate the nature of the fallen condition. Milton's Night is the negative of the created universe and exhibits all the elements of the conditions of sin and of death. It is closely associated with the created hell it contains. Using Night as a type of the fallen womb, I will then examine the other striking example of terrible womb imagery, that of Sin.

In order to proceed with the assumption that Satan, Sin, and death represent together a condition opposite to the creative powers of the Divine Trinity, I will present some established conceptions of the Divine Trinity as they reflect on the nature of the infernal trinity. This discussion will facilitate an equation of the infernal trinity with both lust and death.

The most important step in this argument will be to characterize the infernal trinity as a unit of which the fallen womb is both origin and visible manifestation. I will attempt to locate this manifestation in the ongoing debate concerning paradisal sexuality. The conclusion of this essay will suggest some possible motivations for Milton's sexual characterization of the fallen state.

I

Theologians and poets had long been divided over whether Adam and Eve's error was itself sexual or whether the fall reduced sexuality to its less-than-idyllic state. Both were agreed that, as it stood, sex left something to be desired. "As Donne recorded in his 'Farewell to Love,' sexual consummation is short, depleting, dulling." The Augustinian notion that sexuality would have been ideal in Paradise, like everything else, if there had been time for it before the fall, lay at the root of the libertine tradition. "We conclude, therefore," Augustine explained, "that even if there had been no sin in the Garden, there would still have been marriages worthy of that blessed place and that lovely babies would have flowered from a love uncankered by lust."[1]

The esoteric tradition, on the other hand, argued for a sexual fall. James Turner quotes Browne's *Religio Medici* in its presentation of an "anti-sexual Utopia: 'I could be content that we might procreate like trees, without conjunction, or that there were any way to perpetuate the world without this trivial and vulgar way of coition.'"[3] Jean-Baptiste Von Helmont's words on the same subject, as related by Turner, are especially illuminating: "The Adamical or Beast-like Generation of the Flesh from the Concupiscence of the Flesh and its Copulation, doth naturally contain Death in it." Von Helmont refers to menstruation as "that bloody defilement" whereby "the part wherein the Image of God ought to be conceived by the Holy Spirit, becomes a sink of filths."[2]

There was ample precedent, then, for the notion that sexuality, particularly female sexuality, somehow resembled death and was therefore its origin. Each pregnancy was the operation of the Holy Spirit; each menstrual flow, then, would naturally seem a subversion of that Spirit.

Although Milton inherits and makes use of much of this imagery, he argues for the goodness of created sexuality: "Wisest Solomon among his gravest Proverbs countenances a kinde of ravishment and erring fondness in the entertainemnt of wedded leisures."[3] He argues, as does Leone Ebreo in *Dialoghi d'Amore*, 1535, that "sexuality is not in itself corrupt. . . . the original sin is a kind of libertine eroticism: the serpent represents 'carnal appetite' and sexual connoisseurship, giving them 'much subtle craft and cunning knowledge pertaining to lasciviousness and greed which before they lacked' " (*One Flesh*, p. 70).

In Milton's *Doctrine and Discipline of Divorce,* Turner notes four types of sexual experience:

Two of these—the "mute kindlynes" of sheer animality and its opposite, ascetic renunciation—depend upon the complete separation of mind and body, sexuality and humanity. Two, however, involve a less "mute" and more complex interpenetration of erotic drives and "intellective principles": the "voluntarie" sexuality of true married love . . . and the perverse state—the ideal of libertinism—in which physical desire is enhanced and promulgated by intellectual practice. (*One Flesh,* pp. 203–04).

Milton seeks to justify the third type of sexuality, that of married love, by contrasting it with the fourth, "libertine," type, which is "promulgated by intellectual practice."

## II

Milton's first use of the "fallen" womb image occurs in *On Time.*

> Fly envious *Time,* till thou run out thy race
> . . . . . . . .
> And glut thyself with what thy womb devours,
> Which is no more than what is false and vaine,
> And meerly mortal dross,
> . . . . . . . .
> And last of all thy greedy self consum'd.[4]       (1–10)

Though Milton here is treating a conventional theme fairly conventionally, his use of the devouring womb of time is essentially new. Its precedents in literature are only approximate. In the sonnet sequences of Daniel, Drayton, Skakespeare, Sidney, and Spenser, there are four "devouring time" images. "Devouring Time" and "Sluttish time" occur in Shakespeare; Spenser also uses "Devouring Time," and Daniel uses "Time's devouring rage." Shakespeare's Sonnet LXXXVI uses a similar womb image, "Making their tombe the wombe in which they grew." Spenser uses "cosmic" womb imagery in some of his longer poems: "Great Chaos Wombe," "the great earth's womb," and "the wide womb of the world" all use "womb" in the sense of a hollow cavity. An anonymous poem, "To Time," in Davison's *Poetical Rhapsody* of 1602 associates *womb* with time: "Thy womb, that all doth breed, is tomb to all" and so comes closest to Milton's own time image. But I could discover no other poem that used the idea of a womb that devours its own young and then itself.[5]

Such a unique image cannot be accidental. Milton would use this striking metaphor throughout *Paradise Lost*. The "dross" that time consumes in "On Time" is remarkably similar to the "draff" that Sin and Death consume in Book X of the epic, composed approximately thirty years later. And "self consum'd" would have its echoes in *Comus:* "But evil on it self shall back recoyl, / . . . when at last / Gather'd like scum, and setl'd to it self / . . . self-fed and self-consum'd" (593–6) as well as various incarnations in *Paradise Lost*. Satan and his crew are characterized as "self-begot" (V, 860), "self-tempted, self-deprav'd" (III, 130), and "self-rais'd" (I, 634; V, 860).

Milton intends here to echo ancient theological tradition on the dangers of living for the self. Augustine defends the created human body when he says, "thus the animal man is not one thing and the carnal another, but both are . . . man living according to man" (*City of God*, p. 335). Again, he defines pride: "And what is pride but an appetite for inordinate exaltation? Now, exaltation is inordinate when the soul cuts itself off from the very source to which it should keep close and somehow makes itself and becomes an end to itself" (p. 380). When Milton characterizes time as feeding on human life and eventually on itself, he has in mind a kind of time, the "temporal death" of Book X of *Paradise Lost*. And when he applies the womb to this image, he is deliberately characterizing this "temporal death" in terms of a barren and voracious maw, driven by lust in the absence of divine love. According to Augustine, "The impulse to love, the central constitutive desire of the human spirit, becomes *caritas* or *libido* according as it is centered on God or the self" (*One Flesh*, p. 50).

### III

The word *womb* appears fifteen times in *Paradise Lost*. These images are divided in their use as "cosmic" wombs, that is, wombs which belong either to the earth or the heavens or to "uncreated night," and those which are assigned to an allegorical or real figure. Once the word *womb* is applied to a subject, the subject is thereafter described in terms that evoke the womb. The Oxford English Dictionary cites three meanings of *womb* in Milton's time: as uterus, as a "hollow space or cavity or something conveived as such" (as it is frequently employed by Spenser) and as a "place or medium of conception and development, a place or point of origin or growth." *Womb* was first used in this sense by Shakespeare in 1593. Milton makes use of all of these. He precedes its first use as abdomen (1684) and stomach (1756), but Milton frequently characterizes wombs as devouring, and in many instances he uses *mouth* in a similar way. His purpose is to evoke a deeper and more thoroughly unnatural horror at those things signified by fallen wombs, while at the same time maintaining an associative link with things signified by *mouths*.

The distinction between good and bad wombs, again, depends on its use in the service of God or man.

Of the goodness of creation, many heretics remain unconvinced, on the ground that many things in creation are unsuitable and even harmful to that poor and fragile mortality of the flesh. . . . The heretics mention, for example, fire, cold, wild beasts, and things like that, without considering how wonderful such things are in themselves and in their proper place. (*City of God*, p. 219)

Augustine says even more explicitly, "It is not the body as such but only a corruptible body that is burdensome to the soul" (p. 319).

The good uses of the cosmic womb are usually connected with the creation or the created world. "Thou from the first / Wast present, and with mighty wings outspread / Dove-like satst brooding on the vast Abyss / And mad'st it pregnant" (I, 19–22). Other positive uses appear in Book V (warmed wombs and fruitful wombs) and Book VII (fruitful wombs). Milton here signifies all of God's creation, or the Spirit's fertile powers, as a "type" of good sexuality. Turner comments that the whole of prelapsarian Eden is characterized in terms of this sexuality:

The fruits, the flowers, the liquid "sweets," and above all the fragrances of Eden thus provide an exact counterpart to the movement of the spirits in love. . . . This reciprocity of tenor and vehicle has the effect of extending human sexuality rather than contracting it to a conceit; the reader, too, begins to participate in an eroticized universe. (*One Flesh*, p. 201)

Milton presents God's creative work in terms of sexual activity to define ideal created love as fertile (and thus performing its proper function), erotic, and done in the presence of God.

Night is frequently defined in terms of wombs. This use is developed from "On Time" through *Comus:* "The Dragon womb / Of Stygian darknes" (131–32). In *Paradise Lost*, night is frequently described in similar terms. Belial fears to be "swallowd up and lost / In the wide womb of uncreated night / Devoid of sense and motion" (II, 149–51); Night is "this wild Abyss, / The Womb of nature and perhaps her Grave" (II, 910–11); and death is described as being "plung'd in the womb / Of unoriginal *Night* and *Chaos* wild" (X, 475–76). Other descriptions of Night do not mention *womb* but evoke that image: "farr and wide into the realm of Night" (II, 133), "void profound / Of unessential Night receives him next / Wide gaping / . . . plung'd in that abortive gulf" (II, 438–41), "total darkness should by Night regain" (IV, 665), and "dim Night / Her shadowie Cloud" (V, 685–86).

In what sense did Milton understand his "uncreated" darkness? Is it inherently evil? How was it defined in the theological canon? To answer these questions we should examine the following passage:

> Before thir eyes in sudden view appear
> The secrets of the hoarie deep, a dark
> Illimitable Ocean without bound,
> Without dimension, where length, breadth, and highth
> And time and place are lost; where eldest Night
> And *Chaos*, Ancestors of Nature, hold
> Eternal *Anarchie*
> . . . . . . . .
> For hot, cold, moist, and dry, four Champions fierce
> Strive here for Maistrie, and to Battel bring
> Thir embryon Atoms.                              (II, 890–900)

Night was traditionally characterized as feminine. Jean Bodin's *Colloquium of the Seven About Secrets of the Sublime*, which Milton owned, derives its conceptions of form and matter from the Zohar: "The word man indicates natural form, and woman indicates matter, which is also called in *Proverbs meretrix* (harlot), since as a harlot takes pleasure in a number of men, so matter delights in a number of forms." Walter Clyde Curry explains the traditional view of Old Night as "a feminine divinity who is the receptacle of paternal causes, transmitting into all posterior things the generative powers of the gods."[6]

Night, then, is feminine and is matter. According to this passage, Night is without dimension, length, breadth, height, and time and place. Her "womb" embodies darkness and emptiness. In his divorce tracts, Milton describes the creation of the world in terms of the "divorce" of the created from the uncreated (*DDD*, YP II, p. 273). In Raphael's version of the creation episode, the Spirit of God, "vital vertue infus'd, and vital warmth / Throughout the fluid Mass, but downward purg'd / The black tartareous cold *infernal* dregs / *Adverse* to life" (VII, 236–39, my emphasis). In this passage Night is clearly characterized as hostile, "infernal" and "adverse," even though Night, as proceeding from God, must be ostensibly good.

Much of Milton's thinking on this subject, it seems to me, is derived from Augustine, who sees all of creation as from nothing (*ex nihilo*) by God, and all that is not creation as "nothing." "Nothing," in this view, represents the condition of being without God: "Notice, however, that such worsening by reason of a defect is possible only in a nature that has been created out of nothing. In a word, a nature is a nature because it is something made by God, but a nature falls away from That which is because the nature was made out of nothing" (*City of God*, p. 311).

Milton, however, while inheriting much of his imagery, differed from Augustine on the matter of his *ex nihilo* position theology. Milton was a proponent of the *ex deo* school of creation, a less logical, if more aesthetically appealing, theory.[7] According to this view, God created the universe out of himself. But Milton frequently blurs the distinctions between these two doctrines concerning creation when he refers to the "downward purging of infernal dregs." It is not clear in Book II, for instance, whether it is Milton or Moloc who lapses into the Augustinian system: God's ire "to the highth enrag'd, / Will either quite consume us and reduce / To nothing this essential" (II, 95–97). For the sake of clarity, though, we may say that whereas the Augustinian Night falls from creation into nothingness, the Miltonic Night has fallen into formlessness, at the opposite end of the scale of nature from God, who encompasses all forms. From God "All things proceed, and up to him return, / *If not deprav'd* from good . . . / . . . one first matter all, / Indu'd with various forms, various degrees / Of Substance" (V, 470–4, my emphasis).

Night's womb, then, is matter but not substance, formless, timeless, and shapeless, and is somehow *depraved* from good. As such it is easily associated with hell and with death by proximity and by imagery. According to Regina Schwartz, "In the pseudoepigraphical Book of Enoch there is a remarkable description of the place prepared for fallen angels. It is not hell, but chaos."[8] Most of Virgil's hell imagery is relocated by Milton into Night. Hell is frequently characterized in a similar way, as "profoundest hell" or "the hollow deep." In Books X (288, 636) and XII (42), hell is characterized as having a mouth. Like Night's womb, this mouth also consumes. The difference is one of degree; hell is one state of death, Night is more final, farther from God, the "lower deep." Night's natural desire is to reclaim created matter, her "offspring," but she can do so only through annihilation. She is leagued with Satan in his attempt to "reduce / To her original darkness" (II, 9823–84). Though in some sense of God, her womb is the metaphor for banishment from God and hostility to creation. Milton refers explicitly to this cosmic dualism in his *Doctrine and Discipline of Divorce:* "There is indeed a two-fold seminary or stock in nature, from whence are derived the issues of love and hate distinctly flowing through the whole mass of created things" (YP II, p. 294). The stock of hate, since it is derived from uncreated night, can have only a negative issue.

## IV

Regina Schwartz, in her comparison of the War in Heaven with ancient biblical sources for a heavenly battle against monsters, remarks, "For Milton, the primordial battle with chaos became symbolic of the human struggle with sin" (p. 32). Indeed, the womb of Night very much resembles commonly held theological conceptions of sin. Night, like sin, is a condition. In *Paradise Lost*, Milton's allegory of Sin is, via Satan, the "issue of hate." Her womb is characterized with horrible relish:

> The one seem'd Woman to the waste, and fair,
> But ended foul in many a scaly fould
> Voluminous and vast, a Serpent arm'd
> With mortal sting: about her middle round
> A cry of Hell Hounds never ceasing bark'd
> With wide *Cerberean* mouths full loud, and rung
> A hideous Peal: yet, when they list, would creep,
> If aught disturb'd thir noyse, into her woomb,
> And kennel there, yet there still bark'd and howl'd
> Within unseen.                                   (II, 650–59)

Sin further elaborates:

> These yelling Monsters that with ceasless cry
> Surround me, as thou sawst, hourly conceiv'd
> And hourly born, with sorrow infinite
> To me, for when they list into the womb
> That bred them they return, and howl and gnaw
> My Bowels, thir repast; then bursting forth
> Afresh with conscious terrours vex me round.       (795–801)

Sin is also raped and threatened with extinction by her first offspring, Death, the issue of Satan.

Sin, and through her Satan and death, represents a condition analogous to that of Night's womb. Together they are an "infernal trinity" which is the negative of the creative power of the Holy Trinity. As a unit, they frequently borrow trinitarian imagery and imitate, or parody, God's actions. To understand their relationship as an infernal trinity, it is necessary to be aware of certain commonly held conceptions of the Divine Trinity.

In Book III, line 6 of *Paradise Lost*, Milton invokes the Holy Spirit, "Bright effluence of Bright essence increate." This invocation relies on a fairly standard conception of the Holy Trinity: God the Father is the original essence, existing in eternity. God the Son is the Logos, the medium or act of creation. God the Holy Spirit is the effluence, or outward creative manifestation of both the Father and the Son. In a similar way, Satan is the originator of evil, Sin is the medium or act through which evil is performed, and death is the destructive manifestation, or result, of evil performed.

Evil, however, cannot imitate but only parody creation. Augustine is one of the early sources for the definition of sin as *privatio*, or deficiency, from God:

For, "the true light that enlightens every man who comes into the world" (John 1.9) illumines every pure angel that he may be light not in himself but in God. And, once an angel rejects this light, he becomes impure. Thus, all those who are called unclean spirits are no longer light in the Lord but darkness in themselves, being deprived of a participation in His eternal light. For, evil has no positive nature; what we call evil is merely the lack of someting that is good. (*City of God*, p. 201)

Augustine defines *bad will* as "rather a falling away from the work of God than a positive work itself" (pp. 375–76). Milton echoes Augustine in the divorce tracts when he argues that God did not create sinners: "To banish forever into a locall hell, whether in the aire or in the center, or in that uttermost and bottomlesse gulph of Chaos, deeper from holy blisse than the worlds diameter multiply'd, they thought not a punishing so proper and proportionat for God to inflict, as to punish Sinne with Sinne" (YP II, p. 294). Sin, then, is simultaneously the act and the condition or punishment of *bad will*, falling away from the works of God. Milton enacts syntactically the negative powers of Sin and Night with the frequent formation of words that negate their own root: "Then who *created* thee lamenting learn / When who can *un*create thee thou shalt know" (V, 894–95). In Book IX, Adam doubts the seriousness of God's injunction: God's

> works, which in our Fall,
> For us *created*, needs with us must fail,
> Dependent made; so God shall *un*create,
> Be frustrate, *do*, *undo*, and labour loose,
> *Not well* conceav'd of God.
>
> (IX, 941–45, my emphasis throughout)

And in Book VI, Raphael chooses not to name all of Satan's followers so that they may vanish in obscurity:

> yet by doom
> Canceld from Heav'n and sacred memorie,
> *Nameless* in dark oblivion let them dwell.
> For strength from Truth divided and from Just,
> *Ill*audable, naught merits but *dis*praise
> And *i*gnominie
> . . . . . . . .
> Therefore Eternal silence be thir doom.
>
> (378–85), emphasis added)

Robert White, Jr., uses St. Augustine's orthodox doctrine of the Trinity to develop a new understanding of the infernal trinity. According to White, Augustine's doctrine "attempts to describe the relationships among the three persons of the Trinity in terms of human analogy. The father-son relationship is equated to self-knowledge, and the holy spirit is generated from these two as a sort of divine self-love." Just as the son reflects the perfect image of the father, Sin is Satan's "perfect image" (PL II, 764). White continues, "Milton chose the image of a lustful and incestuous sexual union between father and daughter to serve as the inversion of the love between Father and Son which is personified by the Holy Spirit. . . . Satan's incestuous lust for his daughter is thus characterized as a form of self-love for his 'perfect image' in his child."9 To substantiate White's argument one need go no further than the commonly cited passage in James, i, 15, which states that Lust conceived and brought forth Sin, who conceived and brought forth Death. If Lust and Satan are equated, and Death is the expression of Satan's lust for Sin, then Lust and Death are themselves equated in a very real way. They are a unity which cannot exist independently, as Sin herself explains when she cautions Death not to kill Satan (or herself). Sin looks forward to her reign on earth "At thy right hand voluptuous, as beseems / Thy daughter and thy darling, without end" (II, 869–70). Thus we must conceive of the infernal trinity as characterized by lust: the visible, yet negative act and manifestation of Satan's fallen condition, with each member integrally bound up in the existence of the others.

## V

Stephen Fallon understands the negative nature of the trinity in a similar way: "Sin and Death are metaphysical evil itself, which is the privation of entity. Their actions, as Sin's narration of the fall suggests, unfold within Satan and other fallen creatures."10 To understand more clearly how Sin and Death represent a condition within Satan, let us compare Sin's account of her own genesis with Raphael's account of the same period in time. Sin relates:

> but familiar grown,
> I pleas'd, and with attractive graces won
> The most averse, thee chiefly, who full oft
> Thy self in me thy perfect image viewing
> Becam'st enamour'd, and such joy thou took'st
> With me in secret, that my womb conceiv'd
> A growing burden.                    (II, 761–67)

Raphael does not specifically mention Sin's genesis. He does, however, relate the origin of Satan's envy against the Son of God, and in Book V, line 666–68, relates, "Deep malice thence *conceiving* and disdain, / Soon as midnight brought on the duskie hour / . . . he resolv'd" (my emphasis). No other event that Raphael relates even comes close to Sin's account. Milton must have meant this line to parallel Sin's account of her own birth. It cannot be a coincidence that, even as Death is first encountered in Book II, line 666, Sin is "conceiv'd" on line 666 of Book V.

If we accept this line as corresponding to Sin's account of her origin in Satan's head, we understand that Sin did not merely appear, but was *conceived.* Furthermore, we understand that outside of Satan's mind, Sin has no substance other than as "malice and disdain." Satan's mind is frequently characterized as a place. "The mind is its own place, and in it self / Can make a Heav'n of Hell, a Hell of Heav'n" (I, 254–55). Satan's thoughts stir "the Hell within him, for within him Hell / He brings, and round about him, nor from Hell / One step no more then from himself can fly / By change of place" (IV, 20–23). When Satan is so altered as to be unrecognizable in Eden, he is charged with resembling "now / Thy sin and place of doom obscure and foul" (IV, 839–40). That place of doom, whether Night or hell, is Satan's mind itself. And, just as the Cabala conceives of God in terms of sexual dualism, Satan's mind is here characterized as being the agent and receptacle for Sin's conception.[11] Sin, then, is merely the act of that mind, or essence. She is his perfect image; that is, her womb that is endlessly invaded by dogs is the image of Satan's mental state. Sin is the image, then, of both Satan and hell (or Night). Together, they are the state of deficiency or absence from God, for in order to be consistent with the orthodox definition of sin, this self-conception must be understood as negative or even fictive.

Sin is, ironically, her own punishment. In heaven, she is an Athena figure, sprung full grown from her father's head. In hell, however, she is Scylla, who was punished by Athena for being raped in her temple. Sin's punishment is for the crime of being Satan's agent in the lustful and defiling conception of death in heaven. This defilement is contagious:

> But when lust
> By unchast looks, loose gestures, and foul talk,
> But most by lewd and lavish act of sin,
> Lets in defilement to the inward parts,
> The soul grows clotted in contagion,
> Imbodies, and imbrutes, till she quite loose
> The divine property of her first being.  (*Comus*, 463–69)

Sin and death must both be understood as an inner condition of Satan's deficiency. Christ's redemption shall defeat "Sin and Death, [Satan's] two main armes, / And fix farr deeper in his head thir stings / Than temporal death shall bruise the Victors heel" (XII, 431–33). Death must be viewed, in his role as a parody of the Holy Spirit, as the inward corrosive effect, rather than the outward creative effect, of Satan's sin. Rather than create, he must rape and devour, just as Night does. His offspring, the dogs, must continue that devouring process. He combines sexual lust with greed. Cherrel Guilfoyle remarks that "In action Death, the son of Sin, personifies first lust and then, more significantly, greed. . . . Greed, the intestinal appetite, is for Milton the sin that can best illustrate, and to some extent subsume, the other deathly appetite of lust. He noted in his Commonplace Book, . . . 'Tertullian with nicety of phrase calls gluttony a murderer.' "12

According to this view, all "devouring wombs" are characterized by greed in order to illustrate the exact nature of lust. Lust is the perversion of divinely created things for human use. It is an appetite that cannot be quenched. As such, lust can adequately characterize the fallen condition, and it is for this reason that Milton centers lust in the "fallen" womb. As the manifestation of Sin's womb, which is the act of Satan's mental "womb," now understood as a symbol of privation, Death is *doubly formless*. Images of such doubling occur throughout Milton's work. "Double darkness" (593) and "Prison within Prison / inseparably dark" (153–54) occur in *Samson*. In *Paradise Lost*, Satan fears "in that lowest deep a lower deep / Still threatening to devour me" (IV, 76–77). Together, the trinity is the continual erosion of entity.

In his *Christian Doctrine*, Milton distinguishes four "degrees" of death. The first consists of "all those evils which lead to death, and which it is agreed came into the world immediately upon the fall of man." These evils are guilt, a diminution of countenance, and a conscious degradation of the mind, whence arise total pollution and shame (YP VI, p. 393). The subsequent degrees are the process of dying, the death of the body, and the eternal death of Revelation.

What is this "conscious degradation" of the mind? In the first part of this essay, I referred to the worst of the four types of love, as defined by Milton, as that kind in which "physical desire is enhanced and promulgated by intellectual practice." Death, now equated with Lust, arose as the issue of Satan and Sin. Sin describes Satan's union with her, "thy self in me thy perfect image viewing / Becam'st enamour'd, and such joy thou took'st / With me in secret, that my womb conceiv'd / A growing burden" (II, 764–67). She is describing the fruit of sexual excitement generated intellectually by the stimulus of disobedience or taboo. Satan, Sin, and

Death are thus a clear statement about the nature of fallen sexuality uttered within an established tradition.

As "conscious degradation," then, the infernal trinity represents the condition of the first degree of death. The lower deep constitutes the promise of future degrees, culminating in eternal damnation. Augustine suggests that fallen angels are in one sense dead: "So, too, the rebel angels, by reason of their sin, have died in the sense that, in abandoning God, they gave up the fountain of life" (*City of God*, p. 346). W. B. Hunter locates the beginning of linear time as the point of emanation of the Logos.[13] Sin is conceived on the night of "this day" in which God begets, or exalts, his Son. Her conception marks the origin of fallen time, in which exists the possibility of death. Augustine quotes Paul as saying that the natural body exists in time (p. 336). Sin inhabits that body and through it gives rise to "temporal death."

The entire fall is similarly characterized by Milton's "conscious degradation." Eve's eating of the apple is blatantly sexual and is characterized in terms of Greed, the "murderer," by which Milton implies sexuality: "Greedily she ingorg'd without restraint" (IX, 791). When Adam first sees her afterward, he declares her to be "Defac't, deflowrd, and now to Death devote" (IX, 901). Surely this is not an attractive condition, yet Adam claims to find her more attractive than ever after he himself has eaten:

> Eve, now I see thou art exact of *taste*
> And *elegant*, of *Sapience* no small part,
> Since to each meaning *savour* we apply,
> And *Palate* call *judicious*. (IX, 1017–20, my emphasis)

Turner points out how well this epicurean language corresponds to the intellectual stimulation Milton deplores: "This 'libertine connoisseurship' is obviously corrupt" (*One Flesh*, p. 303). Milton means us to contrast this episode with the unpremeditated "mutual benevolence" of prelapsarian sexuality. And "eating death" is not only extremely sexual, but replicates exactly "On Time" 's fallen imagery by causing Eve to devour what will in turn devour her.

## VI

The question remains as to why Milton chose sexuality as a means to justify God's created beings and to characterize his fallen. It might simply be that, since the publication of the divorce tracts, Milton had been branded a libertine. What is known of his sensitivity and moral seriousness suggests that Milton would have been unable to endure such a charge. Another reason might be that, in Milton's time, the ancient theological debate on sexuality had flowered into genuine libertine abuses. Among the Anabaptists of Munster, lust was forbidden, but polygamy was compulsory and enforced by the death penalty. The idea was that, as the self-proclaimed "elect," these Anabaptists could reclaim lost paradisal sexuality (*One Flesh*, p. 81). Turner points out that, "In *Paradise Lost*, written when the 'Sons of Belial' had truly gained the ascendancy, [Milton] frames the most erotic passages with bold attacks on libertine sexuality" (p. 167).

Or it may be because Augustine himself chose fallen sexuality as emblem and fit punishment for human disobedience since in lust the (male) body is disobedient: "The fact is that the soul, which had taken perverse delight in its own liberty and disdained the service of God, was deprived of its original mastery of the body" (*City of God*, p. 316). It is for this reason that lust alone makes human beings ashamed:

But how is it then, that shame does not seek to conceal what is said and done out of anger or other passions in the way it seeks to hide the lustful excitement of the sexual organs? The answer must be that, in the case of anger and other passions, it is not the passions themselves that move any parts of the body, but the will which remains in control. . . . With the genital organs it is different. There, lust so claims the right to rule that, apart from passion, there can be no excitement except what is spontaneous or artificially induced. It is this tyranny of the body that makes men ashamed. (Pp. 393–94)

In the same way, Satan takes joy with Sin "in secret," and Adam and Eve seek to hide themselves. In this light, the darkness of the fallen womb becomes a metaphor for the human need to hide from God. To Milton, perhaps, the shame of lust, in the light of the possibility of perfect sexual love, might have seemed the fittest and most moving emblem of the fallen condition.

University of Houston

### NOTES

1. William Kerrigan and Gordon Braden, "Milton's Coy Eve," in *John Milton's "Paradise Lost*," ed. Harold Bloom (New York, 1987), p. 140; Augustine, *City of God*, in *The Fathers of the Church*, 65 vols., trans. Gerald Walsh et al. (New York, 1952), vol. XIV, p. 399, hereafter cited as *City of God* in the text.

2. James Turner, *One Flesh: Paradisal Marriage and Sexual Relations in the Age of Milton* (Oxford, 1987), pp. 129, 151, hereafter cited as *One Flesh*.

3. John Milton, "Tetrachordon," in *Complete Prose Works of John Milton*, 8 vols., ed. Don M. Wolfe et al. (New Haven, 1953–82), vol. II, p. 597; hereafter cited as YP.

4. All references to Milton's poetry are from *The Complete Poetry of John Milton*, ed. John T. Shawcross (Garden City, N.J., 1971), with line numbers cited in the text.

5. "To Time," in *Tudor Poetry and Prose*, ed. John William Hebel et al. (New York, 1953), p. 305. There are analogical figures to the devouring womb: the devouring dragon of Revelation, chapter xii, and Chronos, or Saturn, who devours his children. Satan, depicted as eating Judas and Brutus in Dante's hell, is equated with Saturn in *Comus*. A strikingly similar image occurs in Shakespeare's *Richard III*: "From forth the kennel of thy womb hath crept / A hellhound that doth hunt us all to death. . . . this carnal cur / preys on the issue of his mother's body" (IV, iv, 47–57).

6. Harris Fletcher casts some doubt as to whether Milton himself actually knew the Zohar. Alexander Gill, the elder, one of Milton's teachers, probably knew of it. See Harris Francis Fletcher, *The Intellectual Development of John Milton*, 2 vols. (Urbana, 1956), vol. I, pp. 279–83; Jean Bodin, *Colloquium of the Seven About Secrets of the Sublime*, trans. Marion Leather and Daniels Kuntz (Princeton, 1975), p. 94; Walter Clyde Curry, *Milton's Ontology, Cosmology and Physics* (Louisville, 1957), p. 64.

7. J. H. Adamson, "Milton's Creation," in *Bright Essence: Studies in Milton's Theology*, ed. W. B. Hunter, C. A. Patrides, and J. H. Adamson (Salt Lake City, 1971), p. 83.

8. Regina M. Schwartz, *Remembering and Repeating: Biblical Creation in "Paradise Lost"* (Cambridge, 1988), p. 23.

9. Robert White, "Milton's Allegory of Sin and Death: A Comment on Backgrounds," *MP* LXX (1973), 338, 340.

10. Stephen M. Fallon, "Milton's Sin and Death: The Ontology of Allegory in *Paradise Lost*," *ELR* XVII (1987), 343.

11. "Ultimately [the Cabala] conceives of God Himself in terms of sexual dualism which explains his generative power" (Bodin, lviii). Jean Bodin derived his knowledge of the Cabala from Postel, as the editors explain in a note to his *Colloquium*, which quotes from William J. Bouwsma, *Concordia Mundi: The Career and Thought of Guillaim Postel* (Cambridge, Mass., 1959), p. 109.

12. Cherrel Guilfoyle, "If Shape It Might Be Call'd That Shape Had None: Aspects of Death in Milton," in *Milton Studies* XIII, ed. James D. Simmonds (Pittsburgh, 1975), p. 40.

13. W. B. Hunter, "The War in Heaven: The Exaltation of the Son," in *Bright Essence*, pp. 124–25.

# LAUREATE, REPUBLICAN, CALVINIST:
# AN EARLY RESPONSE TO
# MILTON AND *PARADISE LOST* (1667)

## *Nicholas von Maltzahn*

---

U NCERTAINTY ABOUT the welcome which greeted the publication of *Paradise Lost* has long drawn comment from Miltonists. Little
is known about the first reception of the great work and the fragmentary
evidence that remains early acquired the obscuring cast of legend. Thus
Denham's acclaiming "a Sheet, Wet from the Press" in Parliament is
dramatic, can be made plausible, and does not very reliably communicate
the character of his enthusiasm. There are problems, too, with the story of
Dryden's first response—"*that Poet had cutt us all out*"—when the "Earl
of Dorset produc'd" *Paradise Lost:* Richardson's report already seems to
conflate possible events in the late 1660s with probable events in the early
1690s. Shawcross's *Bibliography* (1984) lists a few further entries, but "the
dearth of printed allusions" of which Parker once complained has yet to be
much improved upon with manuscript sources.[1]

Some hitherto unrecorded references to Milton now provide the
earliest direct evidence available for judging the contemporary response
to the publication of *Paradise Lost.*[2] In letters from John Beale to John
Evelyn, successive allusions to Milton and his works indicate some basic
concerns for the first readers of his epic. Beale's comments address biographical, political, and aesthetic matters central to the study of Milton's
early reputation, and point to some critical issues for *Paradise Lost* in
particular.

I

The biographical background suggests not just the individual interest
of these opinions but a social dimension to the intellectual history in
which they have a part. A contemporary of Milton's, John Beale (1608–83)
was an enthusiastic correspondent of the Royal Society, a country minister, horticulturalist, cider maker, and chaplain to Charles II (an honorary
distinction): in brief, a rural virtuoso. His broad range of interests is amply

represented in his extensive correspondence with Evelyn, of which over 120 letters remain, dating from just before the Restoration (28 September 1659) until the last years of Charles II's reign (29 May 1683). To Evelyn, Beale writes about a wide range of subjects, as he had written earlier to Samuel Hartlib, and although his main thrust is scientific, or at least empirical, his freedom with Evelyn contrasts with the narrower focus of his letters to other Fellows of the Royal Society such as Robert Boyle or Henry Oldenburg, first secretary of that body.[3]

Beale's letters reveal him always to have been curious about all manner of natural phenomena—the correspondence provides useful material, for example, for the historian of the Royal Society, of cider making, or of the weather during the Restoration.[4] The letters from the 1660s suggest energies long held in reserve, which he now gratefully and effusively devotes to the New Science. Successful at Eton and King's Cambridge, Beale's calling as clergyman first took him back to his native Herefordshire, where he appears to have suffered much frustration in the Interregnum as a country minister with intellectual ambitions, although he could claim to see God's "providence in it, that, to punish my old pride, in the very flashes of false learning, he hath now placed me under the fact of them, that hate and abhor holy industry and true learning." In the late 1650s, the educational impresario Hartlib encountered Beale's powers of mind and with characteristic enterprise dreamed that Beale could be made "universally use of, to do good to all, as I in some measure know, and could direct" (*Works of Boyle* V, pp. 275b, 280a). Beale's connection was thus forged to the group which would emerge in the Restoration as central to the formation of the Royal Society. This also led to his preferment to a ministry in Yeovil in 1661, where he continued to pursue his avocation as a student of agriculture and where he lived until his death.[5]

With reference to Milton, Beale is most interested in the poet's potential as an unofficial laureate. A country member of the Royal Society—his distant residence preventing closer involvement in London—Beale constantly seeks to benefit that body, chiefly with his scientific communications but also with a number of proposals for enhancing its status. It is with the latter in view that he first mentions Milton to Evelyn as a possible successor to Abraham Cowley. Beale had been deeply impressed with Cowley's greatness, but especially with his gifts as a commemorative poet responsive to social needs. He delighted in Cowley's contributions to the "R Soc," especially the ode "To the Royal Society" which was to grace Sprat's *History* of that institution. In a partial retirement after the Restoration, Cowley had proclaimed his self-dedication to the natural sciences and divinity. Soon, however, this useful and pious service could only be memorialized, for

Cowley suddenly died on 28 June 1667.[6] Beale responded to this loss by seeking to recruit Milton to some similar end, just when Milton was about to publish *Paradise Lost*.

Beale's definition of *laureate* is clearly not that of some self-crowned poet-prophet, whose emerging empire is the egotistical sublime.[7] He summarizes his ambitions for poetry in a later letter to Evelyn, where he asserts the usefulness of laureates in connection with institutions such as the Royal Society and emphasizes the need for royal patronage of poetry and oratory. He could recall the merits of "Old Ben" Jonson and even Thomas May ("though at last dilute & ungratefull"), and suggest ways of recovering those "Royall, & Loyall Inspirations." In prompting Evelyn to canvass for a laureate, or laureates, Beale expresses his belief in "the potent efficacy of the true spirit of good poesy, yea and of comon baladry to modell the Genius of the people, for religion, or for superstition, for sobriety, or dissoluteness; for peace or war; for settlement or disturbance of government" (MS letters 136, 13 May 1677). In 1667 he wishes Milton's powers to be directed to national advantage but remains suspicious of Milton's allegiances: "he wilbe doeing mischeefe, if he be not engagd better," being "too full of the Devill" (MS letters 63, f. 2ᵛ, 31 August 1667). The times were unsettled after the second Anglo-Dutch War, and Beale saw "the leading Sectaryes" as wishing to follow up on their success in obtaining the Treaty of Breda. In Somerset, now notorious for Dissent, he is especially anxious about nonconformity.[8] But he can hope "to engage Milton upon some honest argument," and asserts that "wee should endeavour to draw every potent Inspiration into a right Channell for the noblest uses. This should be the Influence, and will be the glory of the R[oyal] Soc[iety]" (MS letter 67, f. 1ᵛ, 16 October 1667).

It may be noted that such recognition of Milton's strengths was not unusual. In the Restoration others also thought he might prove employable, perhaps even in some official capacity—the example of his fellow-republican Marchamont Needham perhaps suggested that Milton too might prove serviceable.[9] The previous year, Milton himself had in his letter to Heimbach declared a desire to be useful. But his construction of living "ne inutilis" is hedged with the understanding that "politica," "having allured me by her lovely name, has almost expatriated me, as it were," and in here playing on Heimbach's turn of phrase—"it was reported you had been restored to your heavenly *patria*"—Milton acknowledges the seriousness of his situation at the Restoration.[10] His larger reputation was still based on the regicide tracts, and he was reluctant again to expose himself to danger. In further considering Milton as a Latinist, for example, Beale is quick to pronounce "no other fondness" for him "than I should have had for Ovid, Martiall, Petronius, and Lucan, which were all four, either lascivious, obscene, dissolute, or traiterous."[11] But Milton's skills are not in question, in Latin or English, and in view of Beale's preoccupation with reforming English letters it is not surprising that he should attempt to win Milton to his cause.

Milton's laureate talent, as Beale construes it, was that "he was long agoe an excellent Pindariste: Good at all, but best at that straine." That this style might especially serve a national poet was evident in Cowley, who had been the preeminent "Pindarist."[12] Again, Beale's interest lies with the useful encomiast rather than with aspiring Virgils of a Christian stripe; he clearly prefers the celebratory and commemorative decorum of the poet's shorter works to the different laureate claims of the *Davideis* or of *Paradise Lost*. Now that a memorial volume for Cowley seemed in order, Beale wishes "that Mr Spratte would sollicite our choicest poets for their Epicedia, and amongst them Milton for his Ode." Memories of *Lycidas* seem to govern this opinion, since it best displays "the Pindarique way" where, in Dryden's phrase, "the numbers vary and the rhyme is dispos'd carelessly, and far from often chymeing." The formal distinction of that work evidently attracted admiration. But Beale seeks not just to commemorate Cowley, to whom Evelyn had dedicated the second edition of his *Kalendarium Hortense* (1666), and for whom there was a widespread admiration which Milton seems to have shared.[13] Beale had also been vexed by satirical attacks on the Royal Society and thus has an ulterior motive for the Cowley volume, as he explains:

if there be any remaines [in Cowley's papers] which relate to the Inventions or undertakeings of the R Soc they will excellently antidote the scurrilous balladry, which is an oblique Vindication, and not unbecoming the Soc. & doubly effectuall. This in a small print for the Exchanges. (MS letters 64, f. 1ʳ, 11 September 1667; 76, f. 2ʳ, 19 September 1668)

In a similar vein to Secretary Oldenburg, Beale writes that the Society should "make a better use of some greate Names, than is like to be derived from their consent or merite."[14] He seems to think that Milton could prove an unwilling laureate who might nonetheless help with a volume "soe ordered as to asserte the reputation of the R Soc even by their enemyes unawares, & to spread it with dispatch" (MS letters 64, f. 1ᵛ (11 September 1667). How then to persuade this "greate Name"? For Beale not only wants to set Milton to work on behalf of the kingdom and the Royal Society, he also has some innovative ideas for a new scientific poetry in which Milton is to figure.

But Beale's developing plans were now to be frustrated. Milton was moving in another, quite unexpected direction: *Paradise Lost* had been registered for publication on 20 August 1667; by November it had become a talking-point. In one of Beale's responses to Evelyn (11 November 1667), he seems to have been called upon for an opinion on rhyme (more of which below), and in his next letter (18 November 1667), he apologizes for not yet having more to say about the epic. He regrets that "my business hath hinder'd me that I have not fully tasted Milton." But Beale now promises to "give you my free censure in your bosome: Deponam tutis auribus" ("Let me trust a safe hearing"). [15]

Beale's reading of *Paradise Lost* was still governed by his interest in Milton's services as a laureate poet. In first recording his reaction to the larger scope of *Paradise Lost,* or what he calls "the adventure" of that work, his response is mixed, and he states his preference for Milton's earlier work. [16] Apparently unprompted, he perceives the poet to be in decline—"I conceive his first Inspirations to be purer & brighter, than these his last"—but Beale also confides a more personal dimension in his response: "in this glass I see my owne decay, & can weepe at it, that our spirits should share in the debility of our Organs & Vitals, but tis a propheticall note that young men shall see visions, & old men shall dreame dreames." The material dimension of spiritual life much preoccupies him. Where Milton had feared that "years [might] damp my intended wing / Depressed," but could then report the assistance of a "celestial patroness," Beale's more cautious construction "Of things invisible to mortal sight" reflects his customary bias in favor of the natural "book of knowledge." He quotes the Apostle Peter's acknowledgment of prophecy only to express a sense of loss (Act ii, 17; cf. Joel ii, 28). A theologian with some admirers, not least Milton's friend Lady Ranelagh, Beale has been described as "an Erasmian reformist espousing a rational and tolerant religion," if with the millenarian coloring common in his day. [17] The character of Milton's revelation, however, met with a skeptical response from him.

In part this derived from Beale's misgivings about Milton's claims to divine inspiration in his work. In claiming that *Paradise Lost* "is excellent, the other [earlier work] more wonderfull," Beale implies a more secular theory of literary inspiration in which the canons of taste—such as would favor Cowley—are consistent with a poetics that Milton had largely left behind. This critical language is inconclusive, but that the term *wonderful* attaches to the earlier work may testify to its formal interest. It is worth noting the degree to which these distinctions, such as they are, will be inverted in the later, more Longinian valuation of Milton's works: it is exactly the wonders of *Paradise Lost* that Dryden and Dennis and Addison would come to admire, with excellence appearing a secondary virtue. Such high expectations of Milton were of course compounded by expectations for epic. Beale registers the likely response of Milton's readership to his ambitions: "men will be apt to expect great things from the adventure." However, he views *Paradise Lost* as an anomalous production unlikely of final success: "I doubt that this will hardly beare up into a prevalent example." In later references to the poem he articulates such doubts about the poem more fully.

But Beale already has an idea which will help Milton to overcome his decline, and even to surpass the Ancients. His plan is to give him a scientific subject: "I have lett fall my swift pen upon another Argument De Vitris Opticis, & have fostered in my head a designe De Machina Pneumatica intending to traine on our Just Poet to attempt thinges worthy of his force" (MS letters 68, f. 1r[=v], 18 November 1667). Nor did he mean just some celebration of Boyle's famous "Pneumatick Engines," the wonderful air pump to which Shadwell's Virtuoso would be so devoted. His thinking here is obscure, but his "designe" is in part explained by one of his letters to Oldenburg where he hints at a scientific poetry reaching toward metaphysics, in which the poet would elaborate the causal notions or the "spirit" active in nature—his project has an almost Lucretian flavor, further animated by an interest in Boyle. In reading Boyle's *Tracts . . . of a Discovery of the Admirable Rarefaction of the Air* (1671), Beale glimpses an aetiology for many diseases in the elasticity of air or atmospheric pressure. Here too lie some literary possibilities: "A Poet would say, that in the Pneumatical Engine thus managed, wee may clearly discern, how the Prince of the Air, if permitted to Lord it in his own Quarters, may afflict Mortalls more horribly than wee are yet apt to attribute to fascination & Magic."[18] Later, in the letter to Evelyn on laureates, Beale suggests a wide scope for a scientific poetry, although he may now seek only some discursive encomia applauding the discoveries of virtuosi (MS letters 136, f. 2r, 13 May 1677). In the commission for Milton in 1667, however, Beale seems not to wish too much to secularize science. To Boyle he had written of the need for an "operative, practical, and experimental" religion, in which "priesthood" Boyle, for example, might be "by divine endowments consecrated a chief." That this was a gray area, capable of an ill construction, appears in Beale's doubts about Joseph Glanvill's Platonist tendencies and also his suspicions of the Rosicrucian Robert Fludd.[19] Nor at this time did he favor the spate "of polemical writings, which have obtained the mighty titles of theology and philosophy" (*Works of Boyle* V, p. 494b). If he clearly prefers that the poet write uncontroversially from nature rather than Scripture, he could nonetheless entertain much in the way of materialist speculation about the causal operation on the spirit of ordinary providence through natural cause and effect.

Beale's interests seem finally to have led to an approach to Milton, perhaps for this project or the Cowley volume or both. Although tentative in working toward an introduction—"I would make no mention of this my forwardness till I find whether my Introduction be accepted"—Beale a few months later thanks Evelyn for having acted in some such connection:

I am in deepe arreares to you, & can never hope to repay you. Long agoe I red a letter from Mr Milton by your Friendly conveiyance, but by the defect of my sight & other Infirmityes I have bin hitherto discouraged from Attempting to make any reply to you or to him. Only I returning acknowledgements by Mr Oldenburg. (MS letters 71, 2 April 1668)

In this context the expression "long agoe" looks apologetic and thus appears to refer to some quite recent event, especially since Beale's correspondence suggests only this present connection to Milton.[20] It may be supposed, however, that Beale had not just been "discouraged" by his "Infirmityes," since even in this difficult time he sends a number of letters to Evelyn and Oldenburg. Had Milton proven awkward? No trace has been found of his response to this commission, whether as a literary laureate or scientific poet to the Royal Society. Nor does Beale ever return to the subject. A few years later, however, he suggests some lingering fears that Milton might write against the Society. Seeking to restrain the polemical ardor of Glanvill, a fellow-defender of that institution, he notes what a mistake it would be "for Mr G to exasperate Marchamond [Needham], since he, & Milton, with all their Junto, are able to doe us more mischiefe, than millions of S[tubbe] & C[asaubon]."[21] If the terms of Milton's response to Beale's discreet inquiry are uncertain, the evidence suggests that he did not encourage Beale's dreams on his behalf.

## II

Beale, if soon frustrated of his laureate, continued to take note of Milton's works, and his observations point to longstanding critical issues for *Paradise Lost*, as well as for Milton's *History of Britain*. With the epic, Beale shows an early interest in both form and subject. But more pressing political concerns soon take him beyond simply literary issues. Although ready to defend Milton's art, Beale's enduring preoccupation is with the republicanism and finally the Calvinism he perceives in *Paradise Lost*.

From the beginning, Beale reads the epic in light of the contemporary debate on rhyme. This is a frequent topic in early discussions of the poem, and one familiar to students of Milton. But Beale's copy of *Paradise Lost* did not, of course, include Milton's note on "The Verse," which was added to later issues of the first edition in 1668 and after. That Milton so soon came to defend his blank verse has been held to "imply that a good deal of criticism and questioning, of which hardly a trace now survives, has arisen over the poem." Beale's letters prove just how immediate a talking-point this had been since he discusses rhyme a week before mentioning *Paradise Lost*, and thus seems to respond to some opinion or question of Evelyn's on rhyme even before turning to Milton's blank verse.[22]

Much too has been made of the political metaphor with which the note on the verse defends the "ancient liberty" of verse from rhyme.[23] The royalist Beale, however, reveals no misgivings about the political character of Milton's versification and provides no support for any too political reading of the choice of blank verse. His letters only support our received opinion that Milton's versification seemed anomalous to his first readers. Beale sees the blank verse as occasioning "prejudice" which needs dispelling. His defense of the verse rests with the argument "that the best Dramatick writers have ever from Johnsons dayes, & from his paterne, done as well as they could, without the check of Rhime."[24] In the context of Dryden's and Howard's exchanges on the subject this argument from dramatic example seems commonplace, but it should further be noted that the generic distinction between tragedy and epic does not appear to concern Beale, even if Milton, harking back to the example of the dramatists, applies blank verse to an alien literary form. Beale is quick to admire the results: "The best Dramatick writers . . . yet have wanted much of the measure of this flowing grace," which the poet himself would soon advertise as providing "the sense variously drawn out from one verse into another."

Indeed Beale's references to rhyme show the climate of opinion with which Dryden was confronted in developing his critical positions in the 1660s. The favorable view of the earlier English drama was basic to Sir Robert Howard's position and provided a weight of example difficult to counter. The ready association of the versification of drama with that of epic is more surprising. Beale's elision of generic difference anticipates Milton's more self-conscious defense of his innovation in verse. In his note on the verse, Milton needs to cite the example of "Italian and Spanish poets of prime note" since in his native literature only "our best English tragedies" have freed themselves from rhyme. But there was another argument Dryden needed to overcome, that rhyme was barbaric since it had only been introduced into Latin poetry at a late date and was a sign of the medieval decay of classical culture.[25] Dryden acknowledged these origins: "When by the inundation of the *Goths* and *Vandals* into *Italy* new Languages were introduced, and barbarously mingled with the *Latine* (of which the *Italian, Spanish, French,* and ours, (made out of them and the *Teutonick*) are Dialects:) a new way of Poesie was practised" (pp. 70–71). This was familiar enough; Dryden borrows his terms in part from Samuel Daniel's *Defence of Rhyme.* But where Dryden saw this innovation as capable of a new perfection in the hands of the Moderns, even a Modernist like Beale could relapse into styling "Rhime but a Monkish solecisme, or a Gothish charm fetcht from Finland to the tune of—Angelus in penna, pede latro voce gehenna."[26] Having slightingly quoted the medieval proverb—and one singularly apt in conjunction with *Paradise Lost*—he then adds that rhyme is "Like the painted & cloathed Statues in Westminster Abby, & fit for my Ld Mayors pageantry." This preliminary discussion of rhyme reveals that underlying humanist bias to which Milton could appeal, and which Dryden was seeking to correct with a new valuation of the artifice of "like endings."

"Deponam tutis auribus": beyond such literary issues, Milton's political reputation is never far from Beale's thoughts in the autumn of 1667. Even in admiring *Paradise Lost* he is quick to recall Milton's fault as a controversialist. To Evelyn he writes, "You will Joyne with mee to whisper in a smile, that he writes so good verse, that tis pity he ever wrote in prose, & wee wish he had alwayes wanted prose as much as Cicero wanted verse" (MS letters 68, 18 November 1668). Even in jest, the comparison to Cicero recalls Milton's identification of himself with the classical republican, especially in the postscript to the 1658 edition of the *Defensio.* But Beale had more serious misgivings about Milton's politics, past and present. The complaint against Milton's regicide tracts is the most familiar aspect of his reputation in the Restoration. Little evidence remains, however, of the ways in which such political issues colored the first readings of Milton's epic. Beale's comments show a contemporary response to the republican dimension of *Paradise Lost* and the degree to which the epic fulfilled hostile expectations of an old Commonwealth's man.[27] Writing to Evelyn two years after he had first read *Paradise Lost,* Beale maintains that "Milton holds to his old Principle. Lib 10 verse 918 & 927, 954, 972 &c."[28] Thus Beale directly identifies the tyranny of Nimrod and the building of Babel as *the* locus of republicanism in the poem. In Nimrod, Milton had described the

> proud ambitious heart, who not content
> With fair equality, fraternal state,
> Will arrogate dominion undeserved
> Over his brethren, and quite dispossess
> Concord and law of nature from the earth.            (XII, 25–29)

That Milton should again impugn any man "from heaven claiming second sovereignty" (XII, 35) recalls the resistance theory of the *Tenure* and *Eikonoklastes*. So too does his charge that the tyrant "from Rebellion shall derive his name, / Though of Rebellion others he accuse." The further lines cited refer to Adam's response "fatherly displeased," and to Michael's subsequent rejoinder about the reduction to servitude of man "till then free."[29] In Babel Milton portrays the confusion consequent upon such passionate ambition, in which the moral of God's intervention was that "man over men / He made not lord; such title to himself / Reserving, human left from human free" (PL XII, 69–71). In Beale's view, the political passages late in *Paradise Lost* are the most open assertion of Milton's position. A year later he could again cite Milton's "Plea for our Original right" as one of the "great faults in his Paradyse Lost" (MS letters 108, f. 2$^v$, 24 December 1670). Nor does he read any further complexity into these texts—that, for example, it is Cromwell's "proud ambitious heart" that Milton deplores—but instead sees the poet's description of tyranny in history as entirely consistent with the antimonarchical thrust of Milton's "old Principle."

The context of this comment heightens its significance. First Beale adds of Milton, "I wish he were well encouraged about honest worke. Tis the surest way for right Information, & sincere reconciliation." This is in keeping with the line of improvement he had suggested two years before. But all of this appears in the margin (written perpendicular to the text) of a passage in which Beale is urging the stricter control of the press, a frequent theme in his letters of December 1669. The special benefit in now withholding licence followed from the devastation of the London book trade in the Great Fire a few years before:

Since the maine stock of Stationers Bookes are destroyed by Fire, if due care be taken to reprint the best, & to employ all Presses for the best advantages, (for which purpose Mr Lestrange will be as hearty as any of our Clergymen) by this one Single Engine, or Contrivance, you may easily disappoynt the Plotts of our turbulent Enemyes, and insensibly, but Infallibly, reclaime the Giddy Multitude. (MS letters 92, f. 1$^r$, 6 December 1669).

Nor do his plans for the licenser run all one way. In the interests of keeping the peace he thinks it also worth suppressing material too "sharply directed against the Calvinists" (MS letters 91, f. 1ʳ, 1 December 1669). But in the growing backlash against Toleration in the winter of 1669, Beale's proposals sound a dark enough note. In the passage to which he appends the marginal note about Milton's politics in *Paradise Lost*, he first advocates patriarchal political theory and then urges a tighter censorship:

But to our purpose, I hold, that the best & greatest worke that our A[rch] B[ishop of] C[anterbury] &c can doe is to direct & overlooke the Presses vigilantly & severely. You may see in the Merc[urius]: Lib[rarius], what Irrational Stuffe, wrestlings, and Pollutions of Scriptures doe claime the divine Title of Theology.

In Beale's view "our Hierarchy" was failing in its task and appeared in its lenience almost to "conive at the Inundations of Heresyes & Schismes" (MS letters 93, f. 1ᵛ, 18 December 1669). The bold republicanism of *Paradise Lost* leads him to cite it here as typical of laxity in press supervision.

A year later Beale reports with some excitement that "Milton is abroad againe, in Prose, & in Verse, Epic, & Dramatic" (MS letters 108, f. 2ᵛ, 24 December 1670). The sense of Milton's appearing on all fronts in 1670 came from the listing in the Michaelmas Term Catalogue of *The History of Britain* and *Paradise Regain'd / Samson Agonistes*. Beale has "not yet seen his History," and he wonders what Milton "will say to our Cantabrigian"—Edward Chamberlayne of *Angliae Notitiae* fame, briefly active in the Royal Society to which he had been recently elected.[30] Beale's usual preoccupation with the Society emerges in his perennial hopes of Sprat—"We want nothing now for English History, but Dr Spratts promise"—and these remarks are notable chiefly owing to his apparent preference for the society's "own" writers. But two weeks later Beale is reading the *History* and, now beyond such literary gossip, shows himself responsive to Milton's stern censure on an unreforming nation: "Since I wrote I have read much of Miltons History: Tis Elegant, chosen with judgment out of best Authors; And wee needed all, & more than all that I have yet seen of his sharpe checks & sowre Instructions: For wee must be a lost People, if we be not speedily reclaim'd" (MS letters 109, f. 1ᵛ, 9 January 1671). This recalls the less ingenuous response of Thomas Blount, who notes the reputation of the *History* for "not abstainyng from som lashes at the ignorance or I know not what of those times."[31] Beale's interest in the work seems to have proceeded not only from its own merits, but possibly also from some fuller connection between such a publication and the Royal Society; despite its emphasis on natural philosophy, the Society reached out to historians as well. Milton's *History* had been designed as a service to the nation. If he would not serve as the sort of laureate envisaged by Beale, he might prove useful nonetheless. As first published, the *History* featured a rhetoric that moved beyond the narrower language of faction. Beyond Milton's politics lay the religious vision that formed Beale's enduring impression of *Paradise Lost.*

## III

The penitential note in Beale's response to the *History*—"wee must be a lost People, if we be not speedily reclaim'd"—is very much in keeping with the reforming humanist rhetoric of that work. What then of Beale's further response to *Paradise Lost?* Here Milton's call to correction appears to have come through both more and less clearly. The "Plea for our Original right" at the beginning of Book X (*Ed. II,* Book XII) continues to offend Beale. Satan's republican rhetoric, on the other hand, draws no such political comment, although Satan makes a peculiarly lasting impression. Beale counts "the long blasphemies of Devils" among the "great faults in his *Paradyse Lost.*" He sees Satan in more religious than political terms, if the distinction be permitted. Milton's exploration of angelic rebellion against the tyranny of heaven seems to shock Beale, and he does not explain it away as a narrow function of Milton's "old" rebellious political principle, as Dryden and others would soon be doing.[32] His misgivings on this point best inform modern criticism of *Paradise Lost.*

Milton, as Beale perceives him, is here representative not of heterodoxy but instead of a wrong-headed and destructive orthodoxy—Calvinism, in short. Beale had long had difficulties with "Calvinians," as he styled them. These were not just nonconformists (MS letters 108, f. 1ᵛ, 24 December 1670); the whole Church of England hierarchy was, in Beale's view, given to the Calvinism that had once swept the universities.[33] He especially resented this because it led in turn to Beale himself being hounded "for maintaining generall redemption" (MS letters 74, f. 1ᵛ), an unorthodoxy he does not recognize in Milton's work. Others too had questioned the punitive theology of the day and its relation to an elaborate demonology.[34] Beale seems in the case of *Paradise Lost* to have been so struck by the latter that he assumes a "Calvinian" disposition of the work as a whole. His testimony, at least, confirms the hypothesis that a sterner, earlier Calvinism emerges in the poet's description of Satan, whatever the larger Arminian intentions for the theology of *Paradise Lost.* Beale shows that turbulent response to the epic based on the reader's implication in sin, which more modern criticism has postulated as demanding some subsequent self-correction according to Milton's prescription. But Beale seems not much to have experienced this compensation for being "surprised by sin."[35] Instead he objects that Milton "hath no Authority" for his "blasphemies." The slender scriptural support for the literature of hell is recalled to imply a wider critique of Milton's theology.[36]

In Beale's view, Milton also mistook the utility of such satanic threatenings. Instead, these "blasphemies of the Devils . . . beget a bad, or afflict a good Spirit." There are hints in Beale's biography of his suffering such affliction himself, although his letters do not much reveal whether personal fears or pastoral experience in Herefordshire and Yeovil made him so sensitive on this point. He recognizes the dangers, however, of a religious melancholy in which the imagination seizes on the infernal. The Calvinist despair fostered by the "persecutory imagination" was something that he had long struggled against as a minister and theologian. The more peaceful cast of his own doctrine and teaching may be supposed from his assertion that "all our divinity is true excellent, & unquestionable, when it carryes us with the strongest inspirations into the heart of Christianity; & then treates modestly & soberly" (MS letters 114, f. 1ᵛ, 28 April 1681). More shaken by Milton's exploration of despair, Beale can only note that "Blasphemies should be *arreta boulogmata*, infanda [agreed to be things unspeakable], too execrable to be adorn'd with the powre of elegant verse" (MS letters 108, f. 2ᵛ, 24 December 1670). Better the polite wit of Cowley's presentation of Satan in the *Davideis*. His blasphemies had indeed remained largely "infanda," since Cowley had not ventured far into the language of evil but had cut such speeches short in a clever turn—Satan "horribly spoke out in lookes the rest."[37] But Milton had investigated Satan's case much more fully and had hinted at a determination to ruin on the devils' part that sat uneasily with Beale. Was there a *natural* impulse to religion in man? Beale had wondered about this "above these thirty years," and formulated the question in terms borrowed from the suspect, but impressive, Socinus:

I find it very hard to discern, how much or how little of religion we have in the frame of our natures; and to distinguish that from all kind of revelation, or tradition. . . . Yet I incline to conceive, that all the world over there is more of revelation and grace, than we can strictly claim from our natural frame, or any lines written in our hearts.[38]

Beale hoped this last opinion might acquit him "from Pelagianism, which the Calvinians do liberally dash upon all their adversaries." Although interesting to him, the determinism of a merely natural philosophy finally could not sustain his confidence. His attraction to such possibilities seems to have been matched by a corresponding reaction against them and by a fear that nature might prove the source of despair. Was Satan determined or predetermined in his actions?

A decade later, at the height of the Exclusion Crisis, Beale would again make reference to Milton and to Milton's Satan. In a letter to Evelyn on the eve of the Oxford Parliament, he notes that he and Evelyn had "foretold each other of the late Storme" (the turbulent session of the second Exclusion Parliament), and fears that "they stirre every Stone to bring in the same Men for Ox: or worse, if worse can be found betwixt this & Hell" (MS letters 145, f. 1ʳ, 9 March 1681). It had long been evident that the fanatics' "Mouths Water for Sacriledge" in their new and dangerous designs in matters of church and state (MS letters 139, 16 June 1679). Now in his seventies, Beale still likes to propose remedies for such political ills. In the Exclusion Crisis, anticipating the logic of Roscommon's "Academy," he can again imagine an improving use for literature: "I wish all our best Poets would cast in their Symbolls, that every week the Coffee-houses may have some fresh Argument to mingle with their Lectures of Sedition." In this literary *Kulturkampf,* the loyal interest would surely prevail since "I have not yet known one Phanatic that had a Touch of true Poesy, but generally such dull Rhimes, as Touzer in affronting L'Estranges ingenious Masquerade."³⁹ Here Beale is ready to make an exception, however: "Only Milton had a good smack ["of true Poesy"]; yet he mistakes the maine of Poesy, to put such long & horrible Blasphemyes in the Mouth of Satan, as no man that feares God can endure to Read it, or without a poysonous Impression." Cowley's Satan, by contrast, can be again cited as a triumph of wit, although Beale had long known that "there can be no more Cowleyes in one Age" (MS letters 141, f. 1ʳ, 18 October 1679). Again Beale registers his sensitivity to being somehow implicated in Satan's blasphemies. Milton still prompts his suspicion and respect, and Milton's Satan continues to elicit doubt. Even as the English prepared for further struggles, and the longstanding lines of division threatened more serious convulsions still, Milton stands for Beale as the preeminent literary figure of the "faction." Nor, it seems, was the high style necessarily beyond such partisan conflict. Beale himself had sought to enlist Milton for his cause, and saw enduring political and religious claims embodied in Milton's "true Poesy."

University of Ottawa

## NOTES

This essay is part of a wider study on the reception of Milton's works. My thanks to Steven Pincus, historian of the Anglo-Dutch wars, for alerting me to the Milton allusion which initiated this line of inquiry. Materials from the Evelyn Collection at Christ Church, Oxford, are quoted with the permission of Christ Church and the Trustees of the Will of the late J.H.C. Evelyn. Citations from the letter-books in the Evelyn Collection will be abbreviated as "MS letters" in the notes and in the text. The letters are for the most part numbered in chronological sequence.

1. Jonathan Richardson, *Explanatory Notes and Remarks on Milton's Paradise Lost* (London, 1734), pp. cxix–cxx; Vivian de Sola Pinto, *Sir Charles Sedley* (London, 1927), p. 94; *Early Lives of Milton*, ed. Helen Darbishire (London, 1932), p. 295. Malone rejected the Denham story, but it has since been successfully revived: Edmond Malone, *Critical and Miscellaneous Prose Works of John Dryden* (London, 1800), vol. I, pp. 111–15; T. W. Baldwin, "Sir John Denham and *Paradise Lost*," *MLN* XLII (1927), 508–09; J. Milton French, *Life Records of John Milton* (New Brunswick, N.J., 1949–58), vol. IV, pp. 439–40; William Riley Parker, *Milton: A Biography* (Oxford, 1968), pp. 604, 1115–16. William Riley Parker, *Milton's Contemporary Reputation* (Columbus, Oh., 1940), p. 51. The chief exception has been Sir John Hobart's applause for *Paradise Lost*, in letters to John Hobart dated 22 and 30 January 1668, Oxford, Bodleian Library, MS Tanner 45, f. 258; MS Tanner 45*, f. 271. John T. Shawcross, *Milton: A Bibliography, 1624–1700* (Binghamton, 1984), nos. 601, 602; James M. Rosenheim, "An Early Appreciation of *Paradise Lost*," *MP* LXXV (1978); 280–82.

2. Allowance being made for Thomas Ellwood's response to *Paradise Lost* in manuscript, *The History of the Life of Thomas Ellwood* (London, 1714), pp. 233–34, and the licenser Tomkyns's reported misgivings about Book I, 594–99, *Early Lives*, ed. Darbishire, p. 180.

3. Mayling Stubbs, "John Beale, Philosophical Gardener of Herefordshire, Part I. Prelude to the Royal Society (1608–1663)," *Annals of Science* XXXIX (1982), 463–89; "John Beale, Philosophical Gardener of Herefordshire, Part II. The Improvement of Agriculture and Trade in the Royal Society (1663–83)," *Annals of Science* XLVI (1989), 323–63. Stray letters from the series also appear elsewhere (e.g. British Library, Add. MS 15948); Evelyn's responses to Beale have yet to be found. The fullest sequence of letters comes from the years 1664–1671. That Beale's letters were not focused narrowly enough emerges in Oldenburg's comment to Boyle, "I wish, Dr Beale had digested his owne sense to you, and not commissioned me to cull it out of his letters here and there." See *The Correspondence of Henry Oldenburg*, ed. A. R. Hall and M. Boas Hall (Madison and London, 1965–86), vol. III, p. 71 (27 March 1666). Beale's letters selected for publication in *The Works of the Honourable Robert Boyle* (London, 1744), vol. V, pp. 423a–510b, are consistent with the example of over fifty more in *The Correspondence of Oldenburg* (see indices).

4. His two published books represent the strength of his interests, but not their scope: John Beale, *Herefordshire Orchards, a Pattern to all England* (London, 1657), and "Aphorisms Concerning Cider," in John Evelyn, *Sylva [Pomona]* (London, 1664). Note also the second part of Anthony Lawrence, *Nurseries, Orchards, Profitable Gardens, and Vineyards Encouraged* (London, 1677).

5. *The Diary and Correspondence of Dr John Worthington*, ed. J. Crossley and R. C. Christie, Chetham Soc, XIII, XXXVI, CXIV (1847–1886), vol. I, p. 304.

6. See Thomas Sprat, *The History of the Royal-Society of London* (London, 1667), sig. B1$^r$–B3$^v$. On 29 April 1667, Beale had written of Cowley's poem to Evelyn, and noted the thanks owing "for Mr Coweleyes most obliegeing Inspiration," MS letters 57, f. 1$^r$. See also Oxford, Corpus Christi College, MS 332, f. 18. Evelyn had recently discussed with his "very deare friend" Cowley some ways of raising the reputation of (and thus benefactors for) the Royal Society. See John Evelyn, *Diary and Correspondence*, ed. W. Bray (London,

1850–52), vol. III, pp. 194–95; *The Diary of John Evelyn*, ed. E. S. De Beer (Oxford, 1955), vol. III, p. 940. On Cowley's death, see *The Works of Mr Abraham Cowley*, ed. Thomas Sprat (London, 1668), sig. e1; Arthur H. Nethercot, *The Muse's Hannibal* (London, 1931), pp. 194–216.

7. Richard Helgerson, *Self-Crowned Laureates* (Berkeley, 1983), pp. 231–82. For complaint about Helgerson's anachronistic handling of Restoration conditions of authorship, see Dustin Griffin, "The Beginnings of Modern Authorship: Milton and Dryden," *MQ* XXIV (1990), 1–7.

8. N. H. Steneck, " 'The Ballad of Robert Crosse and Joseph Glanvill' and the Background to *Plus ultra*," *The British Journal for the History of Science* XIV (1981), 59–63, 71–72 [59–74]; James R. Jacob, *Henry Stubbe* (Cambridge, 1983), pp. 79–81, 102–03.

9. Parker, *Milton*, pp. 596, 1105.

10. 27 May 1666 (Heimbach), 6 June 1666 (Milton) from *Complete Prose Works of John Milton*, ed. Don M. Wolfe et al. (New Haven, 1953–82), vol. VIII, pp. 1–4; *The Works of John Milton*, ed. Frank Allen Patterson (New York, 1931–38), vol. XII, pp. 112–15, 316–19, hereafter cited as CM.

11. MS letters 67, f. 1ᵛ (16 October 1667). Beale is also speaking of Georg Horn here, author of the "wicked"*Historia ecclesiastica et politica* (London, 1665), "which is in excellent clear Latine." It seems to be Lucan rather than Milton he speaks of when he also notes that "(to my tast) he hath more of a raving Jarr, & of a boysterous strentgh [sic] of wit than of true Poetry, & solemne Harmony."

12. Beale's proposed epitaph for that poet had emphasized this point, MS letters 63, f. 1 (31 August 1667); see also *Works of Cowley*, ed. Sprat, sig. b2ᵛ.

13. *The Works of John Dryden*, ed. Samuel H. Monk (Berkeley and Los Angeles, 1971), vol. XVII, p. 71. Milton's third wife listed Cowley with Spenser and Shakespeare among those English poets of "whom he approved most." See *Paradise Lost*, ed. Thomas Newton (London, 1749), vol. I, p. lvi: CM XVIII, p. 390.

14. Beale to Oldenburg, *Correspondence of Oldenburg*, IV, p. 535 (11 July 1668).

15. Compare Horace, *Odes*, I, xxvii, 18. MS letters 68, f. 1 (18 November 1667).

16. It may be noted that Beale's sense of Milton's earlier work is consistent with a later fiction in which Waller is said to prefer to Milton's epic the "smaller Productions of his in the Scenical and Pastoral way," not least *Lycidas*. John Langhorne, *Letters Supposed to Have Passed Between M. de St. Evremond and Mr Waller* (London, 1769), vol. II, p. 19.

17. Stubbs, "John Beale, Part I," pp. 477, 484–85.

18. *Correspondence of Oldenburg*, VII, p. 407 (21 January 1671). See also British Library, Add. MS 15948, ff. 80, 138. In *Paradise Lost*, of course, Milton had materialist interests of his own. John Rogers, "Milton and the Mysterious Terms of History," *ELH* LVII (1990), 281–305. For more on Beale in this vein, see Michael Leslie, "The Spiritual Husbandry of John Beale," in *Culture and Cultivation in Early Modern England*, ed. M. Leslie and T. Raylor (London, forthcoming), pp. 158–62.

19. Steneck, " 'The Ballad,' " 59–60; Stubbs, "John Beale, Part I," pp. 482–83.

20. Beale's sight had deteriorated only within the last three years. See *Oldenburg Correspondence*, V, pp. 9–10 (10 August 1668). It was about to improve suddenly. See MS letters 75, f. 1ʳ (15 August 1668).

21. *Oldenburg Correspondence*, VII, pp. 439–41 (4 Feburary 1671). The editors observe that "C" might also stand for Robert Crosse, Glanvill's first adversary.

22. French, *Life Records*, IV, p. 436. MS letters 69, f. 1ʳ (11 November 1667).

23. "The political message . . . is clearly conveyed by the diction ('ancient liberty,' 'modern bondage'), and would have been appreciated by the Restoration audience, for

whom classicism would soon give mediation to the political balance struck within the ruling class, symbolizing its comfortable [!] hegemony." Christopher Kendrick, *Milton: A Study in Ideology and Form* (New York, 1986), p. 83.

24. In his note on the verse the next year, Milton fails to cite such native English precedent.

25. From an "ideological" standpoint, a later Whig argument might even be postulated in which the bondage of rhyme is favored as part of some Gothic cultural inheritance.

26. MS letters 69, f. 1ʳ (11 November 1667). "The angel wings his way—so the proverb—a robber walks to hell." No. 1048 in Hans Walther, *Proverbia Sententiaeque Latinitatis Medii Aevi* (Gottingen, 1963); [S.A.I.], *Carminum Proverbialum* (London, 1588), p. 3—there were many English editions, some recent, of this *Carminum*, which had been so dear to Samuel Daniel, *The Complete Works in Verse and Prose*, ed. A. B. Grosart (London, 1885–96), vol. IV, p. 40.

27. The best discussion of republicanism in *Paradise Lost* is A. B. Worden, "Milton's Republicanism and the Tyranny of Heaven," in *Machiavelli and Republicanism*, ed. Gisela Bock, Q. Skinner, and M. Viroli (Cambridge, 1990), pp. 225–45.

28. *Ed II*, XII. 27, 36, 63, 81, etc. The first edition of *Paradise Lost* has line numbers every ten lines, so these references are likely to be accurate. MS letters 93, f. 1ᵛ (18 December 1669).

29. Alastair Fowler, ed., *Paradise Lost* (London, 1968), XII, 80–101n, allows that the whole of the latter passage "may recall the style of the regicide tracts," although he oddly sees it as antithetical that some comparable opinion be available from Augustine.

30. Beale adds that it "is not likely he could take notice of him, time enough": *Angliae Notitiae* (London, 1669) sold out three printings in its first year of publication (19th ed., 1700). The Oxford-educated Chamberlayne could be styled a Cantabrigian because within a month of Beale's writing he was to be honored as a Doctor of Civil Law at Cambridge, later to be "incorporated in this university." See Anthony Wood, *Athenae Oxonienses*, ed. Philip Bliss (London, 1813–20), vol. IV, p. 789; John Venn and J. A. Venn, *Alumni Cantabrigienses to 1751, I.* (Cambridge, 1922–54), vol. I, p. 316.

31. Oxford, Bodleian Library, Wood MS F40, f. 82. Letter from Thomas Blount to Anthony Wood (10 November 1670). Wood lifts this sentence for his "Life of Milton," in *Early Lives*, ed. Darbishire, p. 46. Blount had already noted the appearance of the *History* in a previous letter (1 November 1670), Wood MS F40, f. 80; he would soon cite it with some approval in *Animadversions Upon Sir Richard Baker's Chronicle, and Its Continuation* (London, 1672), pp. 20, 58, 98–99.

32. "Milton [had a better plea], if the Devil had not been his hero, instead of Adam": John Dryden, *The Works of Virgil* (London, 1697), p. 154. Compare the earlier *Vindiciae Carolinae* (London, 1692), p. 3: Milton "was a Person of a large thought, and wanted not words to express those Conceptions; but never so truly, as when the Argument, and his deprav'd Temper met together: Witness his *Paradise Lost*; where he makes the Devil,— *Who, though fallen, had not given heaven for lost,*—speak at that rate himself would have done of the Son of this Royal Martyr (upon his Restauration) had he thought it convenient." The author of this tract may be the nonjuring bishop William Lloyd. See Oxford, Bodleian Library, Tanner MS 26, f. 15.

33. MS letters 72, f. 1ʳ (4 May 1668); MS letters 52, f. 1ʳ (24 May 1666): "I can well remember the fall of Ramistry & doe yet hope to see the fall of Calvinisme."

34. Daniel P. Walker, *The Decline of Hell* (Chicago, 1964). pp. 33–35, 40–42.

35. John Stachniewski, *The Persecutory Imagination: English Puritanism and the Literature of Religious Despair* (Oxford, 1991), pp. 336–38. The best and most elaborate

development of the corrective model remains Stanley Fish, *Surprised by Sin* (London, 1967).

36.  Reading *Paradise Lost* seems also to have moved Beale to check the literature on the geography of Paradise. See British Library, Add. MS 15948, f. 136 (letter to Evelyn, 12 June 1669).

37.  Cowley, *Works* (1668), *Davideis*, I, 144.

38.  *Works of Boyle* (1744), V, pp. 470–71; for similar misgivings about Calvinism and some small indulgence for Socinianism, see also MS letters 31ʳ; Oxford, Corpus Christi College, MS 332, f. 19.

39.  Beale refers to L'Estrange's *The Committee, or Popery in Masquerade* (London, 1680); for an example of "Touzer" poetry, see *Strange's Case, Strangely Altered* (London, 1680).